Seeking Cultures of Peace

Published in association with
Mennonite Central Committee

Seeking Cultures of Peace

A PEACE CHURCH CONVERSATION

Edited by
Fernando Enns, Scott Holland, and Ann Riggs

Foreword by Samuel Kobia

Cascadia
Publishing House
the new name of Pandora Press U.S.
Telford, Pennsylvania

copublished with

 World
Council of
Churches
Publications
Geneva, Switzerland

and
Herald Press
Scottdale, Pennsylvania

Cascadia Publishing House orders, information, reprint permissions:
contact@CascadiaPublishingHouse.com
1-215-723-9125
126 Klingerman Road, Telford PA 18969
www.CascadiaPublishingHouse.com

Seeking Cultures of Peace
Copyright © 2004 by Cascadia Publishing House,
Telford, PA 18969
All rights reserved.
Copublished with Herald Press, Scottdale, PA and

 World
Council of
Churches
Publications

Geneva, Switzerland;
World Council of Churches ISBN: 2-8254-1402-6
Cascadia ISBN: 1-931038-21-X
Library of Congress Catalog Number: 2003027059
Printed in the United States by Evangel Press, Nappanee, Indiana
Book design by Cascadia Publishing House
Cover design by Merrill R. Miller

The paper used in this publication is recycled and meets the
minimum requirements of American National Standard for Information
Sciences—Permanence of Paper for Printed Library Materials, ANSI Z39.48-1984.

All Bible quotations are used by permission, all rights reserved and unless otherwise
noted are from *The New Revised Standard Version of the Bible*, copyright 1989, by
the Division of Christian Education of the National
Council of the Churches of Christ in the USA

Cover background credit: Data courtesy Marc Imhoff of NASA GSFC and
Christopher Elvidge of NOAA NGDC. Image by Craig Mayhew and
Robert Simmon, NASAGSFC. Used by permission.

Library of Congress Cataloguing-in-Publication Data
Seeking cultures of peace : a peace church conversation / edited by
Fernando Enns, Scott Holland, and Ann Riggs ; foreword by Samuel
Kobia.-- 1st ed.
    p. cm.
Includes bibliographical references and index.
  ISBN 1-931038-21-X (trade pbk. : alk. paper)
  1. Peace--Religious aspects--Christianity--Congresses. 2. Historic
peace churches--Congresses. I. Enns, Fernando, 1964- II. Holland,
Scott, 1954- III. Riggs, Ann, 1950- IV. Title.

BT736.4.S435 2004
261.8'73--dc22

                                                            2003027059
        13 12 11 10 09 08 07 06 05 04   10 9 8 7 6 5 4 3 2 1

*To the participants
in the Historic Peace Church
"Puidoux Conferences" of the 1950s and 1960s,
our predecessors in ecumenical peace conversations*

Contents

IV. BUILDING CULTURES OF JUST PEACE

APPENDICES

Foreword

*T*he Decade to Overcome Violence (DOV) calls upon churches to engage in theological reflection to overcome the spirit, logic, and practice of violence. Theological conversation is one of the specific activities the DOV invites the churches to engage in.

This is precisely what the Historic Peace Churches were doing when they met at Bienenberg, Switzerland, in June 2001, just six months into the Decade. The World Council of Churches warmly welcomes such initiatives, and I am happy that the contents of this particular conversation are documented in the present collection of essays. Dr. Konrad Raiser's introductory remarks actually summarize the unfolding process around the questions of war, peace, and nonviolence in the ecumenical movement. This alone is a contribution worthy to be shared widely.

For as long as they have existed, the Historic Peace Churches have presented a challenge to the mainline churches to consider the biblical call to active peacemaking as taking primacy over national, institutional, or religious drives for power or even survival. Some of the motivations and implications of this challenge are documented in this book, and they are as pertinent today as in earlier centuries.

"Churches Seeking Reconciliation and Peace" is the Decade to Overcome Violence theme. The World Council of Churches has from the start emphasized the pertinence of the Historic Peace Churches in the conciliar process within the ecumenical movement. The title of this book, *Seeking Cultures of Peace*, gently points to the UN-Decade for a Culture of Peace and Nonviolence for the Children of the World, to which the DOV is running in complementary parallel.

That process of seeking is a process which we are to engage in together, both as different traditions within the ecumenical movement, and as communities in different cultures and regions around the world. It is in this spirit that I welcome this book as a gift of the HPC to all of us, and that I look forward to the continuation of the conversation, which is planned to take place in Africa, so as to engage more vividly those who come to the table out of the midst of situations of war, protracted violence, and sustained oppression. As we walk the road together, God's Spirit walks among us and inspires us.

—*Dr. Samuel Kobia*
  General Secretary, World Council of Churches
  Geneva, Switzerland

Editors' Preface

September 11, 2001, has become a symbol for a new era of insecurity. Following the terrible terrorist attacks in the U.S.A. people around the globe felt they were facing a new dimension of international non-governmental violence, parallel to the other dimensions of globalization. Surely, horrible scenarios like these have occurred before. But the fact that a symbol of the governing and ruling powers of globalization had been destroyed in a few moments demonstrated a vulnerability which had not been suspected before.

For a few days the world seemed to stand still. People around the globe joined together in mourning and grief, searching for strength in interreligious gatherings of prayer. There was a moment of listening, discerning together how best to react to this terrible act of violence that took the lives of so many. It was a moment of global solidarity, a great historic chance to break the cycle of violence by taking a first step in changing the ruling culture of violence into a culture of self-reflection, trust building, and nonviolence. People around the world were waiting for the Western democracies to react in a way differently than in a thousand situations before.

But nothing changed! Since then we have seen two wars legitimized as defending the so-called "civilized world" through military preemptive strikes. We have witnessed the death of thousands of civilians in Afghanistan and the destruction of the society in Iraq. Both countries were ruled by terrible governments that violated human rights, threatening their own people and beyond. But it is also well known that the very same Western countries had supported both of these governments before. We are witnessing violations of human rights by democracies that—in search of more security for their own—are willing to use violence as a political tool to defend these very rights. Media and press in the militarily and economically strong countries are becoming less critical. And all of this seems to be accepted by the majority of the population in these countries, longing for a life in security and peace.

Peace? The prophet Jeremiah rails against those who cry "'Peace, peace"; when there is no peace" (Jer. 6:14). Nothing has changed if the only reaction to violence is violence. We are captives of this culture of violence. We act as if there are no alternatives, as if we had not realized counterviolence will provoke new hatred, injustice, and insecurity, as if we had not learned anything from history, as if the peace-building power of the Christian story is not meant for this world.

These developments were not in sight when the delegates of the Eighth Assembly of the World Council of Churches in Harare, Zimbabwe (December, 1998), decided to start the new millennium with a "Decade to Overcome Violence, 2001-2010: Churches Seeking Reconciliation and Peace." But the representatives, from different church communities, cultures, and contexts, allowed themselves to be confronted with the simple question: "What do you say?" What is the role of the Church, represented by the ecumenical fellowship of churches, in a globalized world that seems to be dominated by a culture of violence? Is the gospel of the Prince of Peace of any relevance to our witness in this world?

The WCC Central Committee meeting in 1999 took up that commitment to a decade of work against the problem of violence in our world. In their message, giving concrete shape and direction to this work, the Central Committee noted: "There are a number of positive and encouraging examples for congregations and churches around the world. We recognize the steady witness of monastic traditions and the historic peace churches, and we want to receive anew their contribution through the decade" (WCC Central Committee, "Minutes of the Fiftieth Meeting, Geneva, Switzerland, 26 August–3 September 1999," 188).

This book represents a response to that message. The sixteen essays, the Historic Peace Churches' Bienenberg Epistle, and the study-document "Just Peacemaking" collected in this volume are among the first contributions of the historic peace churches—the Mennonite churches, the Church of the Brethren, and the Religious Society of Friends (Quakers)—to the work of the Decade to Overcome Violence.

These three communities have much that draws us together, but also much that is divergent in history, in theological and doctrinal expression, and in community self-understanding. Much of the ecumenical discussion among ourselves in past years has been local and North Atlantic, rather than worldwide in scope. Further, while many Mennonite, Brethren, and Quaker jurisdictions belong to the World Council of Churches, some do not.

To respond to the request of the Central Committee of the World Council of Churches for an offering of our best to the work of the Decade, it was clear that Mennonites, Brethren, and Friends would need first to consult with one another and deepen our own dialogue. This volume is a result of an international consultation among ourselves and with the WCC, held in response to the invitation and opportunity offered in the Decade to Overcome Violence.

Between June 25 and 29, 2001, interested members of the Brethren, Quaker, and Mennonite communities and a few friends met at the Mennonite theological seminary at Bienenberg, Switzerland, and in Geneva at the offices of the World Council of Churches. A list of those participating in the meeting, entitled "Theology and Culture: Peacemaking in a Globalized World," and of the papers presented at the consultation appear in Appendix 3 at the end of this volume. Included is bibliographic information on papers presented at the conference and published elsewhere.

The first section of this book, "Discerning in Ecumenical Context," seeks to locate the texts included here within the work of the WCC, the history of Historic Peace Church relationships, and the globalized reality in which violence occurs in our time. Here are essays by Konrad Raiser, General Secretary of the World Council of Churches; and Fernando Enns, a young Mennonite theologian. These describe the present moment of contextual ecumenical consideration of peacemaking and reconciliation at the beginning of the third millennium and point to the traditional Historic Peace Church preference for spiritual and theological discernment, rather than exclusive reliance on logical argument, in understanding how to be faithful in living out the Christian vocation for peacemaking and reconciliation.

Our present world is one in which all interpretive and truth claims are in cognitive and affective competition with multiple other interpretive truth claims. Questions of power are embedded in the processes of taking in new information, locating that information in the horizon of history and ethics, and the application of traditional theological and ethical commitments in new contexts.

The second section of the book, "Interpreting Globalization: Questions of Power," includes chapters written from three geo-social locations: Neal Blough, author of "Globalization and Claiming Truth," lives and teaches in France; Peter Dula, author of "The 'Disavowal of Constantine' in the Age of Global Capital," lives in the United States; and Alfred Neufeld, author of "The Power of Historiography," writes from his life and work in Paraguay. These articles engage the notion of globalization from three viewpoints: biblical studies, theological ethics, and historiography. They probe the theological foundations for Christian truth claims in service of peace making and reconciliation, and point toward interpretive contributions that could produce a more peaceful future.

Within the Brethren, Mennonite, and Quaker traditions, the construct of being a "Peace Church" has come to operate as an interiorized element of self-understanding and self-definition. In this self-perception, the gospel of peace (Eph. 6:15; Rom. 10:15 KJV; cf. Is. 52:7) is the gospel of our Lord Jesus Christ, the one gospel, and those who follow the gospel will be shaped by this fact. The experiences of these traditions through the centuries are experiences of living out this self-perception in ever changing circumstances, in matters of doctrine and faith (Faith and Order concerns), as well as in action in the world (Life and Work concerns).

The five essays in the third section, "The Gospel of Peace in Context: Shaping Identity" explore this process of reappropriation and ongoing theological reflection. Ann K. Riggs, J. Denny Weaver, Patrick K. Bugu, Scott Holland, and Alix Lozano engage the gospel and our traditions within the context of the present location of our communities in North America, Nigeria, and Colombia.

The theological heritage of the Quaker, Brethren, and Mennonite communities are not, however, our unique property and the gospel is the shared heritage of Christians. The fourth section of the book, "Building Cultures of Just Peace," draws from our traditions and turns outward toward paradigms of, and resources for, action, reflection and critique in building a future of justice and peace with others. Daniel W. Ulrich and Moisés Mayordomo explore the biblical basis of peacebuilding in the teachings and behavior of Jesus and Paul. Debbie Roberts critically engages prevailing notions and influences in the field of conflict transformation studies from the vantage point of a feminist theology and ethic.

In "The Sacred Nature of Places," Elaine Bishop demonstrates how important understanding differences in deeply held religious views about the world can be to healing conflict. Sang Gyoo Lee shares a vision of being peace church from the perspective of a church that has grown into this self-perception in the Korean context, and Alastair McIntosh points suggestively toward connections and points of contact for Christians engaged in peace activism with the peace theology and peace work of others, from other religious traditions or from secular psychological and political thought.

Attached are three appendices. As earlier noted, Appendix 3 lists Bienenberg conference participants and papers. Meanwhile the Historic Peace Churches' Epistle from Bienenberg (Appendix 1) was drafted by the participants to be sent to our HPC constituencies and to the world, reporting on our experience in consultation and committing ourselves to the work of the Decade to Overcome Violence and the process of coming to understand one another more fully. This letter was affirmed corporately by all present.

Appendix 2, "Just Peacemaking: Toward an Ecumenical Ethical Approach from the Perspective of the Historic Peace Churches: A Study Paper for Dialogue with the Wider Church" was also prepared at the consultation. Drawing particularly on the work Duane Friesen presented at the meeting, the text was drafted during our time in Bienenberg and signed by individual participants. It was crafted as a response to a document received by the WCC Central Committee, and recommended for further study among the churches, "The Protection of Endangered Populations in Situations of Armed Violence: Toward an Ecumenical Approach" (Potsdam, Germany, 29 January, 2001). The Bienenberg study paper begins the process of the Historic Peace Churches engaging in direct dialogue within the Decade to Overcome Violence.

The editors thank all those who participated in the deliberations at Bienenberg, and those who have revised their papers for inclusion in this volume. They also offer their thanks to Sara Speicher (WCC staff, Church of the Brethren) and Laura Short (WCC staff, Mennonite) for their logistical support for the conference, as well as to the Mennonite Central Committee (MCC) Europe office and the Bienenberg Theological Seminary staff for so ably hosting the gathering. Thanks also to the planning group, Sara Speicher, Doug Gwyn, Fernando Enns, Robert Herr, and Judy Zimmerman Herr, for their work.

Space constraints have not allowed us to include all the papers we considered together at the meeting at Bienenberg or the taped transcript of the discussions that followed each presentation, now housed in the Mennonite Central Committee's Peace Office, in Akron, Pennsylvania, and in the Decade to Overcome Violence office in Geneva, Switzerland. Nevertheless, the voices of all the participants of our week together in Switzerland impacted the manner in which the papers presented at the consultation have been revised for publication here. This volume was created in a shared enterprise among the Historic Peace Churches and the ecumenical community. It is offered in service to the churches of the world and to the human communities throughout the globe that long for peace and reconciliation.

—*Ann Riggs, Fernando Enns, and Scott Holland*

DISCERNING IN ECUMENICAL CONTEXT

Chapter 1

Remarks to the Bienenberg Consultation

Konrad Raiser

INTRODUCTION

I welcome very much this opportunity to pick up the thread of dialogue between the Historic Peace Churches (HPC) and the churches represented in the World Council of Churches (WCC). Some of the Historic Peace Churches are themselves members of the World Council, so it's actually a dialogue within the family.

The particular context in which this dialogue takes shape is, of course, the initiative the World Council has undertaken by decision of its Assembly in Harare, Zimbabwe. This was prompted by a motion, presented by Fernando Enns, to proclaim the years 2001-2010 as the Ecumenical Decade to Overcome Violence. My task here is to present the context, framework, objectives, and intention of this Decade.

Sometimes in the public presentation of the Decade, this is presented as a dramatic new initiative of the World Council prompted perhaps by the particular circumstances of conflict all around us, certainly within this last decade. Many of you will know that it is actually a part of a much longer history of the WCC. The ecumenical community has been struggling with the question of war and peace, violence and nonviolence, and the ministry of reconciliation ever since the movement began, and that movement was itself a response to violent conflict and all the destruction that followed it. So the whole history of the WCC, of the ecumenical movement at least in the second part of the twentieth century, is inscribed into that context. It is not an additional or an external concern that is thrust upon the churches seeking unity and rebuilding communion among each other, but is integral to the emergence of the ecumenical impulse and the ecumenical movement.

But it is also probably one of the most prominent examples of the ecumenical movement, and the WCC, dealing with a conflict in its own midst—not by exclusion, not by normative decision making, but by engaging a continual process of dialogue. I hope that someone will one day do an analysis of this particular dialogue about violence and nonviolence, about war and peace, as a model for how churches can deal with ethical and other concerns in their midst, in which deeply held convictions growing out of our understanding of the gospel, the central thrust of our Christian witness, stand against each other.

The early church felt obliged to settle some of these disputes by declaring judgments of condemnation and heresy. The ecumenical movement in turn has dealt with such situations, where churches have been divided from each other by earlier condemnations and heresy trials, and where a way had to be found to break those conditions. The way the WCC itself has struggled continuously with the challenge of coming to a more common mind on what the Christian witness of reconciliation is and what it demands of the churches is in itself a model case of a nonviolent approach, from which a number of important lessons can be gained.

The Amsterdam Assembly in 1948, which formed the World Council of Churches, found itself in a dilemma. While there was a reasonable agreement that "war is contrary to the will of God,"[1] the representatives of the churches could not agree on the conclusions about church practice that should be drawn from the churches' basic agreement. In these more than fifty years of ecumenical dialogue, insights and convictions have grown, and there has been an increase of clarity about the central thrust of this Christian commitment on which we should not, and I believe we will not, go back. The fact that we have finally arrived at the point of proclaiming a Decade to Overcome Violence is in itself a witness to this growth, a growth in agreement and in conviction.

GRAPPLING WITH VIOLENCE

The immediate precursor to this Decade was one of the most controversial programs of the WCC. The Programme to Combat Racism included humanitarian support for two liberation movements that were also engaged in armed struggle. The World Council had to respond to the question: How can this be brought in line with a basic Christian commitment to nonviolence? In this conflict, the World Council never crossed the line of justifying violence, and I hope it will never cross that line. It stayed with the statement by the Central Committee in Addis Ababa in 1971 that the WCC does not "pass judgement on those victims of racism who are driven to violence as the only way left to them . . . open the way for a new and more just social order."[2] This is a different statement from one in which violence as a last resort is justified.

That discussion prompted a study process on violence and nonviolence in the struggle for social justice. In 1973 the Central Committee received the report of the study, which I think still remains the most thorough ethical and theological discussion of the issues involved. It contains a lot that remains important even for contemporary discussion.

The report did not try to come out with one normative position. Instead it focused on formulating critical questions for self-assessment to those holding opposing positions. Thus the world saw the WCC precisely not coming to a final magisterial statement, but rather facilitating, engaging, urging the continuation of the critical dialogue of mutual accountability, of mutual questioning. These questions are addressed with equal seriousness to those who have been and continue to be defenders of the principled position of nonviolence, and to those who have been and who continue to be defenders of a just war tradition.

The discussion then took a new turn in 1975 at the Nairobi Assembly, where the World Council was confronted with a motion from the Dutch churches, urging the World Council to start a program to combat militarism. It was obviously inspired by the model of the Programme to Combat Racism, with the feeling that the struggle had to be extended to embrace militarism and its consequences as well. In that particular Assembly the resolution on the world armament situation included the statement that the churches should be prepared to declare that they are ready to live without the protection of arms.

This has become the source of inspiration for some of the new peace movements in the European context. In my own country, Germany, the movement "Living Without Arms (*Ohne Rüstung Leben*)" has been one of the strong allies in the Christian peace movement. The process continued in 1981, when there was a hearing on nuclear arms and disarmament in Amsterdam. This hearing was decisive in preparing the WCC's Vancouver Statement on Justice and Peace that included the rejection of the spirit, logic, and practice of deterrence. It declared not only the use, but also the stockpiling and production, of nuclear weapons as a crime against humanity; and it urged the churches to refuse any act of support that might lead to participation in wars fought with weapons of mass destruction.

That statement, at the height of the peace movement (at least in the European context), marks a significant step forward. It implies that the churches, who expressed the various positions which had been part of the earlier discussion, had definitely moved beyond the traditional attitude of just war and had adopted as a basis of discussion the clear rejection of wars fought with weapons of mass destruction as being incompatible with the Christian teaching, with the spirit of the gospel and the spirit of Christ. That very powerful insight has been the starting point of many of the discussions that followed.

The process of the "Justice, Peace, and the Integrity of Creation" study undertaken by the ecumenical movement included serious discussions about a new understanding of security, which led to a further step forward. The final documents of the World Convocation on Justice, Peace, and the Integrity of Creation in Seoul (1990) included commitments to the banning of war as a legally recognized means for resolving conflict and to the practice of nonviolence. In one of the covenants from Seoul we find a commitment to build a culture of active, life-affirming nonviolence. I think it was the first time that the World Council expressed itself so clearly in defense of nonviolence as the way of building peace.

I still remember the passionate discussions both in the drafting committee and then the plenary of the Seoul convocation around this issue, particularly discussions with those who were still strongly involved in the struggle against apartheid. To have the World Council, which had been seen as leading the struggle against apartheid, suddenly come out with a clear commitment to active and life-affirming nonviolence seemed to disown those who had engaged in a militant struggle against apartheid. In Canberra, during the WCC Assembly of 1991, while the [first] Gulf War was being fought, the time was not quite right, apparently, to make this formulation of the Seoul convocation part of a resolution of the Assembly. But such failures are part of the nature of the discussion in the WCC. You will never move in a straight line, but you move.

A FOCUS ON OVERCOMING VIOLENCE

I am delighted that now, ten years after the Canberra Assembly, the Council has been prepared to launch a Decade to Overcome Violence. In 1994 the Central Committee met for the first time in South Africa, three months before the dismantling of the apartheid system in the first free South African elections. An attempt to relaunch this discussion about alternative ways of conflict resolution had been under preparation. It was then sparked and stimulated by a call from the Methodist bishop, Stanley Mogoba, who was deeply involved in the anti-apartheid struggle and had been in prison for many years. He said that now that we are almost at the point of having succeeded with the Programme to Combat Racism, now is the time to start a program to combat violence. After many debates in the respective committees and then at the Central Committee itself, this led to the decision to initiate a "Programme to Overcome Violence."

This was beyond the experience of many of the churches, and the Council as an organization didn't quite know how to handle it. So it took some time until a focus emerged for this Programme to Overcome Violence. The focus took shape in the Peace to the Cities campaign. And I think it is important to refer to this because here a methodological insight took shape, which I hope will also shape the Decade to Overcome Violence.

The Peace to the Cities campaign started contextually by taking seriously the experience of Christian and other communities in particular situations confronted with manifestations of everyday violence; not so much in the conventional form of war or even civil war, but violence in homes, violence in communities, violence in the streets, violence in places of work. It built on the experience of those who were not prepared to accept such violence as inevitable and, therefore, had begun to develop imaginative forms of resistance, of trying to transform violence. The aim of the Peace to the Cities campaign essentially was to make such endeavors visible, to establish networks among them, to help them learn from each other and encourage each other, and to make their witness known more widely.

The methodological insight was that in our work to overcome violence, we need to build on experience from within concrete situations. We need to focus on networking and coordinating. The focus in the first instance should not be to offer normative definitions of violence. The effort should not be to redraw again the line between nonviolence and violence, or to ask when an act of resistance passes from nonviolence to violence. All of this may be necessary, but it is of little interest to those who are actively involved in situations of resisting violence. A normative definition of violence may be well-supported by sociological, political, and ethical reflection, but it is relatively meaningless for those who are victims of violence. It is the victims who know what violence is, and they also know that you can talk about violence authentically only if you take the specifics of the situation seriously. They know that generalized definitions are likely to pass over many of the most brutal expressions of violence. But they are also the ones who know how to resist in a situation of violence.

This implies a change in the role of the WCC. In the Programme to Combat Racism, the WCC was very much the leader of the program. In the case of the Decade to Overcome Violence, the Council will take a different role. It will serve as the motivator of what will hopefully become a dynamic involving the churches themselves and the Christian communities, in which they will be the ones to determine the specific approaches and not wait for recommendations coming from Geneva.

This approach also means the deglobalization of the discussion. So much of the ecumenical discussion, and, I am afraid, also the Historic Peace Church discussion, has been fascinated by the question of war. But today violence is present in human communities in so many forms that the question of war, traditional war, becomes almost an exception. As long as we stay within these large structural analyses, we will not come close to where violence is experienced by people every day. In particular this is true of violence against women, and that was one of the sources of inspiration for this change of methodology. This emerged as a central concern from the previous ecumenical Decade of the Churches in Solidarity with Women.

Fundamental theological, social, and political challenges are, of course, explicit in the objectives of the Decade. In particular, there is the question whether the Decade is about stopping, resisting, or struggling against violence. In that case, we would remain within the mind-set that has been shaped by the Programme to Combat Racism, where it was essentially a struggle against the system of apartheid—a critical, prophetic struggle.

If, however, we are serious about *overcoming* or *transforming* violence, different demands will be made. You know from the long tradition of reflection among the Historic Peace Churches about that critical transition. Is it a decade *against* violence, or is it a decade *for* active nonviolence? The second part of the title of the Decade is important: Churches Seeking Reconciliation and Peace. It was crucial for the Central Committee in giving shape to the Decade to add this positive direction.

There was a long discussion in Johannesburg on which word to use, because "combating" violence didn't seem commensurate with the objective. When we proposed "overcoming violence," it was with awareness of the significance that this term "overcoming" has in Romans 12:21. And against that background, I am not at all unhappy that we have this term. It has not protected against misunderstanding, as if the World Council pretended that now we know how to eliminate violence from the face of the earth. I have in response to several questions in this regard said, "The main reason for starting the Decade amongst the World Council of Churches is that the churches have a problem at that point." And it is only if we begin to tackle this problem that we can begin to remove one of the sources for continuing the mentality of violent approaches to conflict.

Therefore we need a decade—at least a decade. Not that at the end of a decade we believe that everything will be resolved and we will live in peace and reconciliation. But perhaps we will have contributed to a change of consciousness, a change of mentality among the mainline churches.

That for me is one of the basic objectives of the Decade. At the deeper level, the struggle I referred to earlier will reemerge, i.e. the struggle between (1) those who see violence in the first instance as a manifestation of injustice and accept a commitment to overcoming violence as a special manifestation of the overall struggle against injustice, and (2) those who accept as a new challenge to the churches to become active agents of reconciliation and peace.

THEOLOGICAL STRUGGLES

We know all too well that struggling for justice, in many instances, may be the cause of conflict or disruption, maybe even violence; that struggling for reconciliation and peace may end up in smoothing over some of the deeper issues of injustice we also know. The charge that this is cheap reconciliation needs to remain present in our analysis. The Assembly resolution of 1983 contains the sentence, "There can be no peace anywhere unless there is justice for all, everywhere." After the conflicts in Bosnia, after the genocide in Rwanda, we cannot simply repeat that sentence unless we add that there can be no justice anywhere unless there is a minimum of peace and understanding and readiness to live in constructive dialogue amongst all, everywhere.

But beyond this tension there are further basic theological considerations. Some of the papers written for this consultation point to theological assumptions, images or ways of understanding God, ways of interpreting language about God, and conclusions drawn from the understanding of human nature. Unless we are prepared to go into the core of our ways of understanding God, of understanding the drama of salvation; unless we come to terms with the question of whether, in fact, God required sacrifice to establish justice, the violent sacrifice of Jesus on the cross; we will never come to terms with the religious mentality that occasionally has justified violence.

We have to review the ways in which we talk about *justice*. In reading one of the papers, I became aware that a new understanding of justice, in terms of restorative justice over against retributive justice, is one of the contributions that has come from the Historic Peace Churches—a contribution that I value very highly but that still has to be received within an ecumenical setting of discussion about the demands of justice.

We need a renewed discussion of *power*—power as capacity individually and in community over against power as domination.

And finally, we have to enter the difficult discussion of the *ways religion and religious loyalties have been used to legitimize violent conflict*, and why Christian and other religious communities have had so little ability to resist this political misuse and manipulation of their religious traditions. We must ask what is needed to strengthen the ability of Christian communities not to be manipulated in a nationalist or ethnocentric struggle, as happened in the former Yugoslavia.

These are the kinds of issues that require deeper analysis within the Decade to Overcome Violence. It will certainly be one of the tasks of the World Council of Churches to find ways to initiate this process of reflection, while at the same time continuing to encourage local contextual initiatives that resist and work at transforming violence.

So there is a lot of challenge involved in initiating this Decade. One might ask whether the WCC and its member churches have fully appreciated what they have accepted here— whether, in fact, they have what it takes to respond to this challenge. I hope the answer can be positive, but I think there is a deeply rooted tendency in the churches to consider violence as a phenomenon external to the churches. The churches can comment on it, the churches can try to do something about it, but ultimately violence doesn't touch their own lives. They are ready to mobilize against violence, to offer an analysis of the destructive nature of violence, and then make theological and ethical comments. But it is much more difficult to uncover the hidden roots of violence in the life of the churches themselves, and to challenge those subtle forms of justification of violence in the tradition of Christian teaching about God, Christology, and soteriology.

It's not only the tradition of just war. In fact, I would say that this is a closed chapter and we must move forward beyond this discussion. We must analyze the much more dramatic and contemporary manifestations of violence, even within the church. Therefore, our understanding of sin and redemption will have to move to the center in this continuing discernment. It is in this context that I think the sustained reflection of the Historic Peace Churches can serve as a challenge to the mainline churches in the ecumenical movement.

Finally, what do I expect the final outcome to be? I believe the WCC is ready to face the challenge. But as the challenge evolves, I think we are headed into major new internal difficulties and conflicts. This will certainly not be an easy road, as the road so far has not been an easy one. But that is why the World Council exists—to help churches address precisely those conflicts in our own traditions that we cannot expect anybody else to resolve for us, but that prevent us from rendering a more authentic and critical witness in the world and from being agents of reconciliation.

I think that members of the Central Committee and delegates at the Assembly were aware of the urgency, and also aware of the deficiencies of the World Council as an organization and of the churches at this point. There are hidden tensions, and some of them will become much more obvious.

The debate about violence as a last resort at the most recent Central Committee meeting, sparked off by the report of the moderator of the Central Committee, and the discussion around a paper about the question of protection for endangered populations in situations of violent conflict, or "humanitarian intervention," are indications of the tension that will come to the fore.[3] And it is not yet certain that we will be able to organize the debate so that in the end we will have taken a real step forward. The willingness is there, and I think a strong commitment as well.

It would be presumptuous to believe that, at the end of the Decade, we could have put an end to the culture of violence. But I hope that through the Decade we can initiate a change of consciousness, and move the witness of active, life-affirming nonviolence from the margin to the center of the life and witness of the churches. Here I use language from the framework document for the Decade that also was accepted by the Central Committee, which acknowledged that this would make it necessary that a new spirituality and a new process take shape in the ordinary life of the churches.

As churches, we can make a contribution to building a culture of peace, we can sharpen and make more visible the Christian commitment to peace and reconciliation, as marks of what it means to be church today. We will walk and struggle alongside people who approach the issue of transforming conflict from very different traditions and with varying assumptions. We should embrace them as people engaged in the same struggle for the culture of peace, because this is certainly not a Christian preserve. It is a basic demand for the whole human community at this stage in history.

NOTES

1. This phrase comes from one of the section reports of the founding Assembly of the World Council of Churches, Amsterdam, 1948.

2. Minutes, WCC Central Committee (1971), 55.

3. These remarks refer to discussions at the February, 2001, meeting of the Central Committee in Berlin, in which prolonged discussion took place regarding a study paper prepared on the issue of humanitarian military intervention. The study paper, "Just Peacemaking," which appears as an appendix in this book, was drafted by participants at the Bienenberg Consultation as a response to the WCC study paper.

Chapter 2

Space for Theological Reflection on Being (Peace-) Church

Fernando Enns

THE ECUMENICAL DECADE TO OVERCOME VIOLENCE

At the eighth Assembly of the World Council of Churches (WCC) in December 1998, delegates of the more than 330 member churches called for a Decade to Overcome Violence (2001-2010). During the Central Committee meeting of the WCC in 1999, a message was adopted and sent to the churches inviting them to participate. It included the following: "There are a number of positive and encouraging examples for congregations and churches around the world. We recognize the steady witness of monastic traditions and the Historic Peace Churches, and we want to receive anew their contribution through the Decade."[1]

This is a clear call from the WCC to the Historic Peace Churches (HPC) to share their experience in peace building, their skills in nonviolent peace training, and their theological approach to peace theology. One way of taking up this opportunity and challenge is to renew theological reflection among our own traditions—Brethren, Friends, and Mennonites. Especially in these traditions, theology does not consist first of all in interpreting written historical doctrines, but in a continuing process to explore how to *be* a people of God, the body of Christ, how to be *ecclesia* in changing times; that is, how to live faithfully according to the will of God as peacemakers. Nonviolence in these traditions is one of the continuing axioms in theology, grounded in Scripture and contextual in its application.

In line with this call, representatives from these traditions gathered in an international theological consultation of Historic Peace Churches, to collect and reflect together on their respective peace theologies.[2] The goals were—

- To inform each other, regarding the present challenges in our specific contexts. Being peace church also means constantly to reflect on the societal, political, and cultural context we live in. How do we respond theologically?
- To encourage each other, engaging in dialogue from our different cultural and denominational experiences. The three denominations within the group of HPCs share a common commitment to nonviolence, but they differ in their historic origins and developments and in some of their theological convictions.
- To develop together, as far as possible, common theological axioms for a peace theology at the beginning of the twenty-first century. Is there a common agenda?
- To pursue ecumenical dialogue, nurturing a wider network of Christian contacts within the ecumenical framework and the Decade to Overcome Violence, and welcoming a process of theological dialogue with the Faith and Order Division of the WCC.

Since a first meeting in Kansas (United States) in 1935, the HPCs have met occasionally to make their position on peace theology heard by the wider ecumenical circle. This process of meeting has also had an identity-building effect. After World War II, the so-called Puidoux Conferences (1955-1973) were a forum for discussions between "state churches" and "peace churches."[3] Topics frequently focused on peace theology in times of nuclear threat and the then-developing

Cold War. In 1991 the North American Historic Peace Church and Fellowship of Reconciliation Committee contributed to the ecumenical dialogue through publishing *A Declaration on Peace*.[4] Up to this point, this series of discussions focused strongly on the perspectives and issues of the Northern Hemisphere and the question of "just war theory" versus Christian pacifism.

Today we face a new situation. Violence is not predominantly a threat in the form of nuclear war as during the Cold War era. Rather, we see today how violence presents itself in multiple forms as a threat to human relationships and life — to all of creation — and therefore as a challenge for all Christian churches. The situation of the HPCs has also changed. We find ourselves in many different places and contexts in the world. We live in a globalized world, dominated by an economic system that excludes large parts of our own communities. Some of us live in democratic societies, where the desire for cultural and religious pluralism is a high value. Here HPCs are often called to play a role in public life and engage themselves centrally in the affairs of society. In other places, ethnic and cultural differences lead to violence and strife, and the issue of reconciliation presents itself in challenging and different ways. The issues of violence and peacebuilding can no longer be dominated by the question of just war participation or nonviolent resistance/withdrawal. Being "peace church" certainly implies more.

Today's problems are defined in cross-cultural frameworks where the complexities are different. There is a need for up-to-date exploration. The following issues seem to be core questions for reflection:

- What is the challenge for a peace theology in pluralist societies and a globalized world?
- What does it mean to be a peace church in situations of civil war?
- In what way is nonviolence a key axiom of theology?
- How is ecclesiology shaped by an emphasis on discipleship (*Nachfolge*)?
- What is our stance toward the ordering institutions of our societies?
- How do issues of personal or corporate identity, such as ethnicity and gender, influence our understanding of and calling to peace theology?
- Do we offer particular concepts of reconciliation and justice?

- What is our relationship to other Christian churches when we face similar struggles?
- How does being a "peace church" inform the way we relate to people of other faiths?

Taking up the challenge of these questions implies opening a series of discussions and starting a new process of theological reflection. Often HPCs have rightly been looked to as pioneers in peacebuilding and have been recognized for their practical nonviolent reconciliation work. Unfortunately their theological approaches have not been received with the same appreciation by most of the main-line churches. There likely are historical reasons for the rejection of these traditions. But it is also true that these theologies have not been found to be convincing in their reasoning and arguments, or at least have been found limited, by some who entered into dialogue with a great appreciation for these traditions.

The beginning of an ecumenical Decade to Overcome Violence is an invitation to engage anew in theological discernment, not so much, as I see it, as HPCs over against mainline churches, but by HPCs as family members within the world wide *oikoumene*, with a distinct witness of history and a unique theological voice. This cannot be a one-way mission, but is expected to be a real dialogue. The goal is not to make all theological thinking uniform, which would be a misleading understanding of what consensus means. Rather, ecumenical dialogue will lead to a joint theological exploration. The goal in the end is not necessarily to convince each other, but rather to better understand the other *and* oneself, and at best to identify limitations and find corrections in one's own theological thinking. Different traditions are not a problem for ecumenical Christianity, but instead express the potential and the richness of the worldwide church. It is in this spirit that the contributors of this volume start a new phase in ecumenical learning and sharing.

Today it seems more crucial than ever to look for joint theological reflection in the ecumenical realm. In this essay I will highlight two major theological study-processes within the present ecumenical movement where I see clear points of reference for a fruitful dialogue. I will respond to these study processes from the point of view of a Mennonite, standing in the Anabaptist stream of history, one particular component of the category of Historic Peace Churches.

Mennonites stand in the tradition of the "left wing" of sixteenth century reformation. Their theology is shaped by the Reformed tradition: the exclusive articles (*sola Scriptura, solus Christus, sola gratia, sola fide*) and the concept of the lordship of Christ. In general, peace theology from the Mennonite perspective could be characterized as providing a special correlation between Christology, ecclesiology, and ethics. The reconciling work in Christ is God's act of loving the enemy (Rom. 5: 8-10), and the cross is the sign of God's renunciation of the use of violence. In this revelatory work, the reconciled community recognizes its own vocation to follow the nonviolent way of Jesus, not in the sense of *imitatio*, but as participants.

Living in faithfulness to the Christian message will have consequences for the shape of the church. It is the community of those whose answer to the "yes" of God in the confession in adult baptism includes a declaration of freely chosen discipleship. Through baptism, the individual becomes fully a part of both the local church and the worldwide church of Christ. Mennonites believe the biblical witnesses constitute the central authorities in matters of faith. This does not necessarily lead to biblicism, if the local congregation is understood as a hermeneutical community. This radical view of "priesthood of all believers" has produced a congregational structure for the church and ruled out church hierarchies, although different assignments can always be identified.

A clear separation of church and state is also implied in this model. The church as the community of believers strives to embody a community ethos, which is fully anticipated in the celebration and sharing of the Lord's Supper. The historical emergence of these free church characteristics is explainable on the grounds of the anticlerical mood of sixteenth-century Europe on the one hand and the harsh persecution of the Anabaptists by magisterial and church authorities for decades on the other hand. Mennonites have retained these basic life-oriented beliefs (in various forms) and have at times sought to share them in ecumenical encounters. The two ecumenical study processes of the World Council of Churches, on ecclesiology and ethics, and the trinitarian approach to Koinonia, offer obvious points of contact and conversation with this peace church tradition.

ECCLESIOLOGY AND ETHICS

The Conciliar Process for Justice, Peace, and Integrity of Creation (JPIC), initiated at the WCC Assembly in Vancouver in 1983, and culminating in the world convocation in Seoul (1990), made clear again that we cannot suspend the question of ecclesiology if we want to agree on common ethical commitments within the ecumenical movement. Nevertheless, to start over with ecclesiology would not have been very promising, since the various views of the church differ so much from tradition to tradition, and from context to context. This has been *the* challenge for the ecumenical movement since its beginnings (cf. Toronto 1950). But in the end, the question of ethical commitment must include the question of the quality of the community that commits itself. This was one lesson from Seoul.

The follow-up to this process led to the study project on *Ecclesiology and Ethics*[5] as one of the inevitable consequences of the ongoing JPIC process. Two convictions frame the discussion. First, "ecumenical ethical reflection and action are intrinsic to the nature and life of the church." This tells us that ethics is an expression of ecclesiological convictions and that ecclesiology must be informed by the experience of ethics. Secondly, " . . . ecclesiology and Christian ethics must stay in close dialogue, each honoring and learning from the distinctive language and thought-forms of the other."[6] This implies that an ecumenically oriented understanding of the church takes into account the ethical implications of the concepts of koinonia, memory and hope, Eucharist and baptism.

The study documents stated that "all understandings of the church have affirmed its nature and vocation as a 'moral' community."[7] All of this is very much in line with Anabaptist understandings of ecclesiology; however, the term "moral community" was denounced as too reductionist and too moralistic by some other representatives within the ecumenical family. The second consultation in the study process took this concern seriously by trying to explore the *function* of the term as "moral formation."[8] Especially in today's context, churches are called to provide ethical resources for their members and the wider societies of which they are a part. The challenge remains to describe the relationship between the nature of the church and its social action, which this second consultation stated in a qualified way: "In the church's own struggles for justice, peace and integrity of creation, the *esse* of the church is at stake."

Moral formation is a nurtured process, out of which grow a distinct identity and a unique understanding of community. "To be in the Christian community is to be shaped in a certain way of life." Since, in postmodern societies, identities are formed by a variety of cultural *Lebenswelten* (life-worlds), a critical process of identity-building formation within the church over against general tendencies in the larger society is very much needed. This does not necessarily build a constant counter-culture—church members are also members of the nation state and of society—but identifies and secures the therapeutic function of the church within society. Healthy societies, especially in pluralistic forms, depend on religious institutions that carry within themselves the notion of such a self-understanding.

The study process noted that spiritual aspects of the life of the church play a major role in this, if their ethical implications are understood. The moral community finds its grounding in worship, prayer, baptism, and Eucharist, because it is here that "the story of salvation is reenacted."[9] Spiritual reenaction will prevent the church from sheer activism and moralism. Baptism and Eucharist were suggested as such points of reference: baptism as an initiation into discipleship is a witness to the values of the gospel; Eucharist is the sacrament for the healing of broken community.[10] Here joy, suffering, and hope converge as an answer to God's call for just relationships.

The spirituality of the different elements of worship were seen to serve as "bridges" between ecclesiology and ethics, because in them the eschatological dimension of participating in the kingdom of God is anticipated. It is through the spiritual life—understood as the work of the *Christus praesens*—that the church recalls its very being in relation to God and listens anew to its vocation: to participate in the work of the Holy Spirit. The community we experience in the Eucharist is of the same quality as the community of moral action, since both are anamnesis, active memory. Both are an expression of the certainty that God will fulfill his promises of the kingdom. Eucharist becomes a constant challenge in the search for just, healthy, relationship building in the social, economic, and political sphere. If a eucharistic community does not result in ethical manifestations, it becomes spiritualistic. If an ethical community is not grounded in spirituality, it becomes purely moralistic.

Anabaptists could enter this discussion by contributing their view of the church as moral community as well as their understanding that nonviolent ethics grows from a distinct community. Such a theology does not see the church as the final fulfillment of the kingdom of God, but as a people who anticipate within their community a new quality of relationships. This itself becomes a witness: to live according to the will of God in practicing nonviolent relationships, striving for justice and caring for all creation, *beyond* the boundaries of the small community! Mennonites have never allowed themselves to separate ethics from ecclesiology in their theology. The greater risk has always been to overestimate the possibilities that humans can bring about the kingdom of God and to underestimate the evil within human nature. Here ecumenical encounters can offer a needed corrective, by reminding us that the church is more than the local gathering of its members. It is the worldwide body of Christ, dependent first of all on the forgiving and reconciling grace of God. Only by acknowledging this dependency are the church and its individual members able to participate in the work of the Holy Spirit.

THE NATURE AND THE PURPOSE OF THE CHURCH: A TRINITARIAN APPROACH TO KOINONIA

In its latest study document on ecclesiology, the WCC introduces and proposes anew the term "Koinonia" to explore the nature *and* purpose of the church.[11] The advantage of this term is the possibility it gives us to express different dimensions of community:

- Koinonia with God as participation in the immanent trinity;
- Koinonia with the church;
- Koinonia as a community of churches;
- Koinonia with people of other faiths;
- Koinonia with all of creation.

In the New Testament Koinonia can express participation, sharing, taking part, acting together—a contract-like relationship of mutual accountability.[12] The term is also used in key situations such as the reconciliation between the apostles Paul and Peter, James and John (Gal. 2:9), the contribution for the poor (Rom. 15:26; 2 Cor. 8:4), or to describe the witness of the church (Acts 2:42-45).

Koinonia is an expression of the relation between the members of a community in time and space. Through baptism they become a community with one another, as well as a community with God (Rom. 6:4-11; 1 Cor. 12:13). In listening to God's word and in the celebration of the Eucharist (1 Cor. 11:17-16), they become God's body. This body is a community of discipleship, which finds different expressions:

- Being grounded together in the faith of the triune God (Rom. 4);
- Sharing the apostolic teachings and experiencing community in common prayer and the breaking of bread (Acts 2:42);
- Demonstrating authentic discipleship and readiness to partake in Christ's suffering (Phil. 3:10; 2 Cor. 4:7-11; 1 Pet. 4:13; 5:1);

- Sharing mutual joys and needs (2 Cor. 1:6-7; Heb. 10:33);
- Standing with courage for the truth (Gal. 2:5);
- Serving each other in love and mutual sharing of material and spiritual gifts (Rom. 15:26-27; 2 Cor. 8:1-15; Gal. 5:13);
- Proclaiming the gospel to all people (Matt. 28:19-20; Acts 2:14ff.);
- Caring about harmony within God's creation (Col. 1:14-18, Rom. 8:19-21);
- And anticipating the coming glory (Rom. 8:17).[13]

Koinonia with God is given through the Holy Spirit (1 John 1:3). Paul speaks about the relationship of the believers and their Lord as being "in Christ" (2 Cor. 5:17) and about Jesus Christ as the one who is present in the believer through the Holy Spirit. Therefore, the community is itself a gift of God, "whereby God draws humanity into the orbit of the generous, divine, self-giving love which flows between the persons of the Holy Trinity."[14]

Since the seventh Assembly of the WCC in Canberra (1991), a rediscovered trinitarian theology has become increasingly important in ecumenical thinking. It is an overall framework for doing theology in the ecumenical realm, complementing the christocentric approach of former decades.[15] For the Anabaptist and free-church traditions in general, the doctrine of the Trinity has never played a comparable role. The reasons are manifold. These traditions have emphasized the Jesus-narrative over metaphysical speculations; their priority has been the search for a life of discipleship within the church rather than considerations about the nature of God; and they have read the classical trinitarian thinking in the context of the constantinian shift, which has become a metaphor for the "captivity" of the church by the state. This has led them to downplay the confessions of the early church, not denying their validity, but also not using them frequently.[16]

For the ecumenical discussion, on the other hand, the concept of Koinonia and its trinitarian foundation has now become the leading concept.[17] Here we find a model of community that preserves unity within diversity while at the same time preventing uniformity. The perichoretic relationship of mutual penetration among the three divine persons becomes the model. This idea secures the personhood of the individual, while affirming on the other hand that the individual is constituted by relationship. The quality of community depends on the secured personhood of individuals. But there is no person without relationship and no relationship without persons.[18] It is through this paradoxical form of language that we can speak of the divine persons without hierarchical implications or subordination. Person and society, independence and relationship, definition and openness, identity and communication can be grasped complementarily. From this line of thinking one can then describe the church as a model of "differentiated community."[19]

The quality of relationships in this Koinonia model can also be applied to the relationship between God and human beings. Humans participate in the reality of God and become Koinonia-like creatures. Through this participation our being as a person is constituted and, therefore, we are able to build communities. The individual dignity of humans as well as the reference to community depend on participation in the divine relationship.[20] The Holy Spirit transforms the community of individuals into the body of Christ. The Spirit inhabits the church and stays beyond it at the same time. This constitutes the Koinonia of all people, who become persons to each other in relationship.

With this model we are also able to describe the community of churches in their various contextual and confessional expressions, since the catholicity of the church is present in every local church. This ecclesial quality of Koinonia takes place in the local gathering "in his name" (Matt. 18:20); in every place, universality and particularity are being held together.

IMPLICATIONS FOR THE PEACE CHURCH

For the Anabaptist tradition, the aspect of community is crucial in different dimensions:

- The emphasis on the local gathering as the hermeneutic community,
- The community-ethics of the visible church which claims to live as a prophetic sign in society,
- And the idea of unity in ethical commitment over against an individualistic approach to soteriology, which would neglect the commitment to justice and peace for all of society.

This is an experience-oriented approach, which could be understood as completing the ontological description of trinitarian Koinonia in ecumenical theology. On the other hand, the challenge for an Anabaptist ecclesiology has always been to look beyond the absolute locality of the church and include its visible catholicity. At times one can have the impression that there is almost a sacramental understanding of the local congregation in some Anabaptist groups. How can we prevent a merely voluntaristic approach to ecclesiology, a community of like-minded persons, in which plurality is not really thinkable? How can this Koinonia extend across the boundaries of the small local community, including relationships to others and to all of creation?

Mennonites have tended to ground their ecclesiology in Christology, which at times has led to Christomonism. In this view, the ruling power of Christ provides a relativizing dynamic against all other authorities, upholding the equality of all under the ethical demands of a disciplined community. In the trinitarian model of community, by contrast, the understanding of church as subject is overcome, and a model to relate to others who are different is envisioned. Individuals become visible.

This could offer a corrective while still containing the ethical and communal intentions of being a peace church. The church lives in contrast to its surrounding society because it is founded in a different quality of community. It is not separated from society, but introduces this community beyond its ecclesial boundaries. Ethical commitments find root in the secured dignity of the individual, who is part of the community, but not in uniformity. The congregation is not constituted through a special ministry but by the interdependent *charismata* of its members. Such a community cannot be defined in exclusivist terms, since the in-dwelling Spirit is free from institutions and God the creator is "in Koinonia" with all of creation, the Son incarnated in this world. The local congregation is not limited to itself, although it is still centered around its confession of Christ.

It is here that the peace church can find a foundation for its calling to nonviolence, if violence is in general understood as the destruction of just relationships. In trinitarian thinking one can find a differentiated model of community, not exclusivistic but identity-building, not constituted by ethical behavior, but enabling accountability. From a peace church perspective one must then of course speak against any tendencies to a monarchic, monistic, or modalistic interpretation, but in favor of a perichoretic trinitarian understanding. [21]

On this theological ground, the peace church could understand itself as part of the *una, sancta, catholica et apostolica*, visible in worship (*leiturgia*), service (*diakonia*), and witness (*martyria*). From a peace church perspective these could be described as the constitutive *notae externae* of the church.

In my understanding we are just at the beginning of an exciting process of theologizing in the ecumenical realm. To overcome the simplistic confrontation and comparison of church traditions whose characteristic faith-formulas have been shaped by historical and theological confrontation, we need to develop a common language that enables us to value the treasures that each tradition has kept in its own story and theology. The framework of the Decade to Overcome Violence provides us with a space which invites us to renew our theological encounter. The way we approach each other in our different historical, cultural, and contextual experiences, stories, and theologies will also test our claim to be a faithful, visible peace church.

NOTES

1. WCC Central Committee, "Minutes of the Fiftieth Meeting, Geneva, Switzerland, 26 August-3 September 1999," 188.

2. The ad hoc planning group for the conference at Bienenberg in June, 2001, consisted of Mennonites Fernando Enns, Robert Herr, and Judy Zimmerman Herr, Church of the Brethren member Sara Speicher, and Quaker Douglas Gwyn.

3. Donald F. Durnbaugh, ed., *On Earth Peace: Discussions on War/Peace-Issues Between Friends, Mennonites, Brethren, and European Churches, 1935-1975* (Elgin, Ill.: Brethren Press, 1978).

4. Douglas Gwyn, George Hunsinger, Eugene F. Roop, John Howard Yoder, *A Declaration on Peace: In God's People the World's Renewal Has Begun.* A contribution to ecumenical dialogue sponsored by Church of the Brethren, Fellowship of Reconciliation, Mennonite Central Committee, Friends General Conference (Scottdale, PA: Herald Press, 1991).

5. All documents (*Costly Unity, Costly Commitment,* and *Costly Obedience*) in *Ecclesiology and Ethics: Ecumenical Ethical Engagement, Moral Formation, and the Nature of the Church,* ed. Thomas F. Best and Martin Robra (Geneva: WCC, 1997). Cf. also Duncan Forrester, *The True Church and Morality: Reflections on Ecclesiology and Ethics* (Geneva: WCC, 1997). Forrester notes: "In some cases the same causes that have brought people together in a unity of struggle have also caused divisions in the church, as in the German church struggle in the 1930s or the more recent struggle against apartheid in South Africa, divisions which in some ways may have been necessary, and have pointed the way to a more genuine fellowship or koinonia. . . . This debate . . . is far from concluded and . . . is of the greatest importance for the integrity of the church in its search for unity and faithful discipleship." Cf. also Lewis S. Mudge, *The Church as Moral Community: Ecclesiology and Ethics in Ecumenical Debate* (New York: Continuum, 1998). Mudge strengthens a sacramental understanding of the church, which combines ecclesiology and ethics. He develops this further to a concept of the church as *oikos* and *polis* in eschatological vision.

6. Best and Robra, *Ecclesiology and Ethics,* ix.

7. *Costly Unity.*

8. Cf. *Costly Commitment*, 72ff.

9. *Costly Obedience*, 66ff. Larry Rasmussen had pointed out the original ethical connotation of *leiturgia*: "It meant the public charge to perform a particular public service, or *diakonia*," in Larry Rasmussen, "Moral Community and Moral Formation," *Costly Commitment*, 56.

10. *Costly Obedience*, 64.

11. *The Nature and the Purpose of the Church*, F & O Paper 181 (Geneva: WCC, 1998).

12. Cf. Horst Balz and Gerhard Schneider, eds., *Exegetisches Wörterbuch zum Neuen Testament*, 2. rev. ed., vol. 2 (Stuttgart u.a.: Kohlhammer, 1992, 1981), 747-755. Cf. also *The Nature and the Purpose of the Church*.

13. Cf. *Auf dem Weg zur Koinonia im Glauben, Leben und Zeugnis: Ein Diskussionspapier*, F&O Paper 161 (Geneva: WCC, 1993), 21ff.

14. *The Nature and the Purpose of the Church*, 54.

15. Cf. *On the Way to Fuller Koinonia*. Official Report of the 5th World Conference on Faith and Order, ed. Thomas Best and Günther Gassman (Genera: WCC, 1994) and *The Nature and the Purpose of the Church*.

16. One of the promising reinterpretations within the Anabaptist tradition is James Reimer, *Mennonites and Classical Theology: Dogmatic Foundations for Christian Ethics* (Kitchener, Ont.: Pandora Press, 2001).

17. I have explored this further in Fernando Enns, *Friedenskirche in der Ökumene* (Göttingen: Vandenhoeck & Ruprecht, 2003).

18. Cf. Jürgen Moltmann, *Trinität und Reich Gottes: Zur Gotteslehre* (München: Kaiser, 1980).

19. Miroslav Volf, *Trinität und Gemeinschaft: Eine ökumenische Ekklesiologie* (Neukirchen-Vluyn: Neukirchener, 1996), 179. (English: *After Our Likeness*)

20. Cf. the articles in *Persons, Divine and Human*, ed. Christoph Schwöbel and Colin E. Gunton (Edinburgh: T & T Clark, 1991).

21. Cf. Colin E. Gunton, *The One, the Three and the Many: God, Creation and the Culture of Modernity*, The 1992 Bampton Lectures (Cambridge, England: Cambridge University Press, 1993).

INTERPRETING GLOBALIZATION: QUESTIONS OF POWER

Chapter 3

Globalization
and Claiming Truth

Neal Blough

*T*he Christian story of salvation points us toward helpful clues for how we may engage the questions of peacemaking and globalization. I argue here that peace and peacemaking are a central element of the biblical understanding of salvation, and that this salvation narrative of peace may in large part be understood as a response to the first story of globalization—the account of the Tower of Babel. Following that, I examine how the salvation narrative of peace can be related to our understanding of truth claims.[1]

THE BIBLICAL SALVATION NARRATIVES
IN LIGHT OF GLOBALIZATION AND PLURALISM

The Tower of Babel and the Call of Abraham

The story of the Tower of Babel, recounted in Genesis 11:1-9, provides a conclusion to the biblical account of primeval history. It describes the last great judgment that befell humanity, in a sequence that begins with the Fall in Genesis 3 and the "sons of God" episode in Genesis 6:1-4.[2]

The modern interpreter may find the juxtaposition of the "table of nations" (Ch. 10) and the Tower of Babel story to be incongruous since they seem to offer two incompatible accounts of the origins of the nations and their different languages. Nevertheless, the stories told in Genesis 10 and 11 are to be understood in a complementary rather than a contradictory way. Following the table of nations, where cultural and racial diversity are seen as part of a good creation, Babel represents a continuation of the Fall—a first attempt at human imperialism and the building of a civilization on the basis of a unique and exclusive language, that is, the culmination of the story of primeval rebellion against God.[3]

Various aspects of the narrative reinforce this reading. The people involved in the imperialistic project are migrating and choose to settle at a place called Shinar. Jacques Ellul has argued that Shinar means nothing other than "place of sin."[4] The people of Shinar formulate and pursue their cultural, technological and architectural goals without any reference to God: "Come, let us make bricks. . . . Come, let us build ourselves a city and a tower. . . . Let us make a name for ourselves." According to Ellul, the two main aspects of the project are the city and "making a name."[5] The tower embodies the spiritual pride and rebellion inherent in the project, and "making a name for oneself" could thus be explained as the attempt to construct human identity in relation to our own technological and cultural projects without reference to God.

The Tower of Babel is not the same as globalization in the twenty-first century. But the central themes are unmistakably present: a cultural and political imperialism based on urbanization, technology, and language. The common language does not help communication; rather, it represents an attempt to impose a universal point of view and way of speech upon humanity. It is a totalitarian ideology, enforced through political, moral, and religious centralization—a city with only one way of thinking and talking, reaching heavenward under the authority of a single power.[6]

As history has confirmed many times since, cultural, technological, and ideological imperialism is transitory. At Babel God "came down" and intervened, thus setting limits to the cultural and political processes of creation.[7] At Babel humanity wanted to create its own identity based on its own projects, but the result was confusion. The unique language splintered into many. People no longer understood each other, but were separated, divided, and scattered. The world became a place of "noncommunication," where peoples, cultures, races, and languages were and continue to be a source of conflict and violence.

The biblical version of primeval history thus ends bleakly in a world of scattered peoples, cultures, and languages, prone to continual conflict and incapable of mutual understanding.

From this point on, we find the beginning of the biblical tradition's salvation narrative, told as the call of Abraham, the emerging response to a world squeezed into the mold of the Tower of Babel.[8] The contrasts between the two stories are too numerous and too obvious for us not to recognize a close relationship.[9] Babel represents the scattering of all peoples, the whole world. Genesis 12 is universal: "By you all the families of the earth shall be blessed." Genesis 12 is a universal project being loosed in history by a gracious creator God who refuses to accept humanity's rejection.

The Abrahamic salvation narrative thus originates as a response to a world that is not at peace, a world in which cultural, national, and linguistic barriers are a source of separation and "noncommunication" between families, peoples, and nations. The biblical narrative of salvation promises a blessing to these scattered families who no longer understand one another. Christian theology interprets this narrative in the light of Jesus of Nazareth.

The Peace of the Messiah

Many New Testament salvation texts take on additional meaning when read in light of the Babel-Abraham narratives. Throughout biblical history, the universal and political thrust of salvation overcomes the scattering and confusion of Babel. Indeed, the very reason for the coming of the Messiah and the establishment of the messianic community was to bring "shalom" to the peoples.

One of the most explicit and dramatic examples of this persistent theme is the Pentecost experience in Jerusalem, in which the "noncommunication" between peoples begins to come to an end. Luke, the writer of this account, wanted his readers to understand that the coming of the Holy Spirit to the first community of disciples enabled people who spoke different languages to hear the good news in their own tongue (cf. Acts 2: 6-12).

The coming of the Messiah and the pouring out of the Spirit immediately began to break down linguistic and cultural barriers. In this particular case, the overcoming of barriers occurred not between different races or peoples, but among Jewish believers who spoke different languages. Very quickly, however, the question of different races and classes had to be addressed. "How do we live together with strangers or enemies?" became the first major ecclesiological and missiological question of the first century. The answer to this question was clear in the missionary practice and theologizing of the early communities. Peace had been made through the death and resurrection of the proclaimed Messiah, Jesus of Nazareth. This new peace was to be implemented concretely and visibly in a new social structure called "*ekklesia*," or the body of Christ.

The very meaning of salvation was thereby formulated in relation to the Babel-Abraham tradition. The New Testament epistles point to the Messiah as an altogether new answer. Because of what happened in Christ, divisions that usually separate people—race, class, gender—no longer have the power to separate and scatter. That divisive power has been met and usurped. It is not that race, class, or gender no longer exist or are denied; but they are relativized. A new identity brings into being a new community, and the blessing to the nations becomes a concrete and historical reality. In Jesus, the blessing to the nations promised to Abraham becomes tangible in a distinct way (cf. Gal. 3: 27-28).

In 2 Corinthians (5:16-21), Paul uses a somewhat different vocabulary to describe salvation. In Christ, he writes, there is a "new creation"; God has brought about "reconciliation" and entrusted the "ministry of reconciliation" to the new community. This is not directly related to Abraham, as it is in Galatians or Romans, but "reconciliation" here clearly suggests that boundaries of race, class, and gender are relativized and overcome.[10] The church is a community of reconciliation to whom the ministry of reconciliation has been conferred.

Paul's writings (in Galatians, Romans, and 2 Corinthians) are clear. In these new communities where the discriminating character of barriers was being overcome, the blessing to the nations promised in Genesis was becoming a historical reality. A new way of living, of construing personal and social identity, had been accomplished "in Christ." Salvation in Christ is thus linked to the Abraham narrative. And just as the promise to Abraham came in response to the sociopolitical realities of the ideology of Babel, so the new life in Christ takes on a sociopolitical reality as well.

Other New Testament texts strengthen the links between salvation in Christ, peace, and a new social reality. In Ephesians (2: 14-18), for example, Christ's death and resurrection is interpreted in terms of peace which must be understood in sociopolitical terms. Those who were "far away" and those who were "near" reflect actual boundaries that existed within the sociopolitical structures of the Pax Romana.[11] The creation of this new sociopolitical reality brought about in Christ leads to a very real and concrete expression of peace within history which, in turn, has a mission to extend that peace within the world.

When the New Testament describes salvation in Christ, it gives cosmic significance to that which materializes in human history. As seen in Ephesians, the victory of Christ takes shape through the creation of the new community. This same victory is also posited in universal and cosmic terms, where the resurrected Christ is seated "at the right hand in the heavenly realms, far above all rule and authority and power and dominion" (Eph. 1:20-21).

This kind of cosmic concern, reaching back all the way to creation, is also found in the epistle to the Colossians, where the Christ-event and the cross are spoken of in terms of making peace and reconciliation (Col. 1:15-20). The presence of cosmic elements in this context does not suggest a dehistoricized or nonpolitical version of salvation, peace, and reconciliation. Not only is Babel being healed in the life of the new community, as seen in Galatians, Romans, or Ephesians, but all of creation is renewed and restored once again through the death, the resurrection, and the sending of the Spirit of Christ.[12]

The reuniting of the nations also has eschatological significance in the New Testament documents. Not only do peace and the new community become new realities here and now through the work of Christ in the present, but the healing of the nations is the very goal toward which history is moving. God's final salvation will bring together what Babel separated and scattered. The city of Babel scattered the nations, but the new city of God will bring them together (Rev. 21:23-27). A river of life flows through the city, and the tree of life—which replaces the tree in the garden of Eden—yields fruit for the "healing of the nations."

WHY DOGMA?

Trinitarian and Incarnational Christology

It may be noted that the New Testament texts I have cited are more closely related to "traditional" Christology and soteriology. They speak of Christ's death on the cross *pro nobis* as a source of salvation; of the pre-existent Christ, "the image of the invisible God . . . in whom all things were created," who is "before all things," in whom "the fullness of God dwelt"; and of the resurrected Christ seated "at the right hand of the Father in the heavenly realms, far above all rule and authority." In these texts we find what is often called a "high Christology," even though they cannot be understood outside of or apart from the larger salvation narrative context evoked in the previous section.

Mennonites have tended not to be creedal, if that means that the classical Nicean or Chalcedonian formulas are the automatic point of departure or absolute means of verification for christological statements. In the current debate among Mennonites concerning the usefulness of traditional christological creeds, some have suggested caution in adopting formulas that have their origin in constantinian and violence-accommodating forms of Christianity.[13] This reluctance to use creeds as a starting-point rather than Scripture may be well-founded, but at the same time a "high Christology" is a crucial way of articulating a theology of nonviolence and can provide the spiritual resources necessary to sustain ecclesial nonviolent practice and presence in the world. As Stanley Hauerwas has suggested, "The Mennonite understanding of the church's position toward the world is possible only if such a church is sustained by the kind of theology found in the church fathers, and in particular in that confession we call the Nicene Creed."[14]

The question, however, still remains: Is it possible to elaborate a theology of peacemaking by claiming the uniqueness of Christ and the ultimate meaning of his death and resurrection for the history of the world? How does one make peace among communities while at the same time claiming ultimate truth for your own community's way of understanding the world, for your own theology's understanding of God? Have not the ultimate truth-claims of religions or ideologies encouraged violence among communities and nations? Are such truth-claims any different from the "one-language" imperialism that separates, scatters, and creates the Babel phenomenon of noncommunication?

One clear consequence of the postmodern rejection of modernity is the recognition that our world is divided into communities and groups that live according to their convictions, and that these convictions are inevitably grounded in the history and tradition of any given community.[15] Contrary to the claims of modernity, there is no epistemological starting "from scratch." While reason and logic play important roles in the formulation and justification of our convictions, in the end they are based on premises that cannot ultimately be proven, but only imposed and fought about—or shared, discussed, and respected in a common search for truth. The history of our world can thus be seen as the arena where different convictions and communities live together and where different worldviews come into contact with each other—sometimes in harmony, but more often in conflict and confrontation.

But of course no person or community can function on any basis other than the assumption that its convictions are indeed true. And even though we can and should demonstrate the solidity of our convictions by rational arguments, we eventually come to the place where we need to say: "This we hold to be true. This is what gives coherence and meaning to our experience of history and the world." Ultimately, there are no convictions, secular or religious, without some kind of faith commitment.[16]

The motivation to bring peace among groups, peoples, or religions by relativizing their competing truth claims is an honorable one, but not without its own serious problems. After all, such an approach assumes that violence is wrong and that peace is right, or at least better. Such convictions, however, are not shared by all people or groups. That is, to claim from the outset that violence is wrong and that peace is right is a conviction about the way the world is or should be. But since such a conviction implies that other ways of conceiving the world that justify or permit violence are wrong, it becomes simply another truth-claim. Relativism is therefore not a secure starting point for overcoming violence. We need to find a way to relativize those aspects of convictions which bring about or justify violence without abandoning the search for truth.[17]

If we care about peace and peacemaking, we do so on the basis of convictions about how the world is or how the world is to be. A nonviolent Christology begins in the biblical narrative of Jesus and the cross. It takes seriously the Sermon on the Mount and the teachings of the New Testament. Nevertheless, it recognizes that ethics and narrative alone are not enough. As in the New Testament, a nonviolent Christology needs to integrate an understanding of the incarnation and the Trinity if it is to sustain the faith and practice of peacemaking communities in a violent world. A community that wants to contribute to peacemaking must also pay close attention to the way its convictions are formulated and communicated, and to how they relate to praxis.[18] Jon Sobrino, a Latin American theologian of liberation, has written, "We need words and an authoritative word if we are to give expression to our faith and share it through reciprocal communication. . . . Dogmatic formulations are . . . a historical necessity for a church composed of human beings."[19]

Why dogma? And why christological dogma? Not because it says everything that must be said or because it will be used every day. Certainly not because we yearn for some abstract formulation of our faith that has no relationship to everyday concrete reality. In this essay I purposely started with history and narrative, which is, after all, how the early church arrived at dogmatic or theological formulations, and which offers a model for us as well. Christological dogma does not tell us anything more about Jesus than the New Testament does, and thus needs to be interpreted through the New Testament narratives.[20]

Dogma has to do with the formulation of our convictions and how they relate to the convictions of others, especially those beliefs that we do not share with everyone else. "The intention behind dogma," Sobrino argues, "is not to exhaust the content of faith but to defend some aspect of it, some aspect regarded as basic, against some error that threatens it."[21]

What is the possible error? It is not, at least in the West, the temptation to be "dogmatic" or to impose our faith on others. To the contrary. Precisely because we care about peace; because we respect other people and their convictions; because we remember how doctrinal orthodoxy was used to control, exclude, and kill; because of the embarrassing history of Christendom; because religions do not have a good record of tolerance and nonviolence; because of the postmodern context and its suspicion of truth-claims being used to grab power— precisely because of all this we are tempted to think that a clear christological foundation for peacemaking is an embarrassing relic from the past and probably more of a hindrance than a help.

The possible error is to confuse the notion of "peace" with the idea that "no conviction or tradition may or should make the claim of being true for everyone." Ultimate truth-claims can lead and have led to violence. Nevertheless, a well-constructed and non-constantinian peace Christology allows us to ground peace in an ultimate conviction of "how the world is" while simultaneously denying the possibility of using violence to defend or impose our convictions. It will relativize those causes for which people have readily killed in the past while at the same time allowing us to claim that peace and nonviolence are "true" and correspond to both the intention and goals of human history.

A trinitarian and incarnational Christology makes several key claims about the world and history that are of utmost importance to peacemaking. First, the doctrine of a transcendent creator God relativizes the exclusive claims of those aspects of creation that can easily become idols. The doctrine of the Fall helps us understand how family, race, language, money, country, and self have all become criteria to justify and use violence. The biblical critique of idolatry makes it clear that one may not attribute ultimate meaning to *anything* in the created realm. Believing in a creator God who is related to but "above" the created world means that believers cannot attribute ultimate status to any institution, group, thing, or person that is a part of the created realm. Only God deserves such worship. That is why Abraham and Sarah needed to leave "family and country" to get beyond the logic of Babel. The transcendence of God, the Fall of humanity, and the ensuing critique of idolatry are all fundamental for peacemakers.

Second, a trinitarian and incarnational Christology also help us deal with the question of evil. The narrative of the Fall, which ends up with Babel, tells us that evil has its origin within history and is therefore not part of the original and good creation. Evil entered the world because of human choice and desire. Creation was accomplished by God's Word and not by violence, and therefore violence is neither inevitable nor part of God's intention for human life and history.[22] Nevertheless, evil precedes our coming into the world and has become a power that manifests itself in all realms of life and culture, including nature itself. On the one hand, we maintain that evil has its origin in human choice; yet on the other hand, being born into a world of evil is not something that can be chosen.

The doctrine of the incarnation tells us how God has dealt with evil. Because God is love and refuses to accept human rejection, God chose to enter into history and to become a part of it in God's very flesh and blood. By an act of self-giving love God chose to assume evil, to break the vicious cycle of evil and violence, and therefore to defeat its power. The cross of Jesus demonstrates how God deals with evil, for it is God at work.

No other religion or worldview has this understanding of the world, of evil and of how it has been nonviolently overcome. René Girard's work clearly illustrates how the cross of Christ, especially in relation to violence, offers a unique perspective among other world religions or mythologies.[23]

If God is the ultimate source of reality, if God is fully present and active in the Christ-event and chose to deal with evil in this specific nonviolent manner, it means that nonviolent love is part of the fabric of the universe. And it means that we are to respond to evil in a similar manner. The resurrection of Christ attests to God's approval of the "way of the cross," and demonstrates that the power of evil and death has been defeated. Nothing, not even death, can stop or hinder the working out of nonviolent love in human history.

The resurrection therefore confirms the divinity of Jesus—his ultimate identity with the God who sent him—and is to be understood as God's approval of the cross as the way in which the powers of evil and death are defeated.[24] If we disregard evil, if we are unwilling to confront the dark side of our own selves or to recognize that the solution for evil comes from beyond us, our efforts at peacemaking will probably end in despair.

Our discussion about dogma can now be related to what was previously said about convictions. Convictions are important for how we live and act. Because we see according to our convictions, that is, our Christology, having the right convictions is the first step in formulating our ethics. The incarnation—God's self-giving, nonviolent love on the cross—demonstrates how we become associated with what God has done. It shows how we become "children of God."[25]

Two observations will close this discussion of Christology. First, our doctrine of Christ must be capable of being interpreted anew in each generation. Attending to our convictions implies a constant review of the meaning of dogma in our own context.[26] The questions of Nicea and Chalcedon may not be the most pressing ones for today. The meaning of Christology is always bound to time and space. But if the creeds make valid statements—as the church has confessed throughout the centuries—then they have important contemporary implications as well.

From a peace church perspective, the possibility of historical interpretation also implies that christological dogma has been wrongfully used and interpreted in certain times and places. In Sobrino's words, "The Chalcedonian formula continues to be true insofar as there really continue to be followers of Jesus, people whose concrete discipleship professes Jesus as the Christ. To put it positively, the ultimate verification of the truth of Chalcedon's christological dogma lies in the course of later history."[27]

Second, in the Christian context, our ultimate convictions should lead us inevitably to worship, to doxology. "A dogma," writes Sobrino, "is a doxological formulation that marks the culmination of a whole process of Christian living and Christian reflective thinking."[28]

An incarnational Christology claims that in Jesus we see God. But to claim God as the origin and source of everything, including ourselves and the peace we long for, also means that we are not the ultimate source of our identity and our knowledge. To speak of God in such a way purports that the modern or postmodern ego must be epistemologically relativized. We know because we are known, and truly to know means to acknowledge that we are known: "Thus dogma, insofar as it is a doxological statement about God in himself, presupposes the surrender of the thinking 'I' to the mystery of God."[29]

Ecclesiology: Neither Jew nor Greek

Babel is fundamentally a political problem: the peoples of the world are dispersed and incapable of understanding one another. The good news of salvation in the New Testament—understood as a response to Babel—is also political. Through the peace of Christ racial, social, and sexual barriers are broken down by those living in a new community. For the peace churches this insight into the political nature of salvation extends to include the refusal of violence and the embrace of active peacemaking as essential to the church's mission in the world.

When we think of being peacemakers, we must begin with the concrete existence of the Christian church. The first reason is biblical and theological. The biblical account of primeval history describes humanity as comprising scattered and dispersed peoples who do not understand each other. The Fall, or the introduction of evil into history, is presented as having a concrete embodiment in social and political structures. Biblical salvation history begins as a conscious response to this situation and in Abraham identifies the beginning of a new people, a new sociopolitical reality, called to be a blessing to the scattered families of Babel. The peace of Christ, established through the cross and resurrection of Jesus, finds its most vivid and important expression in the new community of peace ("neither Jew nor Greek, slave nor free, male nor female"). Therefore, a biblical understanding of peace and peacemaking is first of all—but certainly not only—a new community sent into the world with a theology and practice of peace and forgiveness.

Throughout its history the church has not always had this self-understanding of its message, teaching, and practice. Few if any traditional ecclesiologies regard the "neither Jew nor Greek, slave nor free, male nor female" of the epistles as a constituent element of the church's very nature. Mennonites, for example, have defined the church as "people of God" or "community," but have not excelled in the creation of multiracial or multiethnic congregations. Would not such an ecclesiological redefinition be a helpful beginning for understanding the political nature of salvation and the church's existence in the world? Could not this "anti-Babel" peace element of the gospel become part of our ecumenical discussions on the nature of the church? If peace and peacemaking were incorporated in our ecclesiology in this way, the worldwide church could conceivably be one of the most powerful forces for fostering peace on the planet.

Another reason for keeping the church central is that the concrete embodiment of convictions shapes history. Mennonites, Quakers, and Brethren have a long history of being minorities. Sociologists have noted that minorities with strong convictions can make important differences in terms of how a given society evolves or develops, in part because such groups cannot impose their points of view but must rather convince by dialogue and example.[30] The concrete positive effects of embodying the gospel can also be discerned in the history of churches in majority situations. Despite the constantinian perversions of the Christian gospel, many scholars would argue that the concrete embodiment of the gospel in the lives of Christians throughout the centuries of Christendom has made important positive differences in the course of history.[31]

Finally, peace churches—at least the Mennonites—need to be more serious about ecumenical dialogue and relationships. If the church is truly "neither Jew nor Greek," if it is a community of peace, then according to the early creeds it must also be "one, holy, catholic, and apostolic." Church history did not commence on the fringes of the Reformation in Zurich in the sixteenth century. Our own existence and tradition is the result of brokenness and conflict within the western church. Yet I have seen little awareness or lamenting within Mennonite circles about the brokenness of Christ's body in the world. The current dialogue among historic peace churches and the significant contact with the World Council of Churches serves as an important reminder that we have often been absent in peacemaking efforts among Christians and that a considerable number of the world's Christians outside the circles of the WCC (whether Evangelical, Pentecostal, or Catholic) are not yet direct participants in our conversations.

Mission, Peace, and Convictions

Christology and ecclesiology cannot be disassociated from mission. The Abrahamic response to the Babel narrative includes the formation of a new people who will be a blessing to all the families of the world.[32] The new community has received a mission. Peace in Christ, embodied in the community of "neither Jew nor Greek," exists for the benefit of the entire world.

As Mark Gopin has recently demonstrated, such a sense of mission is not evident to all Mennonites involved in peacemaking. At least part of the reticence to be involved in mission is the perceived arrogance of the undertaking itself and a corresponding commitment to pluralism.[33]

Nevertheless, peacemakers become involved in the lives of others. Their desire is to bring "peace" into concrete sociopolitical situations of conflict or war. Only with great difficulty could such efforts not be understood as sharing a truth claim about how the world is or should be. Those who do so believe that peace is better than war (often firmly enough to risk their very lives); they are convinced that mutual understanding is better than violence, that the world would be a better place if people live in peace.

As I have attempted to show, Christian peacemaking flows out of some very basic christological convictions. Of course, it is possible to believe otherwise, and many well-intentioned people do. But alternate approaches arise from other truth claims that also need to be justified in the realms of public discussion and historical reality. If God has not restored peace through the cross and resurrection of Christ, then one needs to find another basis for becoming involved in peacemaking.

Holding a conviction and organizing our lives around it implies testing and sharing that conviction with others. At the same time, convictions always become visible and concrete. This visible and concrete aspect is an important part of how we justify—that is, explain to ourselves and share with others—exactly what our convictions mean.

It is our responsibility, first of all, to be convinced of our own convictions; otherwise, there is no good reason to maintain them. Life itself—and even more, the life of a community engaged in the world—is an attempt to render credible, to ourselves and to others, the convictions that make us who we are. Life within a community of conviction thus implies contact with others and sharing convictions through example, discussion, and all other means of communication. "In the broadest sense," write McClendon and Smith, "one tries to justify one's conviction set (or one's life) by living it. Yet life includes talk, and persuasion, and reflection, and certainly change."[34]

The justification process also includes the history of the community and the kinds of lives it produces over time, across the generations. If a peacemaking community claims that its convictions about peace are only valid for its own members, it effectively removes any reason for entering into the lives of those who do not share those convictions. If peace is "right" or "better," and if we want to share that insight with others in situations of conflict, we are by definition trying to show others that our convictions are well-founded and true. Peacemaking, therefore, necessarily involves "mission," i.e., the sharing of conviction by action, example, or persuasion.

As Christian peacemakers—

- We believe in the God who created the universe and affirm that all human beings reflect the image of God.
- We believe that God causes the sun to "rise on the evil and on the good, and sends rain on the righteous and on the unrighteous" (Matt. 5:45).
- We believe that God deals with evil through self-giving love.
- We believe that love is an essential part of truth, that God is love, and that truth is love—love of God, of self, of the sister and brother, of the neighbor and of the enemy.
- We believe that God's nonviolent love is the foundation of the world as it was made, and that this nonviolent love is God's intention for the world and for history, for how we are to live and to relate to others.

If then we are to be "missionaries" of this conviction, we will need to demonstrate this truth not only through our words but also in our lives and actions, within and among our communities. But by its very nature, the truth we have just described cannot be imposed—and any action of violence or any desire to dominate or manipulate other people is a contradiction of the truth in which we believe and which we want to share. To be part of such a mission means that we need God and we need community, a combination which unites Christology, ecclesiology, and missiology. Thus understood, writes Ron Kraybill, "peacebuilding is only possible as it is grounded in a community of people who share a common vision of reality and who are ready to work actively, even self-sacrificially, to extend that reality to others."[35]

Witnesses, Not Judges

Despite a very painful history of the church—which, if nothing else, proves that Christians are human and that sin is an ever-present possibility—and the postmodern temptation to be tolerant and pluralistic, we do well to recall that no position is finally exempt from some kind of truth claim and that the gospel of peace has always been a stumbling block. Claiming the uniqueness of Jesus has never been easy, and the church has always been tempted either to impose Jesus' uniqueness or to evade its scandal. However, our choices are stark: do we want to proclaim the uniqueness of peace in Christ, or the uniqueness of a worldview that says that the only truth is that there is no final truth? If truth depends only on sociohistorical conditioning and how we view the world, if there is no discernable shared meaning or direction to life and history, do we not end up in a world where Babel is the only real possibility?

History might be compared to a trial where peacemakers are witnesses, not judges. We know what we have seen and what we have been told. But we do not know all that it means or will mean. Ultimate truth is eschatological in nature and therefore not in our possession. Being a "missionary peacemaker" does not necessarily imply that God works nowhere other than in the church, or that we are making a judgment on the "eternal destiny" of non-Christians. That is not my claim, nor do I think it to be the claim of the biblical tradition.

But missionary peacemakers do proclaim that evil and death have been confronted and defeated. Because of that confrontation, we may now enter into that victory, even though it might mean suffering, since the victory itself was won on a cross. Because of that victory, we believe that people can live together, understand and forgive each other. We believe that love is stronger than hate, and that might does not make right. We believe that self-giving love and nonviolence are at the heart of what the world and history are about. If we believe all that to be true, is it not truth worth sharing?

NOTES

1. A more complete version of this text can be found in *Mennonite Quarterly Review* (January, 2002), 7-33.

2. Gordon J. Wenham, *Word Biblical Commentary–Genesis 1-15* (Waco: Word Books, 1987), 242.

3. G. Von Rad, *Genesis: A Commentary* (Philadelphia: Westminster Press, 1972), 151.

4. Jacques Ellul, *Sans feu ni lieu: Signification biblique de la Grande Ville* (Paris:

Gallimard, 1975), 40.

5. Ibid., 42.

6. Michel Quesnel and Philippe Gruson, *La Bible et sa culture* (Paris: Desclée de Brouwer, 2000), 77.

7. Von Rad, *Genesis*, 149, 151.

8. Wenham, *Word Biblical Commentary–Genesis*, 245.

9. Von Rad, *Genesis*, 154.

10 .Cf. John Howard Yoder's discussion of 2 Corinthians in *The Politics of Jesus*, 2ed. (Grand Rapids: Eerdmans, 1994), 221-23.

11. Ulrich Mauser, *The Gospel of Peace: A Scriptural Message for Today's World* (Louisville: John Knox Press, 1992), 154-55.

12. Mauser, *Gospel of Peace*, 147, 148.

13. Cf. J. Denny Weaver, *Anabaptist Theology in Face of Postmodernity: A Proposal for the Third Millennium* (Telford, Pa.: Pandora Press U.S., 2000), 67, and Weaver's paper elsewhere in the current volume.

14. Stanley Hauerwas, *A Better Hope: Resources for a Church Confronting Capitalism, Democracy, and Postmodernity* (Grand Rapids: Brazos Press, 2000), 169.

15. For the rest of this chapter, the term *conviction* will be used in the following sense: "A conviction . . . means a persistent belief such that if X (a person or community) has a conviction, it will not easily be relinquished without making X a significantly different person (or community) than before." James Wm. McClendon, Jr. and James M. Smith, *Convictions: Defusing Religious Relativism*, rev. ed. (Valley Forge, PA: Trinity Press International, 1994), 5.

16. McClendon and Smith, *Convictions*, 118.

17. Ibid., *Convictions*, 149.

18. "Rather it is our . . . conviction that we must attend to the distinctiveness of our language, and to the corresponding distinctiveness of the community formed by that language, because it is true."—Stanley Hauerwas, *Against the Nations: War and Survival in a Liberal Society* (New York: Winston Press, 1985), 5.

19. Jon Sobrino, *Christology at the Crossroads* (London: SCM Press, 1978), 312.

20.Ibid., 334. "Doctrines, therefore, are not the upshot of the stories, they are not the meaning or heart of the stories. Rather they are tools . . . meant to help us tell the story better."—Stanley Hauerwas, *The Peaceable Kingdom* (Notre Dame, Ind.: U. of Notre Dame Press, 1983), 26.

21. Ibid., 317.

22. Cf. Walter Wink's comparison of the biblical creation narrative with other ancient Near Eastern creation myths in *Engaging the Powers: Discernment and Resistance in a World of Domination* (Minneapolis: Fortress Press, 1992), 13-31.

23. René Girard, *Je vois Satan tomber comme l'éclair* (Paris: Grasset, 1999).

24. Sobrino, *Christology at the Crossroads*, 336.

25. Ibid., 340.

26. Ibid., 341.

27. Ibid., 342.

28. Ibid., 324.

29. Ibid., 324.

30. Frédéric de Coninck, *L'Homme flexible et ses appartenances* (Paris: l'Harmattan, 2001).

31. Cf. Jean Delumeau, *Le christianisme va-t-il mourir* (Paris: Hachette, 1977). "L'histoire chrétien face á la déchristianisation," *L'historien et la foi*, ed. J. Delumeau (Paris: Fayard, 1996), 93-94. Girard, *Je vois Satan tomber*, 256.

32. Linda Oyer's careful work demonstrates how the Gospel of Matthew's post-resurrection sending of the disciples can be understood as the formation of an "Abrahamic community" which is a "blessing to the nations" and that nonviolent discipleship and the teaching of nonviolent practice is very much a part of this mission. See Linda Oyer, *Interpreting the New in Light of the Old: A Comparative Study of the Post-Resurrection Commissioning Stories in Matthew and John* (Ph.D. diss., Institut Catholique de Paris, Faculté de Théologie et de Sciences Religieuses, 1997), I:142-86, 193-211.

33. Mark Gopin, "The Religious Component of Mennonite Peacemaking and Its Global Implications," *From the Ground Up: Mennonite Contributions to International Peacebuilding*, Cynthia Sampson and John Paul Lederach, eds. (New York: Oxford U. Press, 2000), 236.

34. McClendon and Smith, 175.

35. Ron Kraybill, "Reflections on Twenty Years in Peacebuilding," in Sampson and Lederach, *From the Ground Up: Mennonite Contributions to International Peacebuilding*, 44.

Chapter 4

The "Disavowal of Constantine" in the Age of Global Capital

Peter Dula

A central theme in peace church (and especially Mennonite) social thought has been "non-constantinianism." While there are many forms of ecclesial failure, leading Mennonite theologian John Howard Yoder was most preoccupied with "constantinianism," the collusion of church and state which occurred with the fourth century Emperor and which continues in various guises.[1] Yoder described and critiqued several current varieties of constantinianism, but they usually involved the church's relationship to the nation-state. It is this focus on the state which suggests that Yoder's account of constantinianism may now require supplementing.

Recent theorists of global capitalism argue that the nation-state no longer wields the sort of power it once did. Whereas sovereignty was once centralized in the capitals of nation-states, and the boundaries of those states were relatively clear, now power seems to operate differently. With the rise of the global economy, sovereignty is de-centered and de-territorialized. The most striking thing about the contemporary situation is movement, from the migrations of large groups of people (whether in search of work or in flight from war) to the migrations of technology and commodities. The nation-state increasingly becomes little more than an instrument for recording the flow of labor and capital.

If these globalization theorists are correct, peace theology is presented with a significant challenge. What should non-constantinianism look like when "Constantine" is no longer the state but instead is global capital? In this paper I will describe the challenge and pose this as a problem. Though not providing decisive answers, I will gesture toward some conclusions. After briefly engaging Richard Falk, I will move to a more lengthy account of the thought of Michael Hardt and Antonio Negri and then bring them into conversation with Yoder. In doing so I do not mean to suggest that they have the last word on globalization or that I uncritically endorse their conclusions. Rather, I only claim that they create space for a creative conversation, an interdisciplinary thought-experiment.

WHAT IS GLOBALIZATION?

The new global economy is characterized by several factors.[2] First, capitalism has been decentered. We can no longer point to one dominant center. Instead we are confronted with a vast network of urban formations (New York, São Paulo, Hong Kong, and so forth) without a clear center and more closely connected to each other than to their immediate hinterlands.

Second, there is now a new "international division of labor." Production has been globalized. The location of production is in a constant state of change and shifts at unprecedented speeds. More specifically, production of goods and merchandise has been relegated to the peripheral regions while the cities are now sites of meta-production, the production of production: of stocks, services, images, and, most importantly, subjectivities. This network is linked together by the transnational corporations and the global monetary organizations that secure their functioning. Neoliberalism has managed to gain an almost global hegemony instead of just a Western hegemony. Fewer and fewer things are able to resist being reduced to exchange value. Everything now seems to have a price.

In this new global economy, there is no longer a useful division between first, second, and third worlds. The second has simply disappeared, and the first is now found in the third, while the third is present in every first world country. In addition, the nature of the nation-state's power is undergoing a significant shift, a shift that some characterize as a decline.[3] That is not to say that the nation-state will just wither away, leaving us ruled by homeless megacorporations, but that the nation-state increasingly functions as an instrument to record and regulate the flow of capital and labor which are set in motion by the demands of the transnational corporation, by forces that lie outside the nation-state's control. Finally, the poor are the victims of this economy. But then that is nothing new.

There is a general, if loose, agreement on the importance of these factors.[4] But now the debates begin. Is globalization a *fait accompli*, an inevitable result of the inexorable march of capital? All agree that it is not just some "invisible hand," but a particular project of the G8 nations (Germany, Japan, Canada, Britain, France, Russia, China, and especially the United States). But can (or should) the nation-state be pried out from under the discipline of global financial interests? I will briefly summarize two competing answers to this question.

GLOBAL APARTHEID AND CIVIL SOCIETY

Richard Falk, in his *Predatory Globalization*,[5] argues that the current situation may be best described as "global apartheid." Imagine, he suggests, that we were to have a world-state. The only conceivable political structure would be that of South Africa before 1994. The world is one-fifth rich and four-fifths poor, and segregated accordingly.[6] Furthermore, this split too often is coextensive with race. The poorer regions are like the South African homelands where the nonwhite population was exiled and exploited. The central difference between global capitalism and apartheid is the international consensus that apartheid was a crime. Global apartheid, by contrast, is a central guideline for foreign policy (13-17).

To change this, Falk argues that globalization-from-above, globalization promoted by neoliberalism and global financial interests, must be resisted by a globalization-from-below. The ideological trappings of neoliberalism (deregulation, privatization, fiscal discipline) are not intrinsic to globalization but only seem so, partly because of the ease with which neoliberalism gained dominance in the years immediately after the Soviet bloc collapse. Falk clearly does not think that the nation-state will or should ever function as it once did, but he does think that it can regain a degree of autonomy and not simply end up a tool of global capital. But "conventional electoral politics" are futile in this regard. The only way to resist globalization-from-above, and restore the nation-state's autonomy, is for grassroots democracy and issue-oriented social movements to generate enough pressure to "rewrite the contract between state and society." The agent of this globalization-from-below is the global civil society, the dominant actor in which is the non-governmental organization (NGO).

I suspect this will be a tempting option for many of us, and for good reason. "Civil society" politics—grassroots democracy and social movements—are an inviting alternative for those of us suspicious of conventional politics (either for theological reasons or because we are just plain weary of the electoral charade). Moreover, Falk's analysis manages to disconnect commitment to democracy from commitment to a particular territorial state. But we should look more carefully at what Falk has in mind before jumping on board. He mentions several activities in the global civil society that have been failures:

- First, *fundamentalism* is a failure because it has not managed to be economically successful and it is not able to win genuine democratic consent from the relevant political communities (142-143).
- Second, the *Roman Catholic Church* has become a "suicidal . . . opting out . . . , a virtual repudiation of life on earth" because of its position on abortion (54).
- Third, the *Green Party* was a failure because it was too marginal and couldn't provide a credible alternative worldview or a sufficiently loyal constituency to pose a threat to the mainstream (143).

The point here has nothing to do with particular judgments about fundamentalists, Roman Catholics, Greens, or even abortion. At issue is the way these examples exhibit the closures in Falk's civil society. To gather around Falk's table, the agent must be economically successful, popular, and credible in the eyes of the mainstream. This civil society isn't a place where difference can be given a voice. The parameters of the debate, what counts as "civil" or as reasonable, have already been set before the conversation has even started. If those are the terms, then it seems clear that the church is a decidedly and unabashedly "uncivil society."[7]

IMMANENT SOVEREIGNTY:
A WORLD OF FLUIDITY AND HYBRIDITY

In exposing such criteria, Falk goes some distance toward verifying the more radical claims of Michael Hardt and Antonio Negri in their recent book, *Empire*.[8] They argue that while the sovereignty of the nation-state is in decline, that does not mean that sovereignty as such has declined. It has simply taken a new form—it has become immanent instead of transcendent. Here they follow Michel Foucault and Gilles Deleuze. Foucault attacked any political theory which concentrated power in the institutions of the state apparatus, insisting that such accounts operated on an anachronistic, monarchical view of authority and that it was necessary to "cut off the head of the king."[9] That meant realizing that power no longer operated simply in a top-down fashion.

One way to express this is to say that the flow of the channels connecting civil society to the state has been reordered. Whereas Falk thinks that pressures generated by civil society flow upward to transform the state, Hardt and Negri argue that the distinction between state and civil society has rapidly become misleading, at least in Europe and North America. Whereas civil society once operated as a mediator between the immanent forces of capital and the transcendent sovereign, all three are now collapsed into "governmentality" or "biopower."[10]

The work of disciplining and normalizing the subject is no longer done by a discrete state. Foucault taught us that the subject is now disciplined and normalized by those institutions that make up "civil society." The schools, the workplace, the hospital, and the church do the work of creating docile subjects. That is what it means to say that power is immanent, not transcendent. It doesn't hover over us in an abstracted "state" but is all around us, in the fissures and striae of the social terrain.

Hardt and Negri go one step further, with Deleuze and beyond Foucault, to insist that in Empire the walls between the various disciplinary institutions (the school, factory, hospital, prison, and the like) have broken down; their logics of subjectification are now generalized across the social field (329).[11] As those walls have collapsed, so have the walls between nations and between self and other, black and white. Exclusion of minorities has been replaced by a finely calibrated attention to the nuances of different market niches. Difference is no longer a threat the way it was in modern sovereignty; it is an opportunity for profit (152). Empire is a world in which difference is celebrated (at least difference with disposable income). Such difference is not simply the much vaunted multiculturalism, but a mixing of those cultures. Empire is a world of fluidity and hybridity. Instead of maintaining essential identities, and binary divisions, Empire does away with them to create a "smooth" terrain upon which commodities can travel unimpeded.

In light of this, recent developments associated with postcolonial theory, particularly the work of Homi Bhabha, are exposed as complicit with Empire. Bhabha's project has been to highlight the ways in which colonialism operated through binary divisions and then to point out how the hybrid, the split and doubled self straddling the colonizer/colonized divide, is a resisting, subversive figure. Hardt and Negri are concerned to point out that this figure is only resistant to modern sovereignty, not to Empire. In fact, this hybridized cosmopolitan figure is a product of globalization. More precisely, it is the product of the great migrations of peoples, the new international division of labor, the expansion of markets, the transnational corporation. Bhabha mistakes the symptom for the cure (143-146).

Global capital operates on all registers of the social order. It is the pinnacle of biopower, where social life is not just regulated but also produced. "Empire not only manages a territory and a population but also creates the very world it inhabits. It not only regulates human interactions but also seeks directly to rule over human nature" (xv). Understood in these terms, the web of power seems inescapable. There are no hiding places. There is no "outside" to this power, as Hardt and Negri repeatedly insist. There is no space from which to mount a critique, no proletariat (or church) to function as a locus of purity. Since this power takes the form of a constantly shifting web or network, it is difficult if not impossible to pinpoint an "enemy" (56-58). Negri goes so far as to say that "the proletariat is everywhere, just as the boss is."[12] In other words, everyone is now both oppressor and oppressed.

It is easy to read Hardt and Negri as utterly hopeless and also as absurdly abstract.[13] On the ground, say in Prague or Capetown not so many years ago, the line between oppressor and oppressed came into focus in a way it can't from the heights of Deleuzian metaphysics.[14] The "borderless economy" announced by both celebrants and critics is unrecognizable to the Arab trying to enter Israel. Civil society becomes more elusive than Hardt and Negri's condemnation (or Falk's approval) suggests.

Such critiques are worth pursuing and my sympathies tend to lie with them.[15] But instead of pursuing them here, I will try to stay with

Hardt and Negri, reading them as generously as possible. Such a reading strips us of the comfort of ideologies marking out spaces of purity or identifying privileged revolutionary subjects. Politics in Empire becomes "much more difficult but in a good way."[16] As good students of Marx, they know that capitalism still digs its own grave. And as good students of Foucault, they know that wherever there is power there is resistance. The wider power spreads itself, the more are the points at which it is vulnerable. Gopal Balakrishnan may be overstating the case when he says Hardt and Negri announce "a springtime of peoples, a world overflowing with insurgent energies . . . a golden age,"[17] but he nevertheless directs our attention to the hopefulness of this book. In doing so, he suggests that it might be unfair to tar Hardt and Negri with the brush so often used, mistakenly, to tar Foucault—that since resistance is never in a position of exteriority to power, no real resistance exists.

This is not naïve hopefulness. It is an optimism based on their reading of past efforts at resistance. In a highly important move, Hardt and Negri insist that the great power of global capital is a reaction to resistance. This is simply the traditional class struggle thesis restated. But in Marxist discussions of imperialism, the argument focused on capitalism's insatiable need for markets as its central engine of growth and expansion. While not denying the importance of that claim, Hardt and Negri write that "the real efficient motor that drives capitalism from its deepest core [is] the movements and struggles of the proletariat" (234). "The history of capitalist forms is always necessarily a *reactive* history" (268). The hope then is that capitalism may yet explode under the pressure of the militant multitude. Like the crust of the earth itself, continually, inexorably penetrated by geological hot spots, the pavement of Empire must buckle. "Globalization . . . is really a condition of the liberation of the multitude" (52).

NON-CONSTANTINIANISM IN EMPIRE

It is important to note the ways in which globalization makes non-constantinianism, the refusal to collapse the church into an arm or servant of the state, difficult. My argument is not that there may now be reason to be constantinian or that the language is no longer useful—it is as necessary as it ever was. Rather, the problem is that if that enormous and amorphous entity, global capital, has transformed the role of the nation-state as much as Hardt and Negri think, then what it means to be non-constantinian has become unclear.

The most obvious form of non-constantinianism was the refusal of helping the state rule, that is, the refusal of military service, of public office, especially at the national level, and sometimes even a refusal to vote. None of this changes because of globalization. The nation-state still exists and is still violent. But concentration on these areas of refusal does seem to presuppose a transcendent sovereignty and leave open the question of non-constantinianism with respect to governmentality—immanent sovereignty. In this sense, the concentration on the state apparatus misidentifies "Constantine" and therefore serves as a smokescreen concealing significant areas of power's operation and our possible complicity with it.

We can identify a second way of being non-constantinian that is still identified with the nation-state but not necessarily with its governing apparatus. Here "Constantine" is not so much the ruler, but the mythology which legitimates his reign. In the U.S. this is often referred to as civil religion which functions to forge a "people" from the multitude. The American dollar bill reads *e pluribus unum* ("out of many, one"). Creating that "one" has meant a series of exclusions and forgettings of those who challenged or just didn't fit the prevailing vision of the people. Non-constantinianism then functions to cultivate the memory of those exclusions in such a way as to reveal how "the people" is a violent construction. This might include refusing to participate in rituals of civil religion such as Independence Day parades, pledging allegiance to the flag, singing the national anthem at ball games, placing flags in church, or letting our sons join the Boy Scouts.

These first two forms of non-constantinianism are the ones we as Peace Churches have thought most about. But I suspect that in doing so we have neglected more central shapes of non-constantinianism. The shape I am concerned with is very closely related to methodological or epistemological non-constantinianism.[19] Central to that is ecclesiological vulnerability.[20] In neglecting this (and I will define it shortly), we have read John Howard Yoder as one more modern purveyor of one of modern sovereignty's central tools—essential identities and binary divisions, in this case, church and world. Such readings undermine the best of what Yoder has to teach us. Yoder first insists on a problematizing of the church/world division. But the question is this: Does the particular way he problematizes those boundaries also mis-identify Constantine?

JOHN H. YODER AND THE PROBLEM OF ECCLESIAL IDENTITY

One of the most regrettable results of the Lutheran and Zwinglian alliance with civil authority was that it made the shape and speed of reformation dependent upon the consent of the government. Because of the need to maintain order, because of the fear of the unruly, the Reformation's initial affirmation of congregationalism gave way to constantinianism. The door was slammed on "the vision of democracy."[21] Or, as Karl Barth might have said, the door was slammed on the Holy Spirit.[22]

A crucial Anabaptist difference, then, was that it "maintained the elbow room to keep on calling for change as new items arose on the agenda of reform."[23] This is the first blurring of the binary division between church and world, the abandonment of what Barth called "an ecclesiological docetism." Elbow room is required by our sinfulness. As Yoder puts it, "In contrast to other views of the church, [the Radical Reformation model] is one which holds more strongly than others to a positive doctrine of fallibility. Any existing church is not only fallible but in fact peccable. That is why there needs to be a constant potential for reformation and in more dramatic situations a readiness for the reformation even to be 'radical.'"[24]

But there is an even more radical destabilizing of church/world in Yoder, because this elbow room means a radical openness to outsiders. According to Yoder, renewal comes when a dissonance is created between Scripture and church practice, when the Bible forces us to confront our sinfulness. That dissonance is created when we bring new sets of questions to the text. Those new sets of questions often, if not always, come from the outside:

> When the empirical community becomes disobedient, other people can hear the Bible's witness too. It is after all a public document. Loners and outsiders can hear it speaking, especially if the insiders have ceased to listen. It was thanks to the loner Tolstoy and the outsider Gandhi that the churchman Martin Luther King, Jr. . . . was able to bring Jesus' word on violence back into the churches. It was partly the outsider Marx who has enabled liberation theologians to restate what the Law and the Prophets had been saying for centuries, largely unheard, about God's partisanship for the poor.[25]

Finally, there is a third way of blurring the church/world distinction. Yoder repeatedly solicited particular sorts of dialogue with those inside the church, refusing the tolerant pluralism of an H.

Richard Niebuhr or a James Gustafson. In their major works, they would carefully describe the various options on the theological landscape and then place themselves alongside them (or above them), but they would never agonistically engage those options. As Yoder read them, their refusal to do so, in the name of tolerance, immunized them from challenge. He wrote, "The same close reading of another person's views that deems the other view worthy of note, as a benchmark, may also assure me that I know all it has to teach me, that I need no longer listen to any claims it might have on me."[26] Inclusive liberalism is exposed as a fear of dialogical vulnerability which closes off the possibility of self-transformation. A church aware of its sinfulness, concerned to cultivate a perpetual readiness for reformation, however, must constantly engage in such dialogue.

It may be useful here to clarify the language of blurring and destabilizing. That puts it far too simply, makes it too easily capable of being co-opted by a banal postmodernism. For Yoder, the church/world distinction is *maintained* by such destabilizations. That is, since vulnerability is constitutive of the church's mission, each of these "destabilizing" moments are in the service of drawing the line between church and world—maintaining the church's identity, not dissolving it. The notion that a community must be distinctly identifiable *or* open to outsiders is just one more dualism that Yoder was able to see through because he knew that difference and motion constitute identity as much as sameness and stability.

It is time to return to Hardt and Negri. Can Yoder's ecclesiology still be non-constantinian vis-á-vis immanent sovereignty? Recall that Hardt and Negri argued that Empire, unlike modern sovereignty, doesn't operate through essential identities and binary oppositions. Empire need not control difference in that way because it now operates through co-option, internalization, neutralization of difference. What was once revolutionary and "outside" is co-opted—commodified—in the space of just a few years. What is avant-garde one day is a television commercial the next.

Global capital does not try to eliminate difference as the nation-state once did. It encourages the proliferation of difference (multiculturalism) because each new difference is another market niche. Furthermore, it encourages the blurring of the lines between niches. So white suburban kids listen to rap, urban yuppies attend bluegrass festivals. Music with strange names like "Afro-Celtic" become hits. Each new "hybridization" helps smooth the social terrain, thereby allowing for the quicker and easier flow of commodities. "Power has evacuated the bastion they [postmodern and postcolonial theorists] are attacking and has circled around to their rear to join them in the assault in the name of difference. These theorists thus find themselves pushing against an open door" (138). Should Yoder be lumped with those theorists?

For Yoder, the proliferation of difference is never a goal in itself. And neither is the way it may liberate the marginalized from hegemonic discourses. Both are good and welcome, but Yoder goes a step further. These are only good things to the extent that they make possible a more fruitful conversation, in which "more fruitful" means transformation, forgiveness, reconciliation. That postmodernism means "we get our voice, too" doesn't mean we get a secure territory which it is then our duty to police diligently. It means that many voices bombard us, all of which Yoder refuses to construe as threat but instead as "providential occasion for clarification."[27] That insistence on seeing the other as opportunity instead of threat is enabled by the refusal of fear. Yoder, instead of being one more theorist pushing against an open door, "makes politics much more difficult but in a good way."

Hardt and Negri have argued that biopower now operates on every register right down to the production of subjectivity itself. But they also insist that "on the terrain of the production and regulation of subjectivity . . . it seems that we can identify a real field of struggle in which all the gambits of the constitution and the equilibria among forces can be reopened—a true and proper situation of crisis and maybe eventually of revolution" (321). So the question hovering in the background of what follows will be: what constitutes a pacifist subjectivity? And how might it—call it "revolutionary subordination"—be resistant? How might it embody the will to "be against in every place" (211) without claiming an "outside" to power?

Ten years ago Ken Surin, drawing on earlier work of Negri, argued that the "fundamental law" of global capital, its "primary way of securing social integration," is "war and the fear of war."[28] The new civil society, the post-bourgeois civil society, will be the collective subject who "deterritorializes the domain of the state by organizing a new kind of social power which cannot be mobilized by war and the fear of war. The state elevates fear into the basic principle which underpins all forms of association. . . . The struggle for peace is thus inextricably linked to countervailing practices which have as their goal the elimination or the demobilization of those fears which motivate the preparation of war."[29]

Hardt and Negri have also identified the importance of fear. Empire, they write, "rules by wielding an age-old weapon. Hobbes recognized long ago that for effective domination 'the Passion to be reckoned upon, is Fear.' For Hobbes, fear is what binds and ensures the social order, *and still today fear is the primary mechanism of control*" (323, italics added). The pleasures which consumption gives us, the desires it creates and fills, are parasitic on the communication of fear. The early modern political philosophers called this sort of fear "superstition." In other words, our sense that in Empire "there is no place left to stand, no weight to any possible resistance, but only an implacable machine" (323) is a superstition created by our fear.

Those of us who are pacifists are good at refusing war, but we forget to refuse the fear of war and the multiple fears that Surin notes create the entanglement of capital and war. In fact, we too often promote such fear to further our nonviolent ends. Moreover, we rarely see how fear motivates our wish for a stable and fixed identity. Yoder knows that identity is constantly in motion, constantly being negotiated, not stable and fixed. He also knows that the stable and fixed identity of the modernist self, or the nation-state's "people," is a fantasy produced by a fear of the dialogical vulnerability he so relentlessly promoted.

This fantasy allows us to escape the difficulty of negotiating with others: the poor, outcast, sinner, leper, tax collector, or prostitute welcomed by Jesus. Yet this is far from unreasonable; it is created by the difficulty we all have understanding others and making ourselves understood. One might even say the fantasy grows commensurately with the difficulty. "In a world where the other endlessly hardens himself"[30] it makes perfect sense to reach out for an essentialized identity which can be preserved, invulnerable to the threat of exchange. It may be better to say that in such a world it becomes more difficult to think of the possibility of vulnerability.

But Yoder's pacifism demands such vulnerability. It is not simply the refusal of war. It is a model of engaging others in such a way that we do not have to fear their difference from us. We don't have to fear the transformation they demand if we are to be in relationship with them. Because we are freed from such fear, we are freed for servanthood instead of violent power over those others, whether that takes the form of war or capital, Mars or mammon. To that extent we are freed from global capital's production of subjectivity. We are freed to make the evangelical invitation to others, to join this community of vulnerable exchange.

We have such freedom, not because we think with Marx that capitalism by its own logic will yet explode, but because we know that at the cross "in Christ God was reconciling the world unto himself" (2 Cor. 5:19). "He disarmed the rulers and authorities and made a public example of them, triumphing over them [in the cross]" (Col. 2:15). For Yoder, ecclesial closures that come from mis-structured hierarchies and diligently policed theologies are rejected for the same reason war is: they are produced by fear of extinction and a refusal of risk. They are attempts to ensure an ecclesial triumph which is already achieved on the cross. The powers cannot win.

Here, of course, is the crucial difference with Hardt and Negri. For Yoder there is always an "outside to power," even if global capital has advanced as far as Hardt and Negri think. That "outside" is Jesus Christ, who is not only outside the powers but rules over them. The mistake would be to conclude that the church is then also outside. Such a move would be missing a central Yoderian point: since Christ is Lord, we are not. All our claims to finality and purity are brought under judgment. The dangers that the church constantly faces elicit, in the hands of Yoder, not defensiveness but dispossession. The powers, then, become the objects of our patience, not our honor. And that patience is cultivated through listening to many, but especially to the witness of the martyrs of our past and those poor whom Sobrino calls "the crucified people," the people whose concern is less to "overcome" violence than to survive it.[31]

The demand Yoder places on us, the ones who are not martyrs but the bearers of the martyrs' memory, is to hear the martyrs' witness and in that listening find new and creative ways to be non-constantinian in an age of global capital. Yoder wrote, in one attempt to outline the shape of the Anabaptist mission, that we are called to proclaim liberation from the dominion of Mars (the god of war), Mammon, and myself. Mammon, he says, "is the only divinity identified in the Gospels by name as being a power which makes people its slave." But then he says that "this is one face of gospel liberty which is not easy to define in the culture of occidental ease."[32] Hence we turn, vulnerably, to "the least of these" in the effort to imagine what it means to be non-constantinian today.

I cannot pretend to know what those ways are. But then Yoder didn't always either, and he didn't think that was a problem. He closed an address to Goshen College students on the arms race by saying

I can't bring answers. . . . If I thought I knew where to go from here, I wouldn't have the right to come and say it, because that wouldn't have been a believers church process. Part of what it means to be the believers church is to believe that there are answers that we don't have yet. And that we get them, not by inviting someone from twelve miles down the road to talk from a distant history, but by working together at specimens, symbols, celebration, studies that say what we can say even though we know that we don't yet know it. That stated hope is all I intend to offer. The rest is for you.[33]

NOTES

1. The theme appears throughout Yoder's work. See for example, "The Otherness of the Church" and "Peace Without Eschatology" in *The Royal Priesthood*, ed. Michael Cartwright (Grand Rapids: Eerdmans, 1994), 53-64, 143-167, and "The Constantinian Sources of Western Social Ethics," in *The Priestly Kingdom* (Notre Dame, Ind.: Notre Dame University Press, 1984), 135-147. My title comes from a Yoder essay reflecting on the tangled legacy of missions and colonialism, "The Disavowal of Constantine: An Alternative Perspective on Interfaith Dialogue," *The Royal Priesthood*, 242-261. That entanglement persists, though in a new shape, and it is an implicit subject of this essay.

2. My list draws freely from several overlapping sources. See Ken Surin, "On Producing the Concept of a Global Culture," *South Atlantic Quarterly* 94:4 (Fall, 1995), 1179-1199; Arif Dirlik, "The Postcolonial Aura: Third World Criticism in the Age of Global Capitalism," *Dangerous Liaisons*, ed. Anne McClintock et al., (Minneapolis: University of Minnesota Press, 1997), 501-528; Jean Comaroff and John L. Comaroff, "Millennial Capitalism: First Thoughts on a Second Coming," *Public Culture* 12:2 (Spring, 2000), 291-343.

3. Ken Surin talks about a "pluralization of the nation-state form." That seems to me a fair and careful way of describing the situation since it avoids the extremes of "decline" or "nothing has changed."

4. But see Robert Gilpin *Global Political Economy* (Princeton: Princeton University Press, 2001) for a strenuous argument against the idea that globalization is leading to a retreat of the nation-state.

5. Richard Falk, *Predatory Globalization* (Cambridge: Polity Press, 1999). All further references will be noted parenthetically in the text. My reading of Falk owes much to the helpful comments of my colleague Scott Williams.

6. And things are just getting worse as globalization intensifies. The share of the poorest 20% in global income has gone down from 2.3% in 1960 to 1.4% in 1991 and 1.1% in 1996. The ratio of income of the top 20% to that of the poorest 20% was 30:1 in 1960, 61:1 in 1991 and 78:1 in 1994.

7. I take the term "uncivil society" from Dan Bell, " 'Men of Stone and Children of Struggle': Latin American Liberationists at the End of History," *Modern Theology* 14:1 (January, 1998), 133.

8. Michael Hardt and Antonio Negri, *Empire* (Cambridge: Harvard University Press, 2000). All further references will be noted parenthetically in the text.

9. Michel Foucault, *History of Sexuality*, vol. 1 (New York: Vintage, 1980), 89.

10. U.S. President George W. Bush's "faith-based initiatives" program, which would give support to church-sponsored social service programs rather than organizing government programs, is only one of the more obvious examples of the collapsing distinction between state and civil society and the subsequent expansion of governmentality under the guise of anti-statist rhetoric. For a perceptive account of similar developments under the Reagan administration see Sheldon Wolin's remarkable collection of essays, *The Presence of the Past* (Baltimore: Johns Hopkins University Press, 1989), especially "Collective Identity and Constitutional Power" and "Archaism, Modernity, and *Democracy in America.*"

11. These same themes are developed with greater historical detail in Michael Hardt, "The Withering of Civil Society," *Social Text* 45 (Winter 1995), 27-44 and in Hardt and Negri, *The Labor of Dionysius* (Minneapolis: University of Minnesota Press, 1994).

12. Quoted in Ken Surin, "Marxism(s) and the Withering of the State," *Social Text* (1990), 46.

13. Stuart Hall writes that the argument that global capitalism is the "final moment of a global post-modern where it now gets hold of everybody, of everything, where there is no difference which it cannot contain, no otherness it cannot speak, no marginality which it cannot take pleasure out of. . . . [is] the form of post-modernism I don't buy. It is what happens to ex-Marxist French intellectuals when they head for the desert." "The Local and the Global," *Culture, Globalization, and the World System*, ed. Anthony King (Minneapolis: Minnesota University Press, 1997), 30.

14. On the realization of radical democratic possibilities among the Charter 77 dissidents see Jeffrey Isaac, "The Meanings of 1989," *Social Research* 63:2 (Summer 1996), 291-344. Peter Euben argues for the relevance of such radical democracies to globalization in *Democracy and Vision*, ed. Aryeh Botwinick and William Connolly, (Princeton: Princeton University Press, 2001).

15. For the postcolonial engagements with globalization that I find most compelling see Hall, "The Local and the Global," and Dipesh Chakrabarty, "Two Histories of Capital," in *Provincializing Europe* (Princeton: Princeton University Press, 2000), 47-71.

16. This is how Hardt characterized the position in his response to a panel on his book at Duke University, March 24, 2001.

17. Gopal Balakrishnan, "Virgilian Visions," *The New Left Review* 5 (Sept./Oct. 2000), 143.

18. See Sheldon Wolin, "Tending and Intending a Constitution."

19. See Chris K. Huebner, "How to Read Yoder," paper presented at the International Historic Peace Churches Consultation, Bienenburg, Switzerland, 25 June, 2001, and published as "Globalization, Theory, and Dialogical Vul-

nerability: John Howard Yoder and the Possibility of a Pacifist Epistemology," *The Mennonite Quarterly Review* 76:1 (January 2002), 49-62.

20. See Romand Coles, "The Wild Patience of John Howard Yoder," *Modern Theology*, (July 2002). I am indebted to Coles' reading for my understanding of Yoder.

21. *The Priestly Kingdom*, 23.

22. See especially Barth's critique of apostolic succession in *Church Dogmatics* IV/1, 723-724.

23. Yoder, *The Priestly Kingdom*, 23.

24. Yoder, *The Priestly Kingdom*, 5. Again, Yoder's similarity (debt?) to Barth is unmistakable. See *Church Dogmatics* IV/2, § 67.4.

25. *For the Nations* (Grand Rapids: Eerdmans, 1997) 93.

26. "Theological Revision and Particular Identity," in *James M. Gustafson's Theocentric Ethics*, ed. Harlan Beckley and Charles Swezey (Macon, Ga.: Mercer University Press, 1988), 86.

27. "Meaning After Babble," *Journal of Religious Ethics* 24 (Spring 1996), 137.

28. "Marxism(s) and the Withering of the State," *Social Text* (1990), 46.

29. Surin, "Marxism(s) and the Withering of the State," 46.

30. Frantz Fanon, *Black Skin, White Masks* (New York: Grove Press, 1967) 229.

31. David Toole's account of the similarity between Yoder's principalities and powers and Foucault's panopticon is of great help here. See his *Waiting for Godot in Sarajevo* (Boulder, Co.: Westview Press, 1998) 218-225.

32. "The Anabaptist Shape of Liberation," in ed. Harry Loewen, *Why I Am a Mennonite: Essays on Mennonite Identity* (Scottdale, Pa.: Herald Press, 1988), 340, 341.

33. "The Believers Church and the Arms Race," *For the Nations* (Grand Rapids: Eerdmans, 1997), 160-161.

Chapter 5

The Power of Historiography

Alfred Neufeld

Translation from Spanish by Jonathan Beachy

INTRODUCTION: HISTORY AND POWER

"Those who recount history maintain power within a society." Although well known, this common expression has not had sufficient priority in theological thinking and in the witness of reconciliation that the church owes the world. History provides identity for communities, ethnic groups, and nations. To justify a war, one must first write history in such a way as to make clear who are friends and who are enemies, and provide historical reasons which justify displacing opponents. Historiography not only reflects the values which the society writing it has, but it simultaneously nurtures values and paradigms as well. History forms basic attitudes about groups outside the history of the community itself. The manner in which history is written determines who was important and who may be omitted in a rewriting of the past.

The Paraguayan Chaco area, where I grew up, hosted a bitter war between Bolivia and Paraguay from 1932 to 1935. The newly immigrated Mennonites found themselves between two lines of fire. Of course, on both sides there had been an intense propaganda machine convincing soldiers that the other side was National Enemy Number One. Official historiography was astounded and bothered by later research that clearly showed that the war had been nurtured by the Rockefellers' Standard Oil Company and other international oil companies on the Paraguayan side. One of the captains and war heroes of that time, Don Enrique Maas, recently told a local newspaper, "The war wasn't worth it, the war was not necessary, and it didn't resolve anything. . . . Now we know that petroleum was a main reason for the war. Bolivian and Paraguayan soldiers did not hate each other, we even didn't know each other."[1]

The facts are different from the official textbook stories. But how shall they teach the real story in public schools? Especially so since Paraguay won the war and many war heroes still live and every year need to be honored on victory day.

THE MISSION OF THE CHURCH
AND THE WRITING OF NATIONAL HISTORY

"Anti-Christian Investment"

In his paradigmatic book, *Faith on the Periphery of History*, John Driver makes an effort to write prophetic history from the perspective of the gospel: "The implications of a gospel, mediated from an inferior position by way of marginalized persons, has rarely been understood by a church which in one way or another is allied with power. The fact that Jesus came as a prophet, priest, and king means that from the incarnation on, Jesus of Nazareth provided us with a definitive model of our prophetic witness, of our sacerdotal intercession, and for exercising real power."[2]

Driver reminds us that Galilee was "located on the periphery of geographic, social, and religious Judaism; it is identified clearly in the Gospels as the starting point of the divine messianic eschatological salvation initiative."[3] Writing history from a Christian perspective means writing history as a stranger. The parish, from which the church nowadays many times exercises influence and power, was the name originally used to indicate the stranger (*paroikos*), characteristic of local Christian congregations.[4]

Enrique Dussel, protagonist of a new way of writing history in Latin America, tells us how he learned to write history the wrong way around. After he told a friend about conquistador Pizarro's feats in subjugating the Inca Empire, his friend asked him, "Are you excited by the conqueror? Is this a Christian interpretation?" Dussel speaks of a conversion experience in his life as a historian and admits, "Shamefully, I understood that all the history I had learned was an anti-Christian investment."[5]

Contexts as Results of History, and the Need for Theological Reflection

National historiography, as an anti-Christian investment which serves to perpetuate historic dislikes, is a subject that has not had adequate priority in theological work. Important advances have been made in the field of hermeneutics in recent decades in favor of the contextualization of the gospel. Today there is a broad consensus that the biblical text and contemporary social context should interact. Elsewhere I have proposed the model of dialysis to illustrate how the biblical text and sociocultural context are related in hermeneutic circulation.[6] I will propose here that we should develop a greater awareness that contexts are always the result of history. Thus the testimony of the church should address not only contemporary contexts but also the historic efforts that formed them. And historic efforts have developed their strength not only by way of events, but even more so by the way in which those events have been chronicled.

For this reason, the church needs to develop a theology of history. It should be present with its prophetic and witnessing voice in all national historiographic settings where history is used to nurture a culture of violence. Terrible and tragic events may occur if the church is absent from those settings because of its failure to have a theology that orients the national historiography.

Such is the case of recent rivalry and violence between rival ethnic groups such as the Hutu and the Tutsi in Rwanda. Protestant pastors and Catholic priests were present on both sides of the bloody confrontations. The clergy, in addition to participating in the violence, also provided theological justification for it. Dalton Reimer of the Center for Conflict Studies at Fresno Pacific University summed up the facts in this emphatic way: "It was more important to belong to a Hutu and Tutsi tribe than to Jesus' tribe."[7] What was important in these recent ethnic rivalries was also important in the great violent events of history in which the church participated on both sides, especially during the last two world wars and the Cold War which followed.

When the church fails to have a theology of history, it cannot assume a prophetic-witnessing role. It then runs the risk of being trapped by one of two forms of betraying its loyalty to Christ. On one hand, the cause of Christ may be reduced to the parameters of a tribal religion. The three foundational points of a tribal religion are territoriality, consanguinity, and ethnic identity. The heart of Christianity has at times resorted to these elements of tribal religiosity to justify religiously the use of violence and the creation and projection of images of enemies.

The other danger facing a church which fails to have a theology of history, and consequently misses the parameters for historiography, is intellectual schizophrenia. This occurs when the church is in no way present or active in the national historiography or when the latter is not integrated into the church's own theological reflection. This also occurs when the "sacred" and the "secular" are existentially differentiated. These phenomena are observed not only in churches where the national flag occupies a predominant place beside the Bible and the pulpit, but also, for example, in Christian educational institutions, at elementary, high school, and university levels, in which social studies and national and universal history are not impacted by the Christian worldview which each institution seeks to promote. This intellectual schizophrenia is emphatically evident in the use of textbooks with minimal criticism, and the almost total failure on the part of Christian historians to provide textbooks with an alternative and Christ-centered worldview.

Violence as an Endemic Evil of a Nation, and the Monotheism of Power

My home country, Paraguay, to which my parents immigrated seventy years ago, has suffered a very violent history. It may well be the only Latin American country in which an indigenous language, Guarani, has attained the status of an official language, and where the Spanish conquistadors were "conquered" by the indigenous women in the process of mixing the races. However, that mixing process itself, the destruction of the Jesuit reservations, the Great War against the Triple Alliance of Brazil, Argentina, and Uruguay, and the periods of dictatorships and anarchy, have all left their violent trails.

Roa Bastos, our best known novelist, who was awarded the highest Spanish literature decoration, the Premio Cervantes, treats violence as an endemic evil of Paraguay's national cultural history. He has dedicated his trilogy of novels *Hijo del Hombre (Son of man)*, *Yo el*

Supremo (I the Supreme), and *El Fiscal (The Attorney General)* to describing what he calls the "Monotheism of Power."[8] He begins his narrative work with an old aboriginal legend:

> Thunder descends and remains among the leaves.
> Animals eat the leaves and become violent.
> People eat the animals and become violent.
> The earth eats the people and begins to roar like thunder.[9]

Many years earlier, a young Spanish author, Rafael Barrett, wrote *El Dolor Paraguayo (Paraguayan Pain)*. He, too, was grieved by violence as an evil impossible to eradicate, and wrote, "The sad fact is that power ages.... We have soldiers to defend the country, and mainly to destroy it from time to time . . . either war, or tyranny. Peace is of no use. Stated in another way: we are not worthy of peace."[10]

Violence is unleashed by the "political virus," according to Barrett. "Those who do not eat from the State, feel the fire of patriotism in their veins and throw themselves into the fight."[11] This agnostic and anarchist concludes that

> the only treatment when confronted by such a colossal cyst (which is impossible to remove surgically or to reduce in size), is to produce a proliferation of normal cells. It is necessary to isolate the tumor, to prevent it from eventually devouring us.... The current generation needs to be disinfected, and the coming generation educated to distance itself from politics and to scorn power.[12]

In 1990, the Catholic Bishops' Conference of Paraguay dedicated a week of studies to trying to grasp the whole destructive dynamic of violence in the national context. They did this because they considered violence in its many forms to be one of the main challenges for the work of the church.[13]

It is important to note that "Monotheism of Power" not only leads to violence, but in many countries to corruption as well. Corruption can be considered a bureaucratic form of violence since it constitutes violent injustice. Once again, in this case the entire Latin American Bishops' Conference (CELAM) issued a declaration called "Convencion Interamericana contra la Corrupcion (Inter-American Convention Against Corruption)," signed in Caracas, Venezuela, March 29, 1996, in which they identify corruption as one of the main topics for Christian ethical reflection.[14]

Historiography for Violence

The endemic evil of violence in Paraguay has been nurtured by a corresponding historiography. Similar processes have occurred in other societies. A friend of mine, who completed his high school studies in Germany following World War II, shared with me that since the German society still did not know how to tell its history beyond 1945, his textbooks ended with the year 1900. We know that subsequently German society sought radical ways to rewrite its textbooks to help the younger generation distance itself from a violent past.

This example notwithstanding, many societies do not find ways to rewrite their history after a violent period. And what is even more serious, many times the church in those societies is not aware that it should give substantial support to historiographies that seek to overcome a violent past.

In my country, after the fall of the dictator in 1989, the Paraguayan Academy of History saw the need to help the Ministry of Education rewrite the textbooks used in public schools. Milda Rivarola, a prominent historian and political scientist, justifies that effort in this way:

> This reform was even more essential since history becomes the mother of human sciences, and knowledge of history has transcendental consequences on the sociopolitical thinking and practice of citizens. . . . The philosophy of history underlying the texts used before the reform in their bibliographical selection, the choice of subjects and personalities, the prioritizing of areas and epochs, and so forth was moralizing, nationalistic, ethnocentric, sexist, centered on warlike episodes and governmental works. The objective appeared to be concentrated on forming nationalistic patriots, and soldiers inflamed with patriotic bellicosity.[15]

Rivarola concludes that to form men and women with liberty and conscience, builders who are lucid about the present, national history should recover its "ethic and scientific dignity," clearly differentiating "what is legend, myth, and ideological trial, from the historical-scientific investigations."[16]

ETHNIC-NATIONAL IDENTITY, CHRISTIAN IDENTITY, AND RECONCILIATION IDENTITY

The subject of identity has recently been rediscovered and explored by theologians who come from areas shaken by ethnic and nationalistic conflicts. That is the case of Croatian Miroslav Volf, as well as Kwame Bediako from Ghana.[17] There is broad consensus that identity is a fundamental theme for social coexistence, civic conduct, daily culture, personal security, and a sense of belonging.

The Primacy of History in the Formation of Identity

But how does identity emerge? Christoph Wiebe maintains that history is the fundamental creator of identity.[18] To form identity without history would be deceit. But, according to Wiebe, historic identity should be conditioned and accompanied by theological reflection and an empirical analysis of reality. He warns that all the talk about identity may deprive the term of its meaning, since the concept of identity is somewhat problematic and barely tangible. In any case, we must recall that identity is never static, but that it may be transformed. It is also important to differentiate somewhat between individual and collective identity.

With a great deal of energy Wiebe argues that the manner in which we tell our history is the most appropriate way to speak of identity: "Identity is encased in history. It can't be had any other way. We cannot isolate and grasp it. We can only tell our history."[19]

It is important to bear in mind that in any state, society, or community, history exercises decisive power—its current traditions, its sociopolitical and economic context, its day to day culture, its worldview and scale of values, its designation of friends and enemies, its guidelines for behavior regarding what is socially acceptable and what is morally rejected, its concepts about God, the creation, and human beings, its cosmology, theology, and anthropology—are all the result of history and how that history was told. The historic events and the way these events are recounted mutually condition each other.

Models of Forming a Christian Identity

The church of Christ establishes itself and grows amid ethnic and national identities. What should the relationship of the church be with the culture in which it is located? Miroslav Volf notes that Christian commitments and cultural commitments at times become fused. There may even be cases, especially in moments of interethnic conflict, in which cultural identity acquires religious strength, and the "sacralization of cultural identity" is carefully cultivated by both parties in the conflict. "Such sacralization of cultural identity is invaluable for the parties in conflict because it can transmute what is in fact a murder into an act of piety." As a response, Volf notes that the answer lies "in cultivating the proper relation between distance from the culture and belonging to it."[20]

In an analogy to the Barmen Declaration, Volf suggests a "Profession of Faith" as opposed to "New Tribalisms" within the people of God. He bases this on the image in Revelation 5 where the sacrificed Lamb opens the book of history, having bought with his blood saints of all tribes, tongues, peoples, and nations. He also refers to Galatians 3:28, where in Christ the identities of Jew or Greek, slave or free, man or woman no longer divide. He supports what he himself calls a "hybrid identity" in which "the blood of the Lamb" has greater identifying force than other blood alliances: "All the churches of Jesus Christ, scattered in diverse cultures, have been redeemed for God by the blood of the Lamb to form one multicultural community of faith. The 'blood' that binds them as brothers and sisters is more precious than the 'blood,' the language, the customs, political allegiances, or economic interests, that may separate them."[21]

Bediako reminds us that theological work and the definition of identity are always intimately related. In addition, theological ideas respond to existential questions and situations of Christians within a given historic and geographic context. And so, for example, we may legitimately speak of African or European theology.[22] John Driver, in his proposal for a radical ecclesiology, suggests that the Christian church should consider itself "countercultural," as an alternative and contrasting society. Christian identity and the praxis of the people of God should have their roots "in Jesus and the messianic community of the first century."[23]

Stanley Hauerwas does a good job of combining the elements of Christian identity mentioned so far. He speaks of the church as a "Christian colony" made up of resident strangers. The church always gets on well in the world, since "there is no other place where the church can be, except in the world."[24] With John Howard Yoder, he identifies three types of churches: the activist church, the conversionist church, and the church with a witnessing presence. He opts for the latter, since the witnessing church seeks to pay homage to Christ in all things. It does not fall into the secularism of activism, or into the individualism of conversionism, but is active and calls for conversion.[25]

If we try to sum up the biblical evidence regarding the formation of Christian identity, I believe Jesus' high priestly prayer (John 17, as well as the thoughts before that, starting with John 14) to be paradigmatic. The church is one because it is immersed in the identity of the

Son, who in turn identifies himself with the Father (John 17:21). The world believes that the Son was sent because the identity of the Son is evident in the life of the church (verses 22 and 23). The permanence of the church in the identity of Christ, and the permanence of Christ in the identity of the church, leads to a fruitful ecclesiastical life (John 15:4,5). "Christ in you, the hope of glory . . . [to] present everyone mature in Christ" (Col. 1:27,28) seems to be the synthesis of Christian identity.

If Christian identity is linked to the person of Christ, this has consequences for the subjects of power and mentality, because Christ has "disarmed the rulers and authorities and made a public example of them, triumphing over them [on the cross]" (Col. 2:15). And followers of Christ are called to have "the mind of Christ" (1 Cor. 2:16). Since culture always has a lot to do with "mental programming" or "mental mapping," having the mind of Christ is a profoundly cultural phenomenon. Since the church is "the body of Christ" (Eph. 1:22-23), being "in Christ" is something corporate. And this body is a new creation that emerges out of a diversity of people (Eph. 2:14). It is a "new humanity" putting hostility to death through the cross (Eph. 2:14-16).

Reconciling Identity in Trinitarian Foundation

Obviously, since the Christian church is identified with the reconciling and recreating work of Christ, it must have a reconciliation identity. Reconciliation is based not only on the mind and work of Christ and on belonging to his body, but also on the fact of Christ's triumph over the powers. "And he has put all things under his feet" (Eph. 1:22); and "disarmed the rulers and authorities and made a public example of them, triumphing over them in [the cross]. Therefore do not let anyone condemn you in matters of food and drink or of observing festivals, new moons, or sabbaths. These are only a shadow of what is to come, but the substance belongs to Christ" (Col. 2:15-17).

The reconciliation and unifying identity of the church has a trinitarian foundation. The Holy Spirit is a spirit who crosses borders. Not only at Pentecost was there a generalized amazement because of the multiethnic and multilanguage presence of the Holy Spirit. The early church also learned to cross ethnic and cultural barriers when the Holy Spirit went before the disciples and fell on the Samaritans, and on the Gentile Cornelius and his family. To speak of the Holy Spirit is to speak of a transnational and transcultural identity.

The body of Christ is an organism that should not be mutilated. The universality of the church as a single body with many members "ransomed for God . . . from every tribe and language and people and nation" (Rev. 5:9) intrinsically contains a reconciliation identity.

The paternity of God the Father creates fraternity within the Christian family. In a list of the unifying elements of Christianity, "one body, one spirit, one hope, one Lord, one faith, one baptism," Paul culminates his argument by saying "one God and Father of all, who is above all and through all and in all" (Eph. 4:6). And before this Father, he bows his knees, because from him "every family in heaven and on earth takes its name" (Eph. 3:15). The sisterhood and brotherhood among Christians is due not to emotional experiences, cultural or ethnic affinity, or affection, but rather to the paternity of God. The same Father makes us sisters and brothers and members of the same family. And God does this independently of national or ethnic identity.

Volf sums up Christian reconciliation identity very well by using three terms: *catholic personality, catholic community,* and *catholic cultural identity.* This type of reconciliation identity "entails a judgment against evil in every culture."[26]

THE MISSION OF THE CHURCH CONFRONTS A HISTORIOGRAPHY OF ETHNIC-NATIONAL IDENTITY

Throughout history, the church has been weak in testifying against the "anti-Christian investments" (Dussel) of secular historiography. But there are biblical witnesses that testify toward the critical reading of national history.

Critical Views of History and National Identity in the Old and New Testaments

Elmer Martens has noted that in the Old Testament, the broader world of nations and their historical sins was always present and was denounced by divine spokespersons. All of the great prophets directed their messages, both of judgment as well as salvation (Isa. 13–23, Jer. 46–51, Ezek. 25–32) to the nations. Those messages have an express purpose: "that they shall know that I am the Lord" (Ezek. 25:5, 11, 17).[27] Reflecting on the title "the Lord of Hosts," and pointing to Amos 1:1–2:3, Martens maintains that the nations should be held responsible before God for their transgressions against general humanitarian principles.[28]

In the New Testament, the church is exhorted not to allow itself to be enslaved by traditions based on customs—food, drink, feast days, new moons (Col. 2:16; see also the entire Letter to the Galatians), but also to distance itself from paying attention to "myths and endless genealogies that promote speculations" (1 Tim. 1:4). Here we have a clear reference to an excluding or even enemy culture of the ethnic identities in the church in Ephesus. The martyrdom of Stephen might well have its roots in the fact that the Christian reading of Jewish history was different from that of the Jerusalem Sanhedrin.

The scroll sealed with seven seals in Revelation 5 is evidently the history of humanity. The early church, by way of John's writing, needed to realize and console itself with the fact that "the Lion of the tribe of Judah, the Root of David, has conquered, so that he can open the scroll and its seven seals" (Rev. 5:5).[29]

Reading History Critically from a Nonviolent, Anabaptist Perspective

One of the most moving documents of early Anabaptist history is the account of the interrogation and martyrdom of Michael Sattler in 1527. In the judicial accusation against Sattler, point nine reads: "He has said that if the Turks would invade the country they should not be offered resistance and that, if wars were just, he would prefer to march against Christians before marching against the Turks; that is very serious, because before us he prefers the greatest enemy of our holy faith." In his defense, Michael responds, "If the Turk should come, we should not offer him any resistance because it is written, 'you shall not kill.' We should not defend ourselves against the Turks and other pursuers, but rather implore God in steadfast prayer, that he assume the defense and resistance . . . . The Turk is a true Turk and knows nothing of the Christian faith . . . . You ([plural], on the contrary, pretend to be Christians . . . and you are Turks in spirit."[30]

John Howard Yoder differentiates between three popular trends in Anabaptist formation literature: the chronicles, the songs, and martyrology.[31] The three trends have historiographic features. The book with the most impact in identity formation for Mennonites has without a doubt been the *Martyrs Mirror*.[32] Among other texts, Yoder notes the "letter to her son Isaiah" by Anabaptist martyr Anneken de Jans:

> For this, my son, do not pay attention to the great majority of the people and do not follow their way. Take your foot from their path. Because they march to hell like sheep to their death. As Isaiah tells it, "Hell opened its jaws wide open," so that both the prince as well as the common people could enter. They are not people with understanding; and so their maker will not have mercy on them. But when you hear that it has to do with a poor

and a simple small rejected group, despised and rejected by the world, join yourself to them! And if you hear them speak of the cross, there Christ will be.[33]

Yoder himself exemplifies seeking a critical posture toward official historiography. Two themes which are most constant in his work are constantinianism in the history of the church, and historic theories on what constitutes a Just War.[34] Both constantinianism and the theory of Just War have been foundational to the history of supposedly Christian civilization. Yoder makes his vehement criticisms based on the grounds that the church is "a new cultural option" amid society. This cultural option distinguishes it from the rest of society, since it emerges from a "radical obedience for which the rest of society is not prepared." As such, the church is a "new phenomenon in history, sharing obediently, in what is humanly possible, the only way of the incarnation." For that reason societies can never have cultures of monolithic unity because the church in their midst always lives a different cultural option.[35]

John Driver has produced a contemporary historiographic alternative. Driver tells the history of those who consciously sought to follow Jesus, even though this placed them on the periphery of history and gave them a "counter-current" or "countercultural" identity. He attempts to write history from a perspective of a renunciation of power.

> The power of the state had been placed at the service of the church; but the church had also placed itself at the service of the state. In the words of English historian, Lord Acton: "All power corrupts, but absolute power corrupts absolutely." Due to the Constantinian changes, the history of the Christian church became what Professor Dussel (in the words with which we began this chapter) termed an "anti-Christian investment." The church's memory was twisted to serve the purposes of established powers and their institutions, rather than the needs of the Christian people. We intend to outline an alternative story, an upside-down history of God's people. We will read the Bible anew, and move through the centuries . . . to recapture a truly radical vision.[36]

This "history in reverse" has only been partly written. In its positive version, it appears in the account of many reconciliation ministries, in peacemaking, in identification with the poor and marginalized persons. In this sense, my colleague Gerhard Ratzlaff suggests that the goal of reediting history can be the glorification of God.[37]

A Metatheology of Peace Confronting History for Violence

If Paraguayan political analyst and historian Milda Rivarola comes to the conclusion that the textbooks of the history of her country should be rewritten to overcome the history of violence, then that constitutes a real challenge for the Christian church in general and an opportunity for the Historic Peace Churches in particular. But what would the objective of an alternative historiography be?

It is obvious that the message of peace the church owes the world should be contextualized according to historic moments, ethnic and national identities, and cultural and geographic realities. Specific contextualizations of the gospel, Paul Hiebert has recently pointed out, should be framed in what he calls "metatheology." According to Hiebert, the hermeneutic community of the priesthood of all believers should contextualize the gospel so that theology is related to daily life, so that it goes beyond certain mental affirmations and leads to a life of discipleship. But, ironically, local contextualizations also run the risk of being blind to certain discrepancies between their culture and the gospel, and so the critical support of believers from external cultural circles is needed. Each local church needs the help of the international community of churches to evaluate whether or not its theology has been excessively conditioned by certain local cultural presumptions. Hiebert encourages us to speak not only of a "metatheology process," but even more of a "supracultural theology."[38]

It seems evident that a peace witness confronting a "historiography for violence" is going to need something like a "metatheology of peace" which is applicable to any cultural context.

Such a theology must start with an appropriate view of God. In cultural contexts where violence exists as an endemic evil caused by a "monotheism of power," a peace theology would do well to recall Jürgen Moltmann's criticism about the religious concept of monotheism. His thesis is that "clerical monotheism" leads to a policy of monotheism. And many times a policy of monotheism is only one step away from the monotheism of power.[39] Moltmann maintains that to counteract this monotheism of power, we need to rediscover the social dimension of the Trinity: the triune God teaches us what human life in communion and harmony is, in which personality and sociality are respected and cultivated simultaneously.[40]

A metatheology of peace will need to be based on the witnessing presence of the church in the world. David Bosch maintains that the witnessing function of the church, thanks to the incarnation of Christ in history, should have an impact on social history:

In this fulfilled historical period, the Church lives and labors; she contributes to the filling of the time by means of her missionary involvement in the world. God does not send ideas or eternal truths to the nations. He sends people, historical beings. He incarnates himself in his Son, and through his Son, in his disciples. God becomes history, specific history, mundane history, in the followers of Jesus en route to the world.[41]

The witnessing presence of the church in the world will point toward an "authentic transformation," to borrow the title of a book that sums up the legacy of John Howard Yoder on the theme of "Christ and Culture." The church as the incarnation of the presence of Christ will not accept or reject the cultural setting, but rather will discriminate between the rejectable elements and the acceptable elements, pointing toward an authentic transformation. Naturally, that church is a church "for the nations," as the title of Yoder's last book states, and it is a church which seeks to live the "wisdom of the cross" in the world, echoing the correctly titled recent collection of essays in homage to Yoder.[42] For his part, Washington Padilla speaks of "integral transformation," outlining a biblical theology for the presence of the church in the world.[43]

The church will witness to "histories for violence" from a perspective of holiness. What Miroslav Volf summarizes under the terms "distance" and "belonging," aptly speaking of "departing . . . without leaving,"[44] is better summarized, in theological terms, with the word *holiness*. Holiness as a characteristic is precisely one of the dimensions of the church the Nicene Creed mentions: one, holy, catholic, apostolic. But holiness does not mean anything other than cultural distance in the measure that loyalty to God and his projects demand. Holiness is always lived within a cultural-ethnic and national identity.

The church with a trinitarian orientation, with a witnessing presence, which points toward authentic transformation and seeks to live holiness within its cultural context, should be a church characterized by peace. But how is that church characterized by peace?

Andrea Lange has summed it up well: "It renounces violence, has voluntary membership, committed participation, service and sharing, celebration and action in favor of justice."[45] This commitment to peace arises, according to Lange, from the apostolic identity of the church that should not be understood as an apostolic succession of offices, but rather a succession of Jesus' way and cause.

This peace testimony is much more than nonresistance. It is a conscious renunciation of the use of power in favor of nonviolent alternatives. The option of suffering because of violent power is always present. Suffering for the sake of suffering does not constitute a value, but such suffering is a possible and natural consequence of the renunciation of violence.

Jesus' way is not a way of weakness, but rather a way that has a great capacity to overcome. For, after all, the cross of Christ is the maximum expression of divine love for one's enemies. For this reason, the church of peace is always going to question any type of enmity creation, and it will oppose any projection of enemy images. But the refusal to project enemy images will be accompanied by concrete initiatives for conflict resolution. Both conflict resolution and peace services will emerge out of a fundamental willingness to promote love for enemies.

In this attempt to witness in favor of Jesus' way, the church will need "exercise camps" to practice peace, and where it is practiced, errors will occur. Within the peace church there is freedom to admit guilt and to repent of erroneous ways.

Since it trusts in God's possibilities, a peace church is a church of hope, and hope is precisely the link that leads the church to be present in history, to edit history, to tell stories of hope and reconciliation. For this reason, Andrea Lange rightly says, "Simultaneously a peace church should be a community of memories and a community in which stories are told that strengthen hope."[46]

The prophetic witness ministry that the peace church owes those drawing up national histories is precisely this: not only to denounce the histories of violence, which perpetrate violence, but also to tell stories that show alternative ways that can serve to nurture hope.

Rewriting national history might well become a Christian investment, an investment for the church to give testimony to the way of Christ, a peace theology investment that helps national and ethnic communities in their efforts to overcome violence.

NOTES

1. "El petróleo fue causante de la guerra, afirma excombatiente. Entrevista al Tte. 1 Enrique Maas sobre vivencias en la guerra del Chaco," *ABC Color* (Domingo, 3 de junio de 2001), 22-23.

2. John Driver, *La Fe en la Periferia de la Historia: Una historia del pueblo cristiano desde la perspectiva de los movimientos de restauración y reforma radical* (Guatemala City: Ediciones Semilla, 1997), 38. Published in English as *Radical Faith: An Alternative History of the Christian Church* (Kitchener, Ontario: Pandora Press, 1999), 25-26.

3. Ibid., 38, (English version, 26).

4. Ibid., 41 (English version, 28).

5. Ibid., 23 (English version, 9).

6. Alfred Neufeld, *Fatalismus als missionstheologsiches Problem. Die Kontextualisation des Evangeliums in einer Kultur fatalistischen Denkens. Das Beispiel Paraguay* (Bonn: Verlag für Kultur und Wissenschaft, 1994), 126-140.

7. Dalton Reimer, Ponencia no publicada ante el claustro de profesores de la Universidad Evangélica del Paraguay, Asunción, Octubre 2000.

8. Augusto Roa Bastos, *El Fiscal* (Buenos Aires: Editorial Sudamericana S.A.,1993), 9.

9. Roa Bastos, *El Trueno entre las Hojas* (Buenos Aires: Editorial Losada, S.A., 1991), 25.

10. Rafael Barrett, *El Dolor Paraguayo: Mirando Vivir* (Asunción: Imprenta Salesiana, 1988), 129.

11. Ibid.,135.

12. Ibid., 111.

13. Conferencia Episcopal Paraguaya, "Equipo Nacional de Pastoral Social. Sociedad Injusta, Sociedad Violenta" (Asunción: XI Semana Social Paraguaya, 1991), 10.

14. Monseñor Mario M. Medina, *Declaración Etica contra la Corrupción. Obispos representantes de las conferencias Episcopales de la mayoría de los países de América Latina y el Caribe*, Serie Fundamentos 2 (Asunción: Konrad Adenauer Stiftung, 1997).

15. Milda Rivarola, "Enseñar Historia desde una perspectiva no violenta," Exposición inaugural, Tercer Congreso Nacional de Educadores Cristianos, manuscrito no publicado, Asunción (Octubre, 2000) 1.

16. Ibid., 4.

17. Miroslav Volf, *Exclusion and Embrace: A Theological Exploration of Identity, Otherness, and Reconciliation* (Nashville: Abingdon Press, 1996); Kwame Bediako, *Theology and Identity: The Impact of Culture upon Christian Thought in the Second Century and Modern Africa* (Oxford: Regnum Books, 1992).

18. Christoph Wiebe, "Geschichte und Identität," *Brücke: Mennonitisches Gemeindeblatt* (Germany), April 1998, 64-67, 64.

19. Ibid., 65: "Identität ist eingekapselt in Geschichte. Anders ist sie nicht zu haben. Wir können sie nicht herausdestilieren und begrifflich fassen. Wir können nur unsere Geschichte erzählen."

20. Volf, 37.

21. Ibid., 54.

22. Bediako, xv.

23. John Driver, *Contra Corriente: Ensayos sobre la eclesiología radical* (Guatemala City: Ediciones Semilla, 1988), 5.

24. Stanley Hauerwas, *Resident Aliens: A Provocative Christian Assessment of Culture and Ministry for People Who Know That Something Is Wrong* (Nashville: Abingdon Press, 1989), 43.

25. Ibid., 44-45.

26. Volf, 51,52.

27. Elmer A. Martens, *A Focus on Old Testament Theology: God's Design*

(Grand Rapids: Baker Book House, 1981), 231.

28. Martens, "Jeremiah's 'Lord Of Hosts' and a Theology of Mission" in Hans Kasdorf und Klaus Müller, *Bilanz und Plan: Mission an der Schwelle zum Dritten Jahrtausend* (Bad Liebenzell: Verlag der Liebenzeller Mission, 1988), 92.

29. Driver, 1997, 29.

30. John Howard Yoder, *Textos Escogidos de la Reforma Radical*, traducido por Nélida M. De Machain y Ernesto Suárez Vilela (Buenos Aires: Asociación Editorial La Aurora, 1976), 172-174.

31. Ibid., 337.

32. This historic collection of martyr stories of the Anabaptists, originally in Dutch, is a central text for Mennonites. Thieleman J. van Braght, *The Bloody Theater or Martyrs Mirror of the Defenseless Christians Who Baptized Only Upon Confession of Faith and Who Suffered and Died for the Testimony of Jesus, Their Saviour, from the Time of Christ to the Year A.D. 1660*, trans. Joseph F. Sohm (Scottdale, Pa.: Mennonite Publishing House, multiple editions).

33. Cited by Yoder, op. cit, 340.

34. John H. Yoder, *Karl Barth and the Problem of War* (Nashville: Abingdon Press, 1970); *Nevertheless* (Scottdale, Pa.: Herald Press, 1971).

35. Yoder, "How H. Richard Niebuhr Reasoned: A Critique of *Christ and Culture*" in Glen H. Stassen, D. M. Yeager, and John Howard Yoder, *Authentic Transformation* (Nashville: Abingdon Press, 1996), 75.

36. Driver, 1997, 33; quoted from English version, 18.

37. Gerhard Ratzlaff, *Ein Leib—viele Glieder: Die mennonitischen Gemeinden in Paraguay* (Asunción: Makrografic, 2001), 16-17.

38. Paul G. Hiebert, "Metatheology: The Step Beyond Contextualization," in Kasdorf and Müller, 392-394.

39. Jürgen Moltmann, *Trinität und Reich Gottes: Zur Gotteslehre* (München: Kaiser Verlag, 1986), 207-220.

40. Ibid., 216.

41. David J. Bosch, *Witness to the World* (Atlanta: John Knox Press, 1980), 70.

42. Stassen, Yeager, and Yoder, *Authentic Transformation* (Nashville: Abingdon Press, 1996); John H. Yoder, *For the Nations: Essays Evangelical and Public* (Grand Rapids: Eerdmans, 1997); Stanley Hauerwas, Harry Huebner, Chris Huebner, and Mark Thiessen Nation, *The Wisdom of the Cross: Essays in Honor of John Howard Yoder* (Grand Rapids: Eerdmans,1999).

43. Washington Padilla, *Hacia una Transformación Integral* (Buenos Aires: Fraternidad Teológica Latinoamericana, 1989), 9-20.

44. Volf, 35-50.

45. Andrea Lange, "Gott ist Liebe: Und woran erkennt man eine Friedenskirche," *Brücke: Mennonitisches Gemeindeblatt* (Germany): März/April 2001, 4-6, 5.

46. Ibid., 6.

THE GOSPEL
OF PEACE IN CONTEXT:
SHAPING IDENTITY

Chapter 6

Inculturation: Building on the Cultures of Our Past

Ann K. Riggs

*I*n an essay, "Considerations on Keeping Negroes," eighteenth-century North American Quaker John Woolman observed and pondered the roots of war and violence within the social fabric of a culture:

> A covetous mind which seeks opportunity to exalt itself is a great enemy to true harmony in a country. Envy and grudging usually accompany this disposition, and it tends to stir up its likeness in others. And where this disposition ariseth so high to embolden us to look upon honest, industrious men as our own property during life, and to keep them to hard labor to support us in those customs which have not their foundation in right reason, or to use any means of oppression, a haughty spirit is cherished on one side and the desire of revenge frequently on the other, till the inhabitants of the land are ripe for great commotion and trouble; and thus luxury and oppression have the seeds of war and desolation in them.[1]

Through this lens offered from the heritage of the Religious Society of Friends (Quakers), questions arise concerning which customs and cultural and ethnic patterns are conducive to the full human flourishing that God intends for all, and which bear within them the "seeds of war and desolation."

The chapter presented here is intended as a theologically based consideration of this theme, written from a peace church perspective but open to the broader Christian community's understandings of the church's two-millennia-long interaction with human culture. We will undertake here first a consideration of the terms and notions of culture and inculturation and will look briefly at the inculturated character of seventeenth century Quaker thought. Second, we will consider Woolman's analysis of the relationship among culture, custom, well-being, and the seeds of violence, and his views on how to respond appropriately and successfully to distorted situations. Finally, noting the biblical roots and congruity of Woolman's thought and lived example, we will reflect on the ecumenical appropriation of Woolman for our present day and for the World Council of Churches' Decade to Overcome Violence.

CULTURE AND INCULTURATION

In *The Open Secret* Lesslie Newbigin, the twentieth-century missionary theologian and ecumenist, defined culture in broad terms: "When we speak of culture in its broadest sense, we are speaking about the sum total of ways of living which shape (and also are shaped by) the continuing life of a group of human beings from generation to generation. . . . From the point of view of the individual member they are given as part of the tradition into which he is born and socialized. But they are not changeless absolutes." [2]

Gaudium et Spes, the "Constitution of the Church in the Modern World" of the Second Vatican Council, offers a similar notion of culture: "It is one of the properties of the human person that he or she can achieve true and full humanity only through culture, that is through the cultivation of the goods and values of nature. Wherever, therefore, there is a question of human life, nature and culture are intimately linked together. . . . Thus its established traditions form the patrimony proper to each human community; thus, too, is created a well-defined, historical milieu that envelops the men and women of every nation and age, and from which they draw the goods needed to foster humanity and civilization." [3]

Drawing on these two ecumenical resources, we may speak, then, of culture as human cultivation of nature as an aspect of God's intention for human life. And we may speak of ethnically specific cultures and subcultures, and of intracultural differences between the lives, activities, and interrelationships of women and men—that is to say intracultural gender differences—as customs, tools, and processes by which we are shaped, that we in turn shape, through which we maintain our physical well-being, and through which we come to be the relational and interactive beings we are.

In Christian terms, "inculturation" might be described as an "integration of the Christian experience of a local church into the culture of its people, in such a way that this experience not only expresses itself in elements of this culture, but becomes a force that animates, orients, and innovates this culture so as to create a new unity and communion, not only within the culture in question but also as an enrichment of the church universal." [4]

One revealing way to make entry into understanding the Religious Society of Friends, for instance, is to think of Quakerism as originating in a deep inculturation of Christian faith into the mid-seventeenth century British common law tradition.

The common law originated in a world familiar with the Roman style law of European mediaeval canon and civil law systems, but developed in a quite different manner historically, theoretically, and practically. English common law may be described as

- a body of general rules prescribing social conduct,
- enforced by ordinary royal courts,
- and characterized by the development of its own principles in actual legal controversies,
- by the procedure of trial by jury, and
- by a doctrine of the supremacy of law.[5]

The development of English common law tradition made heavy use of a pre-Enlightenment understanding of "reason" and "conscience." In the practical development of the common law, reason was often used as a justification for decisions that then became accepted tradition. In these contexts reason meant "good sense" and "giving each his due."[6] Conscience here meant "an inward knowledge or consciousness of right and wrong, a moral sense of the rightness or wrongness of one's actions . . . a knowledge shared, principally by God."[7] It meant to "know with God," "to know the will of God."[8]

Common law incorporated moral expectations and perspectives within its legal system.

While the common law contained important, recurring, and well-known formulas for articulating the law, and the foundation of the entire system can be said to subsist in (but not be) the early royal "writs," over the centuries of common law development no one written version ever emerged as authoritative.[9] Law, in this view, was not "made," it was "declared," as need required, by those familiar with authoritative and accepted custom.[10]

Early and prominent Quaker leader George Fox was so closely connected with a 1640s and 1650s movement to reform but not reject the common law that legal historians cite him in explaining the arguments and views of the time.[11] Meanwhile Thomas Fell was a common law judge who never became a Friend himself but offered his home, Swarthmore Hall, as a kind of retreat center and family hearth for early Friends. And it was his widow, Margaret, whom Fox was later to marry.[12] The structures and processes of authority and decision-making within the Society of Friends still show the effects of this now-ancient common law tradition. Quaker traditional and contemporary structures and processes of authoritative decision-making may be described as

- a body of general rules prescribing social conduct,
- enforced by ordinary Meetings, Committees of Oversight, and Clerks and characterized
- by the development of its own principles in actual controversies or questions needing attention,
- by the procedure of consulting the community or an appropriate subgroup of the community in a decision-making style that goes "beyond majority rule,"[13] a style similar to the workings of the common law jury, and
- by a doctrine of the supremacy of a right order, understood primarily in moral terms and believed, like the pre-Enlightenment conscience, to display within the limits of our present dark-glassed state in the world (cf. 1 Cor. 13:12), the will of God for human life and for specific people and communities at a specific moment.

In Friends' expectation, authoritative decision-making will show "good sense," will give each his due by "answering that of God in every one,"[14] and will be accessed by knowing the will of God.

THE SEEDS OF WAR AND THE LIMITS OF CULTURE

The valuing and appropriation of elements from ambient culture into the thought and life of the Religious Society of Friends is not, however, uncritical. John Woolman's *Journal* and essays and the life and thought that they record are now traditional resources for Friends. Woolman serves for us as a teacher of both analytical insight and faithful response as we seek to evaluate the cultural settings in which we live and respond actively to distortions we find in the social world, especially distortions that contain the "seeds of war and desolation."

Insight

The most obvious and most notable characteristic of Woolman's analytical vision is its sense of the interconnectedness and complexity of difficulties and situations that give rise to violence. In a single four-paragraph passage he notes the interrelatedness of violence and seemingly unconnected aspects of daily life, between the individual and the civil community, individual and family, English and forced African settlers and the indigenous people, misuse of intoxicants, Christians and followers of other religions, errors of judgment, defeat before superior force, multiple and rapidly shifting economies, limits in natural resources, transportation difficulties making necessary or useful trade difficult, loss of traditional ways and inheritances, a deep sense of God's love for all, and the responsibilities of those who enjoy plenty to "a constant attention to divine love and wisdom."[15]

While astute in recognizing connections between interior dispositions, feelings, and attitudes and outward behaviors, Woolman's focus in speaking to others is on their behavior, the building blocks of our social world.[16] This is true even when the behaviors he is seeking to see changed are moving only slowly toward rectification.

In 1760 Woolman was traveling in New England at the time of the Yearly Meeting in Newport. He offered a proposed minute to the Meeting concerning petitioning the legislature to discourage importation of slaves and asked for a more private meeting with some Friends who held slaves. He reported that he wished to engage Friends on the issues of slavery because his "heart yearned toward the inhabitants of these parts, believing that by this trade there has been an increase of unquietness amongst them and the way made easy for the spreading of a spirit opposite to that meekness and humility which is a sure resting place for the soul, and that the continuance of this trade would not only render their healing more difficult but increase their malady."[17] In describing the private meeting on the subject, Woolman reported "the subject was mutually handled in a calm and peaceful spirit." He took "leave of them in a good degree of satisfaction, and by the tenderness they manifested in regard to the practice and the concern several of them expressed in relation to disposing of them after their decease, I believed that a good exercise was spreading amongst them."[18]

Woolman recognized the limits of culture and custom when these work against what is good. Woolman used an organic metaphor, here of vines, to speak of the development of a survival-level dependence upon socially disordered elements within a culture or subculture:

> One person in society continuing to live contrary to true wisdom commonly draws others into connection with him; and where these embrace the way this first hath chosen, their proceedings are like a wild vine which, springing from a single seed and growing strong, the branches extend, and their little twining holders twist round all herbs and boughs of trees which they reach, and are so braced and locked in that without much labor or great strength they are not disentangled. Thus these customs, small in their beginning, as they increase they promote business and traffic, and many depend on them for a living.[19]

Response

For many years, John Woolman has been a role model of active response to social evil for North American Quakers and for others in the ecumenical community.[20] In "Discernment: An Ignatian Perspective on John Woolman's Journal," Jesuit Thomas E. Clarke noted the sense of familiarity and affinity he experienced in connection with Woolman's *Journal*.[21] The evangelical social action journal *Sojourners* lifted up "John Woolman's answer to materialism" in a piece entitled "Plain Living and High Thinking."[22] In 1972 *The Christian Century* published an introduction to Woolman, "John Woolman (1720-1772): Exemplar of Ethics,"[23] so that it abutted an article on the World Council of Churches and its concern that member churches and individuals should use economic resistance and protest to aid in the dissolution of racist civil policies in Southern Africa.[24] The implied connection is most suitable. Woolman refrained from personal use of cane sugar and molasses because these were produced by slaves.[25]

Non-Quaker A. O. Dyson concluded his article on Woolman's ethics of social protest with a list of twelve characteristics of Woolman's protest responses to the social behaviors and conditions he saw to have within them seeds of violence:

- Woolman saw himself as a conduit for God's own protest. His protest was *modest* in scope and self-carriage.
- Woolman's protest showed *optimism* and confidence in human beings.
- He did *not criticize harshly* or fiercely. He was aware that violence in criticism may lead to violence in response. He was aware that those whom he would reprove possess the Light within and should be respected.
- In speaking with others in protest, Woolman relied heavily on *reasoning*, on persuasion.
- Woolman's protest was perceived by others as based in his own *integrity*: his message and his self were one.
- This integrity was grounded and sourced in *worship*.
- Woolman's protests were *steady, long-term, consistent, relentless*.
- He used a *variety of forms* of protest, preferring however personal encounter.
- He was *not unduly preoccupied about successful consequences*. He assumed that God would be at work after he himself had had his say and departed.
- He was willing to *correct* what he believed were misunderstandings or distortions within the Christian tradition.
- He did not rest his protest in fragments of the Christian tradition but on the *central message of the gospel* perceived in its wholeness.
- Woolman *considered carefully and deeply his calling* to a ministry of protest. He struggled, wrestled, discerned his way forward with commitment and hope but also questions and doubts.[26]

To these characteristics we may add that, like Woolman's Quakerism and his social analysis, Woolman's response to the limits of culture and the seeds of war and desolation he perceived in the world around him was offered from within a shared experiential context with those he sought to influence.

When he encountered situations that were beyond his cultural familiarity, Woolman became familiar from within before he attempted intervention. In December, 1761, Woolman was traveling among the native people of North America during a time of rising violence toward the English settlers:

Love was the first motion, then a concern arose to spend some time with the Indians, that I might feel and understand their life and the spirit they live in, if haply I might receive some instruction from them, or they be in any degree helped forward by my following the leadings of Truth amongst them. And as it pleased the Lord to make way for my going at a time when the troubles of war were increasing, and when by reason of much wet weather travelling was more difficult than usual at that season, I looked upon it as a more favorable opportunity to season my mind and bring me into a nearer sympathy with them.[27]

For Quakers, one of Woolman's most enduring lessons is the lesson of this passage. Making a shared culture, a shared community with others, is the first step to a relationship free from the seeds of violence. That process rightly begins with a motion of love and rightly includes a committed search for truth.

CONTEMPORARY APPROPRIATION

Quakers have a deep affection for the saintly figures and thinkers of our community history. We have noted above that in recent decades a wide variety of other believers have found John Woolman a helpful resource. We may conclude with a few reflections on his potential usefulness as a theological resource offered from one of the peace churches to the Historic Peace Churches collectively and to the Decade to Overcome Violence.

Woolman's analytical and responsive styles have a clear congruity with and are self-consciously rooted in Scripture. We may note two passages in particular. In Isaiah 65:21-25, the prophet speaks of the new creation in the peaceable kingdom that God will establish. Like the prophet, in his analysis Woolman connected freedom from violence, fruitfulness of the soil, and well-being of human families with God's nearness to this harmoniously multi-faceted plenty. Woolman spoke repeatedly of seeking and adhering to true wisdom, God's wisdom, in living in and ordering our cultural world. Like wisdom as she is portrayed in Proverbs 8:1-7, 19-21, Woolman's approach to reproof and instruction was generous rather than assaultive in communication, and presupposed that we may learn to be wise.

As biblically based theology, Woolman's thought is potentially useful and appropriate to any Christian setting. But we must be cautious and critically aware in accepting some of his specific analyses—his consideration against wearing dyed hats, for instance. After much careful thought Woolman determined that the use of dyes in hats and other garments was sometimes harmful to fabrics, tended to hide dirt without promoting greater diligence in washing, and was extravagant rather than appropriately plain.[28] The symbolic realism of the undyed garments that Woolman chose to wear has not stood up well to the passage of time. It is difficult for us who wear clothes cut and manufactured in quite a different style from that used in eighteenth-century Anglo-America to see that style of clothing, by which Woolman was untroubled, as being more or less pure and enduring than the use of dyes, by which he was troubled. More seriously, Woolman seems to have been completely unaware of the real damage to the environment and to human health of the mercury-based hat-making processes that he accepted.

In ecumenical terms, we may note that Woolman's analysis of culture and its limits, and his style of response to what he perceived to be participation in violence, are undergirded and shaped by theological presuppositions quite different from some found elsewhere in the ecumenical community. We may note, for instance, a contrast with the widely read theology of Jürgen Moltmann.

Despite his activist stance, Woolman understood the world in the traditionally Quaker manner that emphasizes the "already" of God's reign. In "The Ethics of Social Protest: John Woolman (1720-1772)," Dyson rightly notes that John Woolman's "*Journal* is a sacramental expression of the experience of God. Woolman's actions in the *Journal* are symbolic events that refer to the action of God toward oppression within the present historical horizon. The *Journal* conveys to the Quaker community the victories of the inner Light in the self, in others, in the critical issues of that society."[29]

Where Woolman looks for the renewal of all in the present, Jürgen Moltmann urges believers "to a constant unrest which nothing can allay or bring to accommodation and rest."[30]

In his influential *Theology of Hope*, Moltmann focuses on the "not yet" of God's reign and unfolds his sense of the implications for human life of a resurrection futurity that exists in the present as yet-unfulfilled promise. The rightful stance of Christian faith was described by Moltmann as one that "strains after the future. To believe does in fact mean to cross and transcend bounds, to be engaged in an exodus."[31] Christian faith in the future of God's promise made manifest in the resurrection of the crucified one is called to an exodus from the social context of the ordinary world into a future to be unfolded in hope.

An ecumenical reflection on Woolman's sense of the limits of culture and on his active responses to cultural situations that distort full human development ought to be the occasion of serious consideration of our theological differences, with a view to overcoming them or to reconciling them in a richer and more faithful diversity.

In a recent essay, David Tracy speaks of the five biblical accounts of the passion narrative of Jesus the Christ, those of the four Gospels and of Paul, as offering to us access to the "Word as disruptive, disorienting *Kerygma* and Word as disclosive, manifestory *Logos.*"[32] Tracy's concern in his essay, part of a *festschrift* for the Benedictine theologian Dom Sebastian Moore, is soteriological; that is, it has to do with understanding how we are saved. Tracy concludes his essay with the claim, "as Sebastian Moore has taught us all: Jesus Christ as Word both confronts us in our arrested and self-deluded desires and liberates us to the self-affirming desire for God disclosed in the Word, Logos and Kerygma."[33]

Moore's own theological focus and Tracy's writing in honor of him are turned inward to issues of the "already" and the "not yet" of the reign of God within us. Perhaps Woolman's life and thought, made accessible through the narrative of his *Journal* as well as his more obviously analytical essays, might be seen in related terms. Woolman's probing of the seeds of violence within our cultural environments is a confrontation with "our arrested and self-deluding desires" and our liberation "to the self-affirming desire for God disclosed in the Word, Logos and Kerygma," as these are witnessed and lived in our social and cultural worlds.

NOTES

1. John Woolman, "Considerations on Keeping Negroes (Part 2)," in *The Journal and Major Essays of John Woolman*, ed. Phillips P. Moulton (Richmond, Indiana: Friends United Press, 1989), 227ff.

2. Lesslie Newbigin, *Open Secret: An Introduction to the Theology of Mission*, rev. ed. (Grand Rapids: Eerdmans, 1995), 142.

3. Vatican Council II, *Gaudium et Spes* § 53 in *Constitutiones Decreta Declarationes* (Vatican City: Libreria Editrice Vaticana, 1993), 767ff, my translation.

4. Ary A. Roest Crollius, S. J., "What Is So New About Inculturation?" *Inculturation* 5 (1984), 15-16.

5. Arthur R. Hogue, *Origins of the Common Law* (Indianapolis, Ind.: Liberty Press, 1985), 190.

6. Norman Doe, *Fundamental Authority in Late Mediaeval English Law* (Cambridge: Cambridge University Press, 1990), esp. 119-121.

7. Ibid., 133.

8. Ibid., 133, quoting Fortesque text of 1452.

9. Hogue, 15.

10. Ibid., 9f.

11. Donald Veall, *The Popular Movement of Law Reform 1640-1660* (Oxford: Clarendon, 1970), 128, 132, 144.

12. William C. Braithwaite, *The Beginnings of Quakerism*, rev. ed., Henry J. Cadbury (Cambridge: Cambridge University Press, 1961), 99-104, 107; Hugh Barbour and J. William Frost, *The Quakers* (New York: Greenwood Press, 1988), 27-29.

13. For an insightful introduction to Friends' decision-making process see Michael J. Sheeran, *Beyond Majority Rule: Voteless Decisions in the Religious Society of Friends* (Philadelphia: Philadelphia Yearly Meeting of the Religious Society of Friends, 1996), 214.

14. A famous phrase of George Fox, *Journal,* ed. John L. Nickalls (Cambridge: Cambridge University Press, 1952), 263.

15. Woolman, 128-129.

16. Ibid., 255.

17. Ibid., 110.

18. Ibid., 112.

19. Ibid., 258ff.

20. See e.g. Phillips Moulton, "John Woolman's Approach to Social Action—As Exemplified in Relation to Slavery," *Church History* 35 (1966), 399-410.

21. Thomas E. Clarke, SJ, "Discernment: An Ignatian Perspective on John Woolman's Journal," in *Spirituality in Ecumenical Perspective,* ed. E. Glenn Hinson (Louisville: Westminster/John Knox Press, 1993), 101-114.

22. David Shi, "Plain Living and High Thinking: John Woolman's Answer to Materialism," *Sojourners* 14/10 (November, 1985), 32-35.

23. Phillips P. Moulton, "John Woolman (1720-1772): Exemplar of Ethics," *The Christian Century* 89 (1972), 984-986.

24. Henk Biersteker, "WCC Tugs at the Vines of Investments in Southern Africa," *The Christian Century* 89 (1972), 987-988.

25. Woolman , 156, 162n.

26. A. O. Dyson, "The Ethics of Social Protest: John Woolman (1720-1772)," *Bulletin of the John Rylands University Library* 68 (1985), 115-134, at 133-134.

27. Woolman, 127ff.

28. Ibid., 119, 120-121, 190.

29. Dyson, 132.

30. Jürgen Moltmann, *Theology of Hope: On the Ground and the Implications of a Christian Eschatology,* trans. James W. Leith. (New York: Harper & Row, 1967), 324. Moltmann's theology of disruption of bourgeois life and exodus into an uncharted but purer, truer future bears resemblance to the art theory of the avant-garde. Clement Greenberg's influential 1939 essay "Avant-garde and Kitsch" was republished in *Art and Culture: Critical Essays* (Boston: Beacon Press, 1961), 3-33. Renato Poggioli's *Theoria dellarte d'avanguardia* was published in Bologna (Il Mulino) in 1962. *Theology of Hope* appeared in German in 1964.

Newcomers to Quaker meetings in the U.S. are sometimes surprised by how deeply traditionalist Quakers may seem in contrast to avant-garde oriented forms of religious community life. Friends and others may hold the same views on a social issue, while arriving at those views through quite differing forms of theological reflection and quite differing community processes. One of the most obvious sources of this traditionalism is Friends' corporate decision-making procedure that requires very broad agreement on any action that involves the entire community.

31. Moltmann, 19.

32. David Tracy, "The Gospels as Revelation and Transformation," in *Jesus Crucified and Risen: Essays in Spirituality and Theology in Honor of Dom Sebastian Moore*, eds. William P. Loewe and Vernon J. Gregson (Collegeville, Minn.: Liturgical Press, 1998), 195-210, at 206.

33. Ibid., 210.

Chapter 7

Atonement and the Gospel of Peace

J. Denny Weaver

INTRODUCTION

There is a long history of fraternization and cohabitation between Christianity and war. In the last millennium it runs from the church-sponsored, medieval crusades against Muslims to the Gulf War blessed by Billy Graham and the multiple Christian blessings of George W. Bush's "war against terrorism." While theology is not the only contributor to the long association of violence and Christian faith, the correlation is more than coincidental.

In contrast, I believe that it is nonviolence and the rejection of violence that ought to be understood as intrinsic to Christian theology. This chapter advances that thesis with a twofold argument. First, it demonstrates how the presumed standard theology of Christendom—in particular the formulas for Christology and atonement—has accommodated violence. Second, it provides a brief sketch of a theology that assumes the intrinsically nonviolent character of Christian faith. The argument begins with comments on ecclesiology.

TWO ECCLESIOLOGIES

Believers church ecclesiology is distinguished from Christendom's state church ecclesiology by point of entry to the church. Individuals are born into the state church, whereas the believers church is composed of people who choose voluntarily to belong as adults. Since the believers church is independent of civil authorities, it is also called a free church. Beyond the formal linking of church and state, establishment of a church by civil authorities also assumes identification of Christian faith with the political order. The state church developed from an evolutionary process of several centuries that began in mid-second century. Modern believers church ecclesiology originated with sixteenth-century Anabaptists. Their lineal descendants, the Mennonites and Brethren, and as well as Quakers, who are products of the English reformation, each constitute an expression of believers church ecclesiology.[1]

While the earlier, sometimes lethal, opposition of state churches to believers churches has long ceased, different configurations of these ecclesiological legacies remain visible in the twenty-first century. The United States has an official separation of church and state. Yet its ongoing, strong impulse to identify itself as a "Christian nation" makes it a continuation of Christendom. And while the denominations descended from the state churches of Christendom continue baptismal and other practices that developed in state church contexts, the absence of an official state church makes them all free churches in the United States. Similarly, the heirs of European state churches around the world are frequently minority religions in their societies.

The existence of these ecclesiological motifs, with a history of opposition and confrontation, makes it reasonable to ask whether the different contexts might produce different theologies, both historically and in the present. The question becomes acute when one notes that the formulas of Christology and atonement that comprise supposedly standard Christian theology were finally accepted as authoritative by the churches of Christendom that had abandoned pacifism and that became the erstwhile opponents of early modern believers church people, including the Historic Peace Churches.

For Christology, the formulas in question are the decrees from the councils of Nicea (325 C.E.) and Chalcedon (451 C.E.). In briefest form, Nicea identified Jesus as "one being" (*homoousios*) with the Father. Chalcedon called him "truly God and truly man," thus repeating Nicea's assertion and adding that he was also of the same being (*homoousios*) as humankind. While no atonement image was given official status by an early council, the satisfaction theory of Anselm's *Cur Deus Homo* (1098) in any of several versions has been the predominant image since the medieval period.

The significant point is that these creeds and formulas emerged and were granted authoritative status after the church had evolved into the state church. Every theology develops out of a specific context, and no theology exists apart from a context. The following section suggests ways the standard formulas reflect their context.

SPECIFIC THEOLOGICAL ANALYSES
FROM A NONVIOLENT PERSPECTIVE

Christology

Consider again the classic christological formulas (Jesus as one being with the Father; and Jesus as truly God and truly man). They concern Jesus' ontology, that is, the essence of his being. They compare Jesus' ontology to the ontology of God and of humankind. In those comparisons, Nicea said that Jesus is of the same being as God while Chalcedon repeated that Jesus is of the same being as God and added that he is of the same being as humankind.

It is not as though these formulas are false in what they claim. On the contrary. If in asking about the relationship of the Jesus of the New Testament to the God of Israel, one wants the answer in terms of fourth-century Greek ontological categories and a fourth-century worldview, then Nicea is probably the best answer. At the same time, it is clear that this philosophical context is not our context, and the particularity of the Nicene formula suggests why it cannot float above particularity as a universal statement. This indication of particularities constitutes a preliminary reason why we should not require repetition of that language in our own efforts to give theological expression to what the New Testament says about Jesus.

But more significant is what these abstract, philosophical formulas leave unsaid. These formulas say nothing about the life and the teachings of Jesus. But it is precisely his life and teachings that are necessary if the Christian life is one of discipleship to Jesus. One cannot follow Jesus on the basis of what is given in the classic formulas.

Stated differently, these formulas have separated theology from ethics. They are a way to identify Jesus that is not connected to ethics based on his life and teaching. They enable one to profess a Christian faith based on Jesus that says nothing about such issues as use of the sword. In this way, they seem clearly to reflect the particular context of the church that had accommodated the sword in the fourth century.

It is not that these christological formulas actively advocate violence. They do not. But neither do they challenge violence, and their a-ethical character allowed the accommodation of the sword by those who professed the formulas as the foundation of belief in Jesus Christ.

For the Historic Peace Churches, to accept these classic formulas as the basis of their theology is to accept a foundation that has pushed the ethics of Jesus at least to the margin, if not completely off the map. I suggest that Historic Peace Churches should be slow to espouse this theological foundation as their own. If this foundation really were the foundation on which *peace* churches were built, would not the denominations descended from the established churches of Christendom that espoused these formulas already be peace churches?

Atonement

A parallel analysis reveals multiple levels of violence in traditional atonement doctrines. The standard account of the history of doctrine lists three families of theories or images, each of which attempts to explain the necessity of Jesus' death. *Christus Victor*, the predominant image of the early church, existed in two forms. In the *ransom* version, the devil held the souls of humankind captive. Jesus was killed when, in a seemingly contractual agreement, God handed him over to Satan as a ransom payment to secure the release of captive souls. In the *cosmic battle* version, Jesus was killed in the struggle between Satan and God for control of the universe. In either case, the resurrection turns the apparent defeat of death into victory for the reign of God, hence the name Christus Victor.

Satisfaction atonement has been the predominant image for most of the past millennium. In satisfaction atonement, the death of Jesus is aimed Godward. In Anselm's version, Jesus' death was necessary to satisfy the offended honor of God and restore order in the universe. In a later version, Jesus bore the punishment that sinful humankind deserved, and thus satisfied the divine law's requirement that sin be punished.

In the *moral influence* image, the death of Jesus is a loving act of God aimed toward sinful humanity. God the Father shows love to us sinners by giving us his most precious possession, his Son, to die for us. The impact of Jesus' death on the psychological or moral character of humankind identifies this view as the moral influence theory.

The later theories respond to earlier ones. In the first book of *Cur Deus Homo*, Anselm specifically rejected the idea that Jesus' death was a ransom payment to the devil. Satan has no contractual rights that God need honor. And even when humankind deserves punishment, Satan has no right to administer it. These considerations make it unworthy of God to deal with Satan, and Anselm deleted the devil from the salvation equation.[2] Instead of humankind being Satan's captives, Anselm made humanity directly responsible to God. Human sin offended the honor of God, and thus disturbed order in the universe. Jesus' death then satisfied God's honor and restored order in the universe.

Abelard followed Anselm in rejecting the idea of Jesus' death as a ransom payment to the devil. But Abelard's moral influence view also rejected the idea of Jesus' death as a payment to God. It made God seem vengeful and judgmental. Instead, Abelard saw the death of Jesus aimed not at God but at sinful humankind, who stand in a state of rebellion against God. Giving Jesus to die was a loving act of God designed to get the attention of these rebellious sinners, and reveal a loving God rather than a vengeful God to be feared.

Each of these images attempts to explain why Jesus died "for us" or "for me." But recalling the object or direction of the death of Jesus makes clear that these images suggest entirely different approaches to atonement and to understanding the death of Jesus. For Christus Victor the death of Jesus has the devil as its object. For Anselm, it is aimed at God's honor, while for penal substitution, the object is God's law. Finally, for moral influence, the death of Jesus targets "us," sinful humankind, as its objects.

Developing the implications of Anselm's (and Abelard's) removal of the devil from the salvation equation brings to the fore the violent assumptions in both satisfaction and moral theories of atonement. Since human beings cannot save themselves, they are obviously unable to offer the required payment to God's honor that is visualized in satisfaction atonement. Thus in Anselm's equation, it is God who organizes the scenario whereby the God-man makes that penalty payment. With the devil removed from the equation, it is only extending the interior logic of Anselm's own move to say that this scenario makes God ultimately responsible for the death of Jesus. In penal substitution, Jesus is punished by death, in place of killing us.

Thus God's law receives the necessary death that it demands for justice. But again, since sinners cannot pay their own debt, God is the one who arranged to provide Jesus' death as the means to satisfy the divine law.[3] The image of God is that of chief avenger or the one who oversees lethal punishment.

Possible defenses against making God responsible for the death of Jesus are to argue that Jesus volunteered to die, or that the devil, the mob, or the Romans were responsible for killing Jesus. However, having Jesus volunteer leaves in place the framework in which God arranges to have Jesus volunteer to pay what God requires. And making the devil, the mob, or the Romans responsible means that those who oppose the reign of God by killing Jesus are also doing the will of God by killing Jesus to provide the payment that God's honor or God's law requires.

The moral theory fares no better. Remember that while Abelard rejected the idea that Jesus' death was a payment directed toward God's honor, Abelard agreed with Anselm in removing the devil from the equation. The result is that God is the Father who has one of his children—the beloved Son—killed to show love to the rest of the Father's children, namely to us sinners.

The conclusion from these observations about classic atonement doctrine is that they portray an image of God as either divine avenger or punisher and/or as a child abuser, one who arranges the death of one child for the benefit of the others. This is hardly the image of God that supports nonviolence, nor of the God who is revealed in the nonviolent story of Jesus. Does it surprise that through the centuries, people following a God of this stripe, where violence belongs intrinsically to the divine working, might justify violence, under a variety of divinely anchored claims and images?

Another path leads to similar conclusions. The various versions of satisfaction atonement function under the assumption that doing justice or righting wrongs depends on retribution. Satisfaction atonement assumes that righting wrong depends on the violence of punishment. Sin creates imbalance. That imbalance is righted or balanced by the punishment of death.

The atonement assumption that imbalance or injustice is righted by the punishment of death is reflected by capital punishment in contemporary society and in the feudal system of Anselm's medieval time frame. Since the assumption that restoring order or righting injustice requires retribution or the violence of punishment is virtually universal, satisfaction atonement can seem self-evident. The argument here, however, is that satisfaction atonement is an intrinsically violent, and violent-modeling, atonement image.

Related to the observation that satisfaction atonement puts God in charge of retribution is a third way that satisfaction atonement accommodates violence. It structures the relationship between humankind and God in terms of an ahistorical, abstract legal formula. Salvation based on an abstract legal formula does not challenge violence and injustice, nor is it a salvation that is expressed in how one lives.

A fourth component of the violence in classic atonement images is the model of Jesus they present. In satisfaction atonement, Jesus models voluntary submission to innocent suffering. Because Jesus' death is needed, whether to satisfy divine honor and restore the order of creation or to undergo the punishment required by divine law, Jesus models being a voluntary, passive, and innocent victim, who suffers for the good of another. Similarly the Jesus of moral influence theory who dies to show the Father's love, and the Jesus who dies as the innocent ransom payment to the devil, also appear as innocent victims who voluntarily submit to unmerited violence.

It is important to underscore for whom these images of Jesus as innocent and passive victim may pose a particular problem. It is an unhealthy model for a woman abused by her husband or a child violated by her father, and constitutes double jeopardy when attached to hierarchical theology that asserts male headship.[4] A model of passive, innocent suffering poses an obstacle for people who encounter conditions of systemic injustice, or an unjust status quo produced by the power structure. One example is military-backed occupation and confiscation of land, with indigenous residents crowded into enclosed territories, called "reservations" in North America, "bantustans" in South Africa and "autonomous areas" in Palestine. For these people, the idea of "being like Jesus" as modeled by satisfaction atonement means to submit passively to that systemic injustice.

A victim is controlled by forces and circumstances beyond himself or herself. A victim surrenders control to others and accepts the injustice imposed by others. In satisfaction and substitutionary atonement, Jesus models victimization. When this atonement motif is the model for people who have experienced abuse or exploitation, this model underscores their status as victims.

The observations in this section reveal multiple ways in which the classic christological and atonement formulas inherited from Christendom have accommodated or condoned or contributed to violence, starting with the sword. Before proceeding to a sketch of Christology and atonement specifically shaped by nonviolence, it is important to see that theologians beyond the Historic Peace Churches have also made such observations.

MORE VOICES

The "inherited history" of James H. Cone, founder of the black theology movement, is the enslavement of Africans who were brought to North America against their will. While Cone's history differs in many significant ways from that of the Historic Peace Churches, he offers critiques of Christendom's theology that are remarkably parallel to the critique from a nonviolent perspective.

If enslaved people became Christians, they did not accept the proffered Christianity outright. When the white owners read the Bible aloud, they stressed "Slaves obey your masters," and made a future home in heaven dependent on that obedience. This slave-holder theology depicted Jesus as a spiritual savior who delivered people from sin and guilt but said nothing about conditions in this world. This spiritual salvation did not challenge the master-slave relationship, nor the exclusion of free African-Americans from white churches.[5]

But when owners read the Bible to them, the slaves actually "heard" something else. They heard the exodus as a story that placed God squarely on the side of slaves. The story promised that as God had freed the Hebrew slaves, so one day God would also free the Africans enslaved in America. These enslaved people saw Jesus as a liberator, whose salvation included freedom from the physical bondage of slavery, and support in the struggle against the continuing evils of segregation and racism in post-slavery America.[6]

In Cone's analysis, the white reading of the Bible rested comfortably on the christological formulations of Nicea and Chalcedon and Anselm's satisfaction atonement. In themselves the abstract categories of "humanity" and "deity" of classic Nicene-Chalcedonian theology lacked an explicit ethical or justice content, which reflects their location in the church that was growing in favor with the Roman state. Cone writes:

> Few, if any, of the early Church Fathers grounded their christological arguments in the concrete history of Jesus of Nazareth. Consequently, little is said about the significance of his ministry to the poor as a definition of his person. The Nicene fathers

showed little interest in the christological significance of Jesus' deeds for the humiliated, because most of the discussion took place in the social context of the Church's position as the favored religion of the Roman State.[7]

White theologians could claim Jesus as defined by Nicea and Chalcedon, thus claiming "correctly" to stand in the orthodox theological tradition, but at the same time owning slaves and later continuing racial segregation and discrimination.

Cone emphasizes that reconciliation is "primarily an act of God,"[8] but that the link between reconciliation and God's liberating acts has been cut for most of the history of Christian thought.[9] He applies this critique specifically to Anselm's satisfaction theory, which depicts salvation in terms of a spiritual transaction with God that spoke neither to the social conditions of Africans in slavery nor to the oppressive character of racism in modern society. Cone calls it "a neat rational theory but useless as a leverage against political oppression. It dehistoricizes the work of Christ, separating it from God's liberating act in history."[10]

Cone's critique of Christendom's Christology and atonement are parallel to my critique from a nonviolent perspective. Where I describe abstract and ahistorical categories that accommodated the sword, Cone says that they accommodated slavery and racism.

Womanist theologians, African-American women, represent another dimension of the black church in North America. Womanists emphasize their particular social location as people who have confronted the threefold experience of racism, sexism, and classism.

Kelly Brown Douglas' analysis of Christology echoes that of James Cone. Douglas notes several aspects of the Nicene-Chalcedonian formulation that appear inconsistent with her reading of Jesus as presented in the Gospels. Focusing on incarnation "diminishes the significance of Jesus' actions on earth. His ministry is virtually ignored." Further, the confession "moves directly from the act of incarnation to the crucifixion and resurrection," which implies that "what took place between Jesus' birth and resurrection—the bulk of the Gospels' reports of Jesus—is unrelated to what it means for Jesus to be the Christ." And, finally, emphasizing the uniqueness of Jesus' metaphysical nature "makes what it means to be Christ inaccessible to ordinary Christians. There becomes little reason to strive to be an example of Christ in the world, because to be Christ requires a divine incarnation, which happened only in Jesus. . . .He is seen as someone to be worshipped, believed in, but not followed or imitated."[11] In another place Douglas notes that focus on incarnation apart from Jesus' ministry to the poor and oppressed implied that little was required for salvation. One had merely to accept the belief that God had become human in Jesus, which meant that "white people could be slaveholders *and* Christian without guilt or fear about the state of their souls," and blacks could be Christians without challenge to their status as slaves. A second implication was that slavery actually served a good purpose since it "provided the opportunity for Africans to attain this salvific knowledge" about the incarnation.[12]

Nonetheless, Douglas does not remove Nicene-Chalcedonian speculation entirely from the picture. Rather this "formulation is seen as a part of a continuing tradition in which those who confess Jesus as Christ attempt to discern the meaning of that confession. It does not, however, have any normative significance as womanist theologians attempt to articulate Christ's meaning for the black community."[13] Womanist particularity points to the particularity of Nicea-Chalcedon. Rather than allowing Nicea-Chalcedon to float in a presumed authoritative and normative status that transcends particularity, the womanist critique makes it one conversation partner among several.

Womanist Delores Williams has focused much of her work on issues surrounding atonement. Williams uses the story of Sarah's exploitation of Hagar as the biblical model of black women's experience and as the point of entry for womanist critique of feminist theology. Hagar's treatment by both Sarah and Abraham foreshadows how white women as well as white men have participated in the oppression of black women. The experience of African-American women has frequently been that of surrogates: as coerced sex partners of white men when white women were elevated to a sexless ideal; as physical laborers and wage earners when the white power structure suppressed black men after the Civil War; as surrogate mothers— "mammies"—for the children of white women.[14] Such observations become the basis for the womanist charge that feminists, who have assumed that the experience of white women is normative for all women, have contributed to the exploitation of African-Americans.

Examining the role of Hagar as surrogate provides Delores Williams with a fundamental critique of Anselmian atonement theology. In the version of European Christendom exemplified by what Williams calls "mainline Protestant churches,"[15] sinful humankind was redeemed because Jesus died on the cross as a substitute for humans, taking their sin and punishment upon himself. Viewed from Williams' womanist perspective, this means that in substitutionary atonement "Jesus represents the ultimate surrogate figure." When attached to Jesus, surrogacy "takes on an aura of the sacred." Given the exploited experience of black woman as surrogates in both white and black contexts, womanist theologians do not want to endorse any understanding of Jesus' work that models surrogacy. "If black women accept this idea of redemption," Williams asks, "can they not also passively accept the exploitation that surrogacy brings?"[16]

This brief look at black and womanist theologians reveals problems with the presumed standard theology of Christendom that are parallel to the issues raised earlier from a peace church perspective. In each case, speaking from different social locations, the presumed standard theology accommodated violence or exploitation.

African writer Kwame Bediako of Ghana further indicates the significance of social location in critique of Christendom's theology. Bediako notes three reasons why the nineteenth- and early twentieth-century missionary contacts with African peoples were negative. First, these contacts between Europeans and Africans revolved primarily around the slave trade. Second, the Europeans held racist assumptions that placed the African peoples at the lowest end of the evolutionary scale and considered Africans to be destitute of civilization. Third, developments in European history "had brought about the virtual identification of 'Christian' with 'European.'"[17]Consequently, little thought was given to the possibility that these supposedly primitive religions might serve as a preparation for Christianity. The general missionary thinking was that African religions had to be uprooted, and "Africans could only receive and articulate the [Christian] faith insofar as they kept to the boundaries and models defined by the Christian traditions of Europe."[18]

In contrast, Bediako suggests a Christology from an African perspective. This means involving Jesus in an African spiritual universe, which includes the belief that who Jesus is cannot be separated from what he does and can do in the world. Bediako's suggestion builds on African reverence for the ancestors, which provides an image of how Jesus participates in every aspect of our experience, including annulling any terrorizing influence that evil powers may have over the living ones.[19]

Bediako's analysis is much more detailed and profound than the minimal sketch here. But alongside the analysis of black and womanist theology, it makes clear that the kind of issues raised from a nonviolent, peace church perspective extend far beyond the confines of the Historic Peace Churches.

NONVIOLENT CHRISTOLOGY AND ATONEMENT

This section shifts from critique of the supposed standard theology of Christendom to sketching a proposal that both reflects the nonviolence of Jesus and understands ethics as an integral dimension of salvation. I propose narrative Christus Victor as an image of Christology and atonement that displays the reign of God in nonviolent confrontation of and triumph over evil and that understands salvation based on a nonviolent reign of God and separated from the violence of retribution.

My construction of narrative Christus Victor is anchored at both ends of the New Testament. The book of Revelation portrays multiple versions of the classic imagery of Christus Victor, namely a cosmic struggle between the forces of God and the forces of Satan. The reign of God is triumphant in the resurrection of Jesus.

Observing the potential historical antecedents of Revelation's symbols locates the confrontation in the arena of human history, with Rome as the representative of Satan's realm and the church as the earthly manifestation of the rule of God. Although the reign of God has triumphed in the resurrection of Jesus, the aftermath of the struggle continues. James Cone locates the contemporary powers of evil that resist the rule of God in "the American system" that can "make heroes out of rich capitalists"; "the Pentagon, which bombed and killed helpless people in Vietnam and Cambodia and attributed such obscene atrocities to the accidents of war"; and a system of "police departments and prison officials, which shoots and kills defenseless blacks for being *black* and for demanding their right to exist."[20] But for Christians, the point is that although evil still resists, the reign of God has triumphed through the resurrection of Jesus, and Christians are thus freed to live in and celebrate salvation in the reign of God.

At the front end of the New Testament, the Gospels depict the same confrontation between the representative of the rule of God, namely Jesus, and everything and everyone that is not under the rule of God. The Gospels portray a Jesus who challenged violent or exploitative or oppressive conditions in a number of ways—through Sabbath healings, challenging conventional treatment of Samaritans and women, confronting temple desecration, and more.

In place of the violence-accommodating theology of Christendom, this brief sketch based on a reading of Revelation and the Gospels suggests a theology that takes Christian identity from the narrative of Jesus. This theology understands that Jesus is the norm of ethics for Christians. One can call this reading of the Bible a narrative

Christology with an atonement motif of narrative Christus Victor. Faith shaped within this theological reading of the Bible is Christian faith as embodied nonviolence. It is lived theology. Stated another way, ethics and theology are two versions—one written, one lived—of the story of Jesus. To be Christian is to live this story of Jesus.

CONCLUSION

Space has permitted only the briefest of sketches of atonement and Christology from a specifically nonviolent perspective.[21] This discussion about violence in Christian theology has clear ecumenical implications. One set of those deals with the theological relationship between Historic Peace Churches and those churches that are descended from the established church traditions of Christendom. Concerning relationships between those entities, the question is whether the theological foundation that peace churches and Christendom churches try to agree on will be one with or without an explicit reference to the nonviolence of Jesus.

Equally important, I suggest, is the theological relationship between churches of Europe and North America, and those of the so-called third world, who have often borne the brunt of European and North American exploitation. Will the relationship between these churches be based on a theological foundation of specifically imperial, European origins, or will it be one that is based more centrally in the narrative of Jesus, which has the potential to confront the domination of Europeans and North Americans?

How we answer these questions and the basis on which we understand our relationships will go far, I believe, in showing how serious the peace churches are in remaining peace churches and how serious all Christians are about the World Council of Churches' Decade to Overcome Violence.

NOTES

1. For an introduction to the concept of the believers church, see the classic history, Donald F. Durnbaugh, *The Believers' Church: The History and Character of Radical Protestantism* (Scottdale, Pa.: Herald Press, 1985); the collection of papers from the first believers church conference, ed. James Leo Garret Jr., *The Concept of the Believers' Church: Addresses from the 1968 Louisville Conference* (Scottdale, Pa.: Herald Press, 1960); and John Howard Yoder, *The Priestly Kingdom: Social Ethics as Gospel* (Notre Dame, Ind.: University of Notre Dame Press, 1984).

2. Anselm, "Why God Became Man," in *A Scholastic Miscellany: Anselm to Ockham*, edited and trans. Eugene R. Fairweather, The Library of Christian Classics (Philadelphia: Westminster, 1956), 107-10. Portions of this and following sections draw on my article, "Violence in Christian Theology," *Cross Currents* 51.2 (Summer, 2001), 150-76.

3. It is this observation, which is implied from Anselm's deletion of the devil from the equation, that has led feminist and womanist writers to speak of this atonement motif as an image of "divine child abuse." See Joanne Carlson Brown and Rebecca Parker, "For God So Loved the World?" in *Christianity, Patriarchy, and Abuse: A Feminist Critique*, ed. Joanne Carlson Brown and Carole R. Bohn (New York: Pilgrim Press, 1989), 1-30; Julie M. Hopkins, *Towards a Feminist Christology: Jesus of Nazareth, European Women, and the Christological Crisis* (Grand Rapids: Eerdmans, 1995), 50-52; Rita Nakashima Brock, *Journeys by Heart: A Christology of Erotic Power* (New York: Crossroad, 1988), 55-57; Carter Heyward, *Saving Jesus From Those Who Are Right: Rethinking What It Means to Be Christian* (Minneapolis: Fortress Press, 1999), 151; Delores S. Williams, *Sisters in the Wilderness: The Challenge of Womanist God-Talk* (Maryknoll: Orbis Books, 1993), 161-67.

4. Brown and Parker, "For God So Loved the World?"; Hopkins, *Towards a Feminist Christology*, 50-52; Brock, *Journeys by Heart*, 55-57; Heyward, *Saving Jesus*, 151.

5. James H. Cone, *God of the Oppressed*, rev. ed. (Maryknoll, NY: Orbis, 1997), 42-52.

6. Cone, *God of the Oppressed*, 57-76.

7. Ibid., 107.

8. Ibid., 209.

9. Ibid., 211.

10. Ibid., 211-12, quote 212.

11. Kelly Brown Douglas, *The Black Christ*, The Bishop Henry McNeal Turner Studies in North American Black Religion, no. 9 (Maryknoll, NY: Orbis, 1994), 112-13.

12. Douglas, *The Black Christ*, 13-14.

13. Ibid. 112-13.

14. See the discussion of surrogacy in several chapters, as well as specific discussion of feminist-womanist dialogue in Delores S. Williams, *Sisters in the Wilderness: The Challenge of Womanist God-Talk* (Maryknoll, NY: Orbis Books, 1993), 178-99.

15. Williams, *Sisters*, 161.

16. Ibid., 162.

17. Kwame Bediako, "Biblical Christologies in the Context of African Traditional Religions," in *Sharing Jesus in the Two Thirds World: Evangelical Christologies from the Contexts of Poverty, Powerlessness, and Religious Pluralism*, ed. Vinay Samuel and Chris Sugden (Grand Rapids: Eerdmans, 1983), 83-84, quote 84.

18. Bediako, "Biblical Christologies," 85-87, quote 87.

19. Ibid., 94-104.

20. Cone, *God of the Oppressed*, 212-13.

21. For more complete development of this argument, as well as extended discussion with black, feminist, and womanist writers, consult J. Denny Weaver, *The Nonviolent Atonement* (Grand Rapids: Eerdmans, 2001).

Chapter 8

Reconciliation or Pacifism? The Nigerian Experience

Patrick K. Bugu

INTRODUCTION

Every true Christian who reads his or her Bible carefully will, without being instructed, come to understand that Jesus, the founder of the Christian faith, was a peaceful person who through his pacifist position defeated and even transformed his enemies. Peace is one of the fundamental teachings maintained throughout the Bible. It is clear from both the Old and New Testaments that peace is a universal longing in the life of all humankind and all other creatures. The desire for peace with God, peace with human beings, and peace with other creatures is echoed from every book of the Bible. Peace therefore is an indispensable requirement of life.

Like any word, "peace" is not a religious term. It is a human term subject to the interpretations of individuals and corporate bodies. The longing for peace is in the heart of every creature. It is the desire to enjoy freedom in life. It is a state of being secure from harm, free to live, free to enjoy both physical and spiritual life. It is an indispensable desire of every living thing. When anybody or anything tampers with it, the natural reaction is to stage a defense. Such defense is what we call fighting or war. Defensive fighting or wars are not something any creature would like to engage in, but for the sake of peace every creature fights, because peace is so dear to life that few condone disrupting or losing it. War and other disruptive, defensive situations are often efforts to regain peace.

Peace can be many things for many people. The pursuance of peace by Christians cannot be limited to just some churches; all Christian faith groups must be concerned about peace, but the path to peace differs from individual to individual and from denomination to denomination. Peace, it seems, is like the belief in God. People do not have the same concept of God, but a belief in the existence of God as the creator and sustainer of the universe is, nevertheless, basic to all theists. In the same way, the pursuit of peace may have different expressions but few living creatures can deny the desire for peace. Peace is life and without peace there is no life. Nevertheless, from the Christian point of view there is a difference between general peace and the special peace revealed in Jesus Christ.

DEFINING PEACE

The understanding of peace in Islam and other religions is somewhat different from peace in Christianity. In Islam, for instance, peace does not mean only social justice; rather, it embraces the whole of life. Islamic concepts of peace include: "to be well," "peace and health," "peace in this world as well as in the next." The Muslim uses "Peace be upon you" as a greeting as well as a farewell. Like the Jew of Old Testament times, the contemporary Muslim sees peace as harmony, integration, and a total way of life. It is both internalized and externalized. It embraces past, present, and future.[1] Nevertheless, Moslems only see peace through the lenses of their faith. Anybody that does not belong to the Islamic faith can only enjoy a temporary peace. To enjoy peace in Islam one has to submit to the beliefs of Islam or submit to the Islamic government by agreeing to pay tribute.

The Christian biblical basis for wholistic ministry and *shalom* can be examined by reflection upon two interlocking concepts: the kingdom of God and the covenant of peace. The kingdom is God's sovereign rule in nature and in history. The covenant of peace is not mere absence of conflict; it is the condition of well-being, peace, and harmony wherever God reigns. It characterizes the state of appropriate relationships under God's kingship. Therefore, in simple terms, the kingdom of God is also "the reign of right relationships."[2] The message of peace in Christianity is based upon the call to love your neighbor as yourself and on the extraordinary call to love your enemies. This call to love even the enemy is perhaps the most difficult demand of Christian peacemaking.

THE HISTORY OF THE
CHURCH OF THE BRETHREN IN NIGERIA

The purpose of this chapter is to explain the position of the Church of the Brethren in Nigeria, Ekklisiayar Yan'uwa a Nigeria (E.Y.N) on the issue of peace and pacifism. The Church of the Brethren in Nigeria is a mission branch of the Church of the Brethren in the United States. It began in 1922 when two Brethren missionaries, Albert Helser and Stover Kulp, arrived in Nigeria. These men were sent on a trial mission among the Bura people of western Borno.

Borno was the first area to accept the Islamic religion in Nigeria. Before the coming of the British, the Borno empire had existed for many years as the main power in the area. Through jihad, the Islamic holy war, they had expanded Islam to a radius of more than a hundred miles. Those who rejected Islam but wanted to remain on their lands were enslaved by the Moslems. Those who objected to being slaves to the Moslems fled into the mountains and remained there until the coming of the British government, which imposed conditions that forced the Moslems to maintain peace and order.

However, the British peace initiative in this area was mainly for their own interest, not for that of the people under oppression. The British government, through their hideous system of indirect rule, imposed the Moslems as rulers over the non-Moslems, not because they respected Islam but because that was the only way they thought they could make the people pay their taxes and have them work on the roads and anywhere else they needed cheap labor.

Although the British and the Moslems had different interests, they worked together to exploit the non-Moslems. The British officers in Borno and the Muslim leaders deliberately created tensions among the tribes. If they knew of a tribe or tribes that were too difficult to control, they would create some problems between these tribes which would often push them into fighting with one another until both tribes became weak. Then, the Moslems with their British allies would jump in to take control of both tribes. This was the situation in which the first Brethren missionaries found themselves.

In light of this situation, it was not easy for the Brethren missionaries to establish their mission work in the Biu region. Neither the British officers in Borno, nor the Moslem leaders, consented to the establishment of a mission center in Biu area. But through a series of struggles with the resident (British commissioner) of Borno and the British offices in Lagos, it was finally agreed that the Brethren would be officially permitted to begin their work, under some defined conditions, but not in Biu. The missionaries were sent to Garkida, a place known for its venomous snakes. Thus, they started the church among snakes, scorpions, and many dangerous animals, coupled with firm opposition from both the secular and religious groups.

Exhausted by a series of warnings and threats, the Brethren mission began in Garkida in 1923 among people struggling with all sorts of life situations. It was not long before the missionaries discovered that the need of the people was not first the need for salvation from sin, but rather salvation from practical situations such as diseases, hunger, war, poor hygiene, illiteracy, and domination by the Moslems.

As explained by Chalmer E. Faw, these Brethren missionaries were representatives of the Church of the Brethren in America, but they were not leaders of the church.[3] They were members of the church who willingly gave up everything to share their lives with an "unknown, distant, colored race." In terms of traditional Brethren doctrines and practices, the majority of them knew enough to share with others equal to or below their rank but not enough to really represent the denomination. Faw describes them as "middle Brethren," which they were. While they did not shy away from their distinctive tenets of faith as Brethren, they did not see that as the most needed aspect of their work. True, the missionaries promoted such tenets as "the historical Brethren love feast (with feet washing, simple meal, bread and cup) as well as the triune immersion mode of baptism for believers."[4] And they emphasized simple living, tolerance for others, and the problem of misuse of authority. However, of all these Christian teachings, the Brethren missionaries valued and cherished the heritage of brotherly love more than anything else.

Unfortunately, and for reasons best known to them, the early missionaries did not emphasize the other Brethren tenets such as the wearing of special garb, the holy kiss, rejecting war through teaching peace and pacifism, and several other marks of the Brethren tradi-tion.[5] The missionaries, it seems, did not intend to make Brethren of the Africans. Their main concern was to make them followers of Christ, not Brethren. Thus, they focused their attention more on what the Bible said in the African context rather than on what the denomi-national beliefs and practices demanded.

Why, one may ask, did they not teach the full range of Brethren beliefs and practices? Why did they ignore the peace position of the Church of the Brethren? Did they not believe in the peace position of the church? Yes, these missionaries were ardent believers in the tenets of the Church of the Brethren. In fact, Stover Kulp and many other missionaries were at one time conscientious objectors to war and therefore pacifists. The truth is that missionary churches were shaped by the situation in which the missionaries found themselves contex-tually, not by what the mother denomination believed. Thus, it was not surprising that the brothers and sisters who went to Nigeria to preach the gospel established a church not fully dependent upon Brethren beliefs and practices but on what they felt the Holy Spirit was leading them to do in that particular context.

PACIFISM OR RECONCILIATION? THE NIGERIAN CONTEXT

The church established by the Brethren in Nigeria was centered more on the love of God for humanity than on a doctrinal under-standing of peace. It was the missionaries' conviction that once the message of God's love was planted in the hearts of the people, it would be natural for them to see the importance of peace. Conse-quently, rather than preaching the *gospel of peace and pacifism*, Stover Kulp and Albert Helser (and most of those who followed later) preached with sincerity and vigor the *gospel of God's love and reconcili-ation* through Christ. Through this gospel of love and reconciliation, the missionaries were able to reconcile the warring tribes and to es-tablish cordial relationships with the Moslem leaders.

Although the Brethren in Nigeria did not teach peace and paci-fism in the way of the Brethren in the United States, their way of peacemaking was very practical. It was seen and understood by be-lievers and unbelievers alike. It was not a peace centered simply on nonviolence vs. violence, but a peace deeper than external conflicts. Christianity for them was a way of life, advocating the worth of the individual and the importance of home and family, which they be-lieved was the way to peace and reconciliation.

The Brethren missionaries not only preached Christianity as a new way of life, they demonstrated it practically in their daily relationships with all people. They displayed that witness to reconciliation through the practice of hospitality, in their care for patients at the hospitals, in their rural health and education programs, and anywhere they worked and witnessed. The Brethren demonstrated practically what it meant to be a Christian to such an extent that even those who once hated them, like the king of Biu, later felt regret and eventually pressed gallantly and successfully to have the Brethren schools built in Waka, just a mile from his house. Some Moslems even sent their children to learn from the missionaries.

What was even more amazing was the recognition of the Brethren Bible school by the Emirs of Yola. For many years, and to this day, the Lamido of Adamawa has a high respect for the Church of the Brethren. During the time of the early missionaries, the Emir came to Kulp Bible School to inspect the farms of the Bible school students and to visit with the missionaries. Although some did not consider this behavior appropriate for the Emir as the grand leader of the Moslem faith in that region, he so trusted and respected the missionaries that he feared nothing at all.

Peace theology was not part of the curriculum of any of the Brethren schools. Even the Kulp Bible School did not have peace or nonresistance as part of its curriculum, not to mention pacifism. How then is the Church of the Brethren in Nigeria a peace church? How did they know about peace? How can they be a peace church without being pacifists?

For some people, peace is not known until a podium is mounted and a long sermon on peace is given. For the Nigerian missionaries, peace was not understood primarily through preaching nonviolence but through practical acts of loving and serving in life. Peace, in the Nigerian context, is to know Jesus as the Christ. Peace is to love God with all your heart, with all your mind, with all your soul, and to love your neighbor as yourself. Peace is to be free from poverty, hunger, disease, ignorance, and domination. Peace is not the absence of war; instead, it is a war against evil and injustice. Peace is the refusal to compromise with injustice, sin, or evil acts. Peace is the courage to face evil in all dimensions through the Spirit of God.

As members of the Church of the Brethren in Nigeria (E.Y.N.), we claim with our fellow Brethren in the United States that we are a peace church. In fact, even if we do not voice that, our connection with the Church of the Brethren mission in Nigeria has made us known as a peace church by both Christians and Moslems in Nigeria. The Brethren missionaries believed in the New Testament concept of peace, not in its specific historic interpretation, and so do we. They taught brotherly love as recorded in the New Testament without necessarily concentrating on things like war, pacifism, nonviolence, and the like.

This reflects the current position of the church in Nigeria. We hate war, and many Nigerian brothers and sisters will defiantly refuse to consent to go to war or to kill. The Church of the Brethren at present is well known in Nigeria for this one thing, the concern for peace through reconciliation. The church has helped in reconciling sister churches within the TEKAN (Nigerian Council of Churches) fellowship and between churches and the government. It has confronted the government many times around issues relating to peace and justice. The church is more aware of itself as a peace church now than ever before. Nevertheless, this is not because we are pacifists but because we have learned to love our neighbor as ourselves. It will take a long time for the church to recognize pacifism, but some are now moving in that direction.

The main concern of the early Brethren in Nigeria was the gospel of reconciliation rather than the gospel of peace. They emphasized reconciliation as the main path to peace among the brothers and sisters in Christ. The main biblical texts cited were Matthew 18, John 13, and 1 Corinthians 13. Through their biblical teaching and practical life witness, the EYN Church in Nigeria has come to know peace as the source of life. We have come to recognize reconciliation as the only source of peace.

We are peacemakers without claiming to be pacifists. We have learned about the value of life, about justice, and about freedom, which we cannot obtain through war and injustice but only through love and reconciliation. Through the gospel of reconciliation we believe that we will, through the grace of God, succeed in experiencing peace and order in the church and within the broader society with our Muslim neighbors.

We in Nigeria are still studying the peace venture of the Church of the Brethren, a venture we feel is worth emulating, but we are still on a journey. With constant visits to the Nigerian church by leaders and members of the Church of the Brethren in the United States to discuss peace and pacifism in light of political, tribal, and religious violence, there is hope that the two sister churches will reach together for a just peace. The recent visit by Scott Holland to Nigeria to talk to the Ministers' Annual Conference on peace is timely, and it is my hope that visits by peace church theologians will continue.

Finally, since the desire for peace does not rest exclusively with humankind but also with the other creatures around us, all peace ventures should not only concentrate on peace within humankind, but should also extend to other creatures and to all of God's creation. Christianity is not only a peace religion; Christianity is peace in itself. Let us go forth therefore to preach, to teach, and to practice genuinely the gospel of peace and reconciliation to the whole world.

NOTES

1. *The World of Islam: Resources for Understanding* 200 (CD-ROM) Colorado: Global Mapping International.

2. Ibid.

3. See Chalmer E. Faw, "Profile of Brethren Mission: An Evaluation of Fifty Years in Nigeria," *Brethren Life and Thought,* vol. 19, no. 2 (Spring, 1974), 85-96.

4. Ibid., 88.

5. Ibid.

Chapter 9

The Gospel of Peace and the Violence of God

Scott Holland

I rest my case on the rights of desire. . . . On the god who makes even the small birds quiver. —André Brink, The Rights of Desire

On January 6, 2001, I flew out of the Pittsburgh International Airport bound for the Federal Republic of Nigeria. January 6 is Epiphany on the Christian calendar and it has always been my favorite holy day. Epiphany, of course, celebrates the manifestation of God to the magi from the East. Those wise men followed neither the voices of the angels nor the paths of the Hebrew shepherds to Bethlehem. They were guided instead by the stars. With the strange scents of Babylon on their bodies, they entered the house of Mary and Joseph with exotic gifts for the Christ child.

The magi from Persia, like Persian mystics, sages, and poets who followed them, such as Rumi, understood that the breath of the divine touched the primordial elements of life: earth, water, fire, wind. Many Christian mystics throughout the ages have likewise understood well how the metaphors and rituals of religion return us not merely to a text or tradition; indeed, they return us to our elemental passions. The waters of baptism are wet with the longings and losses of life. These mystics have taught us that religion, like life, is a tremendous and terrifying mystery.

I traveled to Nigeria at the invitation of the pastors of the Ekklesiyar Yan'uwa a Nigeria, the EYN, which is the Nigerian denomination started by the educational and medical missions of Church of the Brethren early in the twentieth century.[1] The Church of the Brethren, along with the Mennonite Church and the Society of Friends, is one of the Historic Peace Churches. The EYN is now an indigenous West African peace church in partnership with the Church of the Brethren.[2] The EYN Church had seen much violence the previous year and I was invited to address the Pastors' Majalisa or Synod in a number of lectures on peace, pluralism, and religious tolerance.

I flew into Kano, a Muslim city in the north. I spent my first night in the country there before traveling on to Jos for an orientation to Nigeria presented by EYN church leaders along with American and European church workers. I was awakened before dawn by a sound that was more chilling than comforting. It was a call to prayer that pierced the silent night like a sword:

> God is most great!
> God is most great!
> I testify that there is no God but Allah.
> I testify that Muhammad is the prophet of Allah.
> Arise and pray, arise and pray!
> God is great.
> There is no God but Allah.

I found this voice crying out of the darkness chilling not because I don't value inter-religious encounters and dialogues but because of Kaduna. Let me explain.

Kaduna is a city in the north of Nigeria that was the site of what Nigerians call "the crisis." It is one of the Nigerian cities that truly embodies the ethnic, religious, and class diversity of modern Nigeria. Churches and mosques, beer parlors and Koranic schools, stand side by side on the city's active streets. The crisis of Kaduna in February 2000 was a bloody clash between Muslims and Christians that left churches, mosques, schools, libraries, homes, and businesses burned to the ground. At the end of several days of bitter fighting—both in public riots and in violent private acts of retaliation—it is estimated that the crisis led to the deaths of as many as three thousand people, both Christians and Muslims. [3]

What led to this crisis? I regret to say it was religion—fundamentalism, which is to say totalitarian religion.[4] It had only been two years since Nigeria shifted from a military government to a fragile democracy. President Olusegun Obasanjo is a Christian committed to the formation of a democratic, pluralistic, secular state. However, Muslim fundamentalists, of which there are many in Nigeria, sought to impose Sharia law, theocratic Islamic law, on the state and city of Kaduna. Thus, these words of religious law would become civil law—including their penalties of amputations and floggings, their ban on alcohol, art, and cinemas, and integration of the sexes—for the citizens of Kaduna:

> God is most great!
> God is most great!
> I testify that there is no God but Allah.
> I testify that Muhammad is the prophet of Allah.
> Arise and pray, arise and pray.
> God is great.
> There is no God but Allah!

How calls to prayer can become calls to war! We must quickly concede that this is likewise true of The Lord's Prayer. "May thy kingdom come, may thy will be done, on earth as it is in heaven," has inspired imperialistic violence from the followers of the crusading Christ of constantinian expressions of Christendom.

Nigeria is a multireligious, democratic state.[5] Therefore, in response to the threat of Sharia, on February 21, 2000, Christians in Kaduna state, under the umbrella of the ecumenical Christian Association of Nigeria (CAN), staged a peaceful demonstration at the State House of Assembly and Governor's House. It was a King-style nonviolent march to protest the imposition of Sharia. As the march moved from the Governor's House to its conclusion, a number of Muslims who were offended by this public display of resistance began to attack the Christian marchers and several were killed. Many Christians retaliated and responded in kind, and during the next few days the violence escalated across Kaduna. EYN Pastor Iyasco Taru, married with seven children, was assassinated in his parsonage when he refused to confess to his attackers, "There is no God but Allah and Muhammad is his prophet."

I felt that I needed to visit Kaduna before I attempted to lecture at the Pastors' Synod on peace, pluralism, and religious tolerance. After all, Christian ethics is grounded in an incarnational theology; therefore, a poetics of place must inform all textual interpretation. Thus in January, 2001, almost a full year after the crisis, I found a city with large slices of destruction that still looked like a war zone in the aftermath of the clash of fighting gods. Entire neighborhoods had been "religiously cleansed."

In the remainder of this chapter, I will explore a central question or problem that emerged during four intense days of theological conversations at the Pastor's Synod held on the campus of Kulp Bible College near the Nigeria-Cameroon border. The problem was stated pointedly by the EYN pastors: "How do we reconcile a gospel of peace with the violence of the life-world, indeed, with the violence of God?" However, before I examine this question, I want to summarize three ancillary issues we worked on together at the synod in light of the call to peace and the reality of violence: the importance of strangers, the problem of purity, and the problem of totalitarianism.

THE IMPORTANCE OF STRANGERS

There is a great temptation in any religion or spirituality to domesticate the divine and thus make God our family, churchly, tribal, or national deity. The genius of the Judeo-Christian tradition's representation of God is its insistence that God is both immanent and transcendent. God is indeed present, yet God is "other." In Christian thought and spirituality it may at times be quite appropriate to imagine Jesus as a friend and even sing these sentiments in songs of popular piety such as "What a Friend We Have in Jesus." Other times, however, it is important to be reminded that God comes to us as a stranger.

The Nigerian pastors and I explored this tension together through the astonishing figure in the Hebrew Bible of Melchizedek.[6] He is presented as a prince of Salem, a prince of peace. He is a rather mysterious and distant figure, without genealogy, a stranger priest from the far country. He is not of the tribe or faith clan of Abraham. Yet he greets Father Abraham carrying bread and wine. Not only does Abraham receive Melchizedek and commune with him; he also pays him a tithe! When the writer of the New Testament book of Hebrews provides an extended commentary on the Melchizedek narrative, he likens Jesus to Melchizedek and contends that Jesus is more like this priest than a priest in the proper line of Levi and Aaron.

At times Jesus is indeed a friend. At other times he comes to us as a stranger priest from the far country. This legacy of the strangeness or otherness of God in the biblical tradition is undoubtedly one reason why the writer of Hebrews exhorts his readers to treat strangers well, for in doing so, some have entertained angels unawares (Heb. 13:2).

THE PROBLEM OF PURITY

We continue to live in a world of ethnic, ideological, and theological cleansings in quest of a kind of "purity." In my lectures for the synod I turned to several examples of this problem. Most compelling to the EYN pastors was the work of Croatian theologian Miroslav Volf. Like these Nigerian pastors, Volf has seen too many of the terrors and tragedies of a politically and religiously driven ideology underwritten by claims of purity. His book, *A Spacious Heart* (coauthored with his spouse Judith), addresses this powerfully. He suggests that sin is not so much a defilement as it is a certain form of *purity*—the exclusion of the other from one's heart and world. Volf turns to the story of the Prodigal Son. In this biblical narrative, the sinner was the older brother—the one who expected exclusion and withheld an embrace. Volf writes, "Sin is a refusal to embrace others in their otherness and a desire to purge them from one's world, by ostracism or oppression, deportation or liquidation. . . . The exclusion of the other is the exclusion of *God*." [7]

I told my Nigerian colleagues and friends about a striking sculpture on the campus where I teach. At the Earlham College Friends Meetinghouse an image of a woman solemnly greets worshipers as they approach the chapel. Her name is Mary Dyer. The bronze plate by artist Sylvia Judson Shaw reads: "Mary Dyer, Hanged on Boston Common, 1660." Dyer was a Quaker free thinker in Puritan Boston. When in dissent from Puritan theology, morality, and politics she declared, "Truth is my authority, not some authority my truth," she was hanged by the Puritan fathers for heresy. A terrible violence attaches itself to quests for purity.[8]

THE PROBLEM OF TOTALITARIANISM

Like the desire for purity, the longing for totality is likewise violent. Many Nigerian pastors were quite familiar with the story of the life, work, and witness of Dietrich Bonhoeffer. They admired his agonizing struggle of Christian conscience in the face of Nazism. They recognized his difficult choice, as a pastor involved in the ecumenical peace movement, to join the violent resistance to Hitler. Most saw this decision as a genuine dilemma of tragic necessity and faithful compromise, reflecting what it meant to be a Christian and a man in a moment of profound historical horror and crisis. No attempt was made by these pastors to baptize this individual decision as normative Christian ethics. Instead, it was understood more as an exceptional act of faithful compromise under God's grace in a blessed, fallen world.

Drawing from my work on Bonhoeffer's theology and ethics, I suggested that this movement of resistance was made possible by Bonhoeffer's intellectual evolution from the purity of discipleship (*Nachfolge*) to an understanding of theology as *polyphony*.[9] Bonhoeffer spent a year in a black Baptist church in Harlem, worshiping and serving as the youth group leader and teaching Sunday school. He also became well acquainted with the art, music, and literature of the Harlem Renaissance. As a classical pianist, Bonhoeffer would have been familiar with the musical phenomenon of polyphony, but this was a musical style embodied daily in the life and in the jazz music of Harlem. A polyphony—literally "many sounds"—is not a symphony, neither is it a harmony. Instead, it is a musical piece in which two or more very different melody lines come together in a satisfying way. There is not an even harmony in polyphonous pieces, but there is nevertheless a satisfying aesthetic coherence.

In his final writings, *Letters and Papers from Prison*, Bonhoeffer confesses in a letter to his dear friend Eberhard Bethge that he has finally come to understand theology, like the life-world of life from which it must come forth, as a *polyphony*. It is in these final writings that we see a shift in Bonhoeffer's thought from grounding theology in largely moral metaphors to locating it instead in musical metaphors. A polyphony resists the artificial harmonies of all totalistic systems, and thus rejects all totalitarianisms, whether political or theological.

Even in a country as religious as Nigeria, where most Muslims, Christians, and animists take their faith quite seriously, religion's best hope for peace and prosperity is in a polyphonous, secular state. An increasing number of Christian pastors and theologians are concluding that the old heresy of "constantinianism," whether of the Christian variety or of the Muslim variety, only incites violence toward the other through its implicit or explicit longings for totality.

THE GOSPEL OF PEACE AND THE VIOLENCE OF GOD

Let me turn now to a problem the pastors and I explored together with the most intensity during the synod. It is a problem, a dilemma, beyond the theological exposition of our response to strangers. It is a problem beyond the ethical criticism of the desire for purity. It is even a problem beyond the political critique of totalitarianism. It is truly a classic problem of "the Holy."

There is a great temptation in modern and late modern Christendom to tame and tutor the mystery of God and the terrors of nature with our favorite selected texts. We tend to edit and even censor texts that conflict with our needs or longings for a peaceful divinity and a friendly and harmonious creation.[10] This is especially tempting for those of us who are suburban or small town theologians in North America. The trees are nicely trimmed, the lawns are well groomed, and God is a pacifist in Goshen, Bluffton, Richmond, North Newton, and Waterloo.[11] It is different and otherwise in Kaduna, Kano, and Lagos. Thus, linking the gospel of peace to a notion of the benevolence of nature and the pacifism of God, as some contemporary peace church theologians are tempted to do, is unthinkable and unbelievable to most Nigerian pastors and theologians.

My engaging dialogues, and sometimes debates, with my Nigerian brethren invited me to ponder again a model of religious reflection I first encountered years ago in the classic work by the pietistic Lutheran, Rudolph Otto. His book, *Das Heilige*, or *The Idea of the Holy*, is both a phenomenology of religious experience and an apologetics for a complex view of divinity that does not collapse the mystery of existence into rationality; nor does it pretend that the experiential dimension at the heart of all religion can ever be completely conceptualized or moralized.[12] The *holy* or the *numinous*, for Otto, is beyond mere morality or philosophical argument and demonstration; it is an experience, a feeling (*das numinose Gefühl*), that must be encountered and evoked. Further, Otto insists that God's transcendence, *das ganz Andere (the Wholly Other)*, cannot be fully known in God's immanent presence. This phenomenological description of religion in many ways echoes Luther's theology of the hidden and revealed God.[13] Even in revelation, indeed even in incarnation, there is something of the transcendent God that remains hidden.

Rudolph Otto's description of the holy is rather well known. The experience of the holy is described and developed in Otto's thought as *mysterium tremendum et fascinans*. The *tremendum* is the awe-evoking, unapproachable, overpowering, transcendent, tremendous yet also terrifying presence of the divine. It is encountering God as wholly other. It is an encounter—indeed a *tremor*—that is not only spiritual but physical and psychological as well. The *mysterium* evokes not *tremor* as much as *stupor*: a silence and yieldedness before the divine mystery. The *fascinans*, on the other hand, carries with it the revelation of God's tender mercy, grace, and love. The holy, like the life-world, is never reducible to one attribute or limited by finite theological or theoretical descriptions. Infinity must never be collapsed into any finite totality. *Das Heilige* is *mysterium tremendum et fascinans* at one and the same time.

This idea of the holy could indeed be more important to ethical reflection than early phenomenologists of religion might have suspected. There is a striking suggestion of this in Jacques Derrida's funeral oration for Emmanuel Levinas. The Jewish philosopher Levinas is known for his understanding of ethics as a first principle: ethics before ontology, the state, or politics. Yet Derrida recalls an illuminating conversation with the philosopher in which Levinas declared, "You know, one often speaks of ethics to describe what I do, but really what interests me in the end is not ethics, not ethics alone, but the holy, the holiness of the holy."[14] The project of Levinas, because of this understanding of the holy or the infinite, seems not only to place ethics before and beyond ontology, but also pushes thought and action toward an ethic beyond ethics. Thus, the idea of the holy, "limits" all ethical, theological, or political doctrines or dogmas.

The EYN Church, and most of the Christianity I encountered in Nigeria, had a much more profound sense of this "idea of the holy" than we Christians in North America seem to be at ease with in our theological imaginations.[15] In fact, this image of a tremendous and transcendent God is very difficult for many peace church pastors and theologians. We are comforted more by a God who is a lot like a Mennonite, Brethren, or Quaker pacifist. We are happier when God is one thing, when the holiness, otherness, mystery, transcendence, and even terror of God are eclipsed by the politics of Jesus. We are tempted to substitute the wonder of a sacramental universe for a churchly ethic. More than one of my Nigerian brother-preachers said to me, "God is love but not a pacifist!"

Some years ago I was having a conversation with the Canadian Mennonite theologian James Reimer. We were talking about the work of John Howard Yoder, which we both admire, respect, and teach. As our conversation picked up momentum and passion, in what seemed like a whirlwind of emotion, Reimer declared, "Behold the Lamb indeed, but I fear there is no lion in Yoder's theology!"[16] Other Christian thinkers have struggled deeply with this problem of the gospel of peace and the violence of God.

In 1939 in New York City, Dietrich Bonhoeffer was praying and pondering about what direction his resistance to Hitler and European fascism might finally take. He had a conversation with the poet W. H. Auden.[17] We have no record of what was said in this conversation, but we do know Bonhoeffer and Auden discussed not only poetry but also international politics. Auden had been a pacifist, but the rise of Hitler had him thinking otherwise and differently. He had been at work on a book exploring, among other things, the difficult images of the divine presented by the artist and mystical poet William Blake in his classic, *The Marriage of Heaven and Hell*. Blake asks a difficult but necessary question in his poem, "Tyger": "Did he who made the Lamb make thee?" This poetic question is addressed to the tiger and cannot be avoided by any honest theologian: "Did he who made the Lamb make thee?"

Of course we know the answer is "yes," but what do we do with this understanding? James Reimer and Miroslav Volf, along with a number of Nigerian pastors and theologians, would suggest that it might serve us well, as people longing for peace, to dwell within the assertion that "God is love but not a pacifist."[18] To do so is not to perform a radical deconstruction of classical Christianity. On the contrary, these theological thinkers insist that such a confession returns us to the mystery of the triune God, a God who is revealed but also hidden, transcendent and immanent, loving and terrifying. Consider James Reimer's description of this God:

> This God is no Mennonite pacifist. This God is beyond all human ethical systems, beyond our rules of good and bad. This is the God one meets not in the living room but on the boundary, at the abyss, at the point where one is faced with the threat of non-being. Does this mean God the Creator is arbitrary, like the Greek and Roman Gods? No, the pagan arbitrariness is precisely what the Jews and the Christians rejected. God is not arbitrary—God is just, righteous, good, and loving, but in ways that are not fully transparent.[19]

Reimer writes that God's revelation through Jesus Christ is a revelation of this mystery. It is not a revelation of all that is hidden but rather the revelation of a mystery—"the mystery that despite the reality of violence and evil in the world there is a moment of divine redemption and reconciliation in the cosmos."[20] Yet Reimer insists that God's means of achieving ultimate reconciliation of all things are not immediately evident to us.

More than a few members of the Historic Peace Churches worry that if we do not make God as ethically earnest as our most committed disciples and as theologically correct as our best theologians, then anything will be permitted in the moral universe! So, in this scenario, we tend to make God in our image and thus in the process make ourselves like God. Indeed, if we do not edit the biblical claim that "Yahweh is a warrior," will it not follow logically that God's servants will feel obligated to be like the divine and fight to the death on behalf of righteousness? Or unless we cleanse the atonement of all traces of violence, will we not feel compelled to sacrifice ourselves and perhaps even others for the causes of just wars or violent liberation movements?[21]

Not necessarily. In fact, Miroslav Volf has suggested that the primordial temptation—the desire to be like God—may indeed be a far greater impetus for violence in the world.[22] Those of us in the Anabaptist tradition can testify to the history of terrible cruelty and emotional terrorism that emerged when the church through its leadership became a proxy for God in the process of disciplining the erring or dissenting member through shunning or the use of the "ban." The ban was an ecclesiastical sword that cut members off not only from the church but often from family, friends, and even from the source of one's livelihood. There is a great temptation in restorationist, primitivist, or perfectionist religious movements to be "godly" or even "godlike." Ah, but the Wholly Other still declares: "I saw Lucifer fall from the sky like lightning!"

James Reimer has wisely written: "Our commitment to the way of the cross (reconciliation) is not premised on God's pacifism or nonpacifism. It is precisely because God has the prerogative to give and take life that we do not have that right. Vengeance we leave up to God."[23] This is a theology of peacemaking that my Nigerian colleagues articulated and found compelling. It is a theology that refuses to domesticate the Infinite, and it likewise reflects the spirit and the letter of the biblical witness.[24]

I would suggest that this understanding of God is not only good classical theology, but also good psychology and spirituality for the work of conflict transformation and peacemaking in a blessed but fallen world. We will never completely escape the violence in our world or in ourselves. The violence is not only out there— it is in here; it is internal. Conversation with my Nigerian colleagues around this issue led me to consider in a new way the deep therapeutic value of imaginatively holding together the gospel of peace and the violence of God. Of course, pop therapists who fill the terrifying shadows of the unconscious with glib and gleeful self-help books will see this proposal as "unhealthy." Likewise, theologians who cloak the dark night of the soul in a Jesus story that turns too quickly from the bloody tragedies of history and from the unapproachable, overpowering otherness of the divine to an easy, ideological resolution of conflict will certainly reject this paradoxical and poetic intellectual therapy.

I will not quarrel with them. I will only ask them to join me in Kaduna to visit the widow of Pastor Taru and his seven fatherless children. We will walk by the terrible rubble from the destruction of churches, mosques, schools, homes, and businesses. We will drive to the site of the largest Christian theological library in northern Nigeria, burned to the ground by Muslims during the crisis, with only the charred spines of books now remaining. I will ask them to lean into their feelings, not only into their properly tutored thoughts of pacifism, but into the inescapable feelings of shock, sorrow, anger, outrage, judgment, and perhaps even vengeance. These are feelings that come from souls conflicted by the paradoxical desire for love *and* justice, and emerge naturally from psyches throbbing from the bodily chemicals and emotions of human aggression, judgment, and justice. These are elemental passions.

What are we to do with these intense, inescapable feelings? We could address and release these tensions by reaching for a sword. Or we might instead find a deep theological therapy through reflecting upon a rather terrifying revelation. I propose the latter. As we consider this astonishing revelation, I propose that we ponder a very strange question as an exercise of deep theological therapy: could it be that a theopoetic acknowledgement of the violence of Hidden God might indeed transform the aggressive energies in the human psyche, soul, and body into active and nonviolent expressions of peacemaking on earth?

Consider the Revelation of Saint John the Divine:

And I saw when the Lamb opened one of the seals, and I heard, as it were the noise of thunder, one of the four beasts saying, Come and see. (Rev. 6:1, King James Version)

And when he had opened the fifth seal, I saw under the altar the souls of them that were slain for the word of God, and for the testimony which they held: And they cried with a loud voice, saying, How long, O Lord, holy and true, dost thou not judge and avenge our blood on them that dwell on the earth? (Rev. 6:9-10, KJV)

And he saith unto me, Write, Blessed are they which are called unto the marriage supper of the Lamb. And he saith unto me, These are the true sayings of God. And I fell at his feet to worship him. And he said unto me, *See thou do it not*: I am thy fellowservant, and of thy brethren that have the testimony of Jesus: worship God: for the testimony of Jesus is the spirit of prophecy.

And I saw heaven opened, and behold a white horse; and he that sat upon him was called Faithful and True, and in righteousness he doth judge and make war. His eyes were as a flame of fire, and on his head were many crowns; and he had a name written that no man knew, but he himself. And he was clothed with a vesture dipped in blood: and his name is called The Word of God.

And the armies which were in heaven followed him upon white horses, clothed in fine linen, white and clean. And out of his mouth goeth a sharp sword, that with it he should smite the nations: and he shall rule them with a rod of iron: and he treadeth the winepress of the fierceness and wrath of Almighty God. And he hath on his vesture and on his thigh, a name written: KING OF KINGS AND LORD OF LORDS.

And I saw an angel standing in the sun; and he cried with a loud voice, saying to all the fowls that fly in the midst of heaven, Come and gather yourselves together unto the supper of the great God; That ye may eat the flesh of kings, and the flesh of captains, and the flesh of mighty men, and the flesh of horses, and of them that sit on them, and the flesh of all men, both free and bond, both small and great.

And I saw the beast, and the kings of the earth, and their armies, gathered together to make war against him that sat on the horse, and against his army.

And the beast was taken, and with him the false prophet that wrought miracles before him, with which he deceived them that had received the mark of the beast, and them that worshipped his image. These were both cast alive into a lake of fire burning with brimstone. And the remnant were slain with the sword of him that sat upon the horse, which sword proceeded out of his mouth: and all the fowls were filled with their flesh. AMEN. (Rev. 19:9-21, KJV)

I ask again a question I found disturbing yet also theologically and psychologically profound during my visit to Nigeria. Could it be that because Yahweh is a warrior, we can be a people of peace?

NOTES

1. See Chalmer E. Faw, "Profile of Brethren Mission: An Evaluation of Fifty Years in Nigeria," *Brethren Life and Thought* 19:2 (Spring 1974), 85-96.

2. For a discussion of the EYN's understanding of its identity as a "peace church" in its West African context see Patrick K. Bugu, "Reconciliation or Pacifism? The Nigerian Experience," ch. 8 in this volume.

3. B.E.E. Bedki, *The Tragedy of Sharia, Cry and the Voice of Masses: Kaduna Crisis from An Eye Witness* (Jos, Nigeria: Distributed by the EYN Center, 2001).

4. I of course don't mean to suggest here that "religion," whether fundamentalism or liberalism, is ever disentangled from economic, ethnic (tribal), political, or other social realities. Indeed, the deplorable poverty and corrupt economic politics of contemporary Nigeria (where even a gallon of petrol must be bargained for on the black market in an extremely oil rich nation) destroys public hope as it undermines even the most eloquent rhetoric about political democracy and thus fuels the fires of religious resentment and sectarian retreat. For an excellent treatment of contemporary Nigerian politics, economics, culture, and religion see Karl Maier, *This House Has Fallen: Midnight in Nigeria* (New York: BBS Public Affairs, 2000).

5. For a helpful collection of essays and articles on political and cultural transition in Nigeria in particular, and in Africa more generally, see the work of Nigerian historian J. F. Ade. Ajayi, *Tradition and Change in Africa* (Trenton, N.J.: Africa World Press, 2000).

6. A more extended discussion of the significance of the Melchizedek narrative for Christology will appear in my forthcoming published lectures from Nigeria, *Lafiya: A Wholeness Without Harmony?*

7. Judith M. Gundry-Volf and Miroslav Volf, *A Spacious Heart: Essays on Identity and Belonging* (Harrisburg, Pa.: Trinity Press International, 1997), 49.

8. The new work by Harvard sociologist Barrington Moore studies the human tendency to divide the pure "we" from the impure and polluting "other" or "enemy." Moore's investigation into why groups of people kill or torture each other concludes that there is a driving tendency for people to persecute those they perceive as polluting due to their "impure" religious, political, or economic ideas. Barrington Moore, *Moral Purity and Persecution* (Princeton: Princeton University Press, 2000).

9. See Scott Holland, "First We Take Manhattan, Then We Take Berlin: Bonhoeffer's New York," *Cross Currents* 51:4 (Winter 2002), 470-483.

10. The Summer, 2001, issue of the journal *Cross Currents* is devoted to this problem. Jewish and Christian thinkers reflect upon not only the problem of religion *and* violence, but also upon the more difficult and disturbing problem of violence *in* religion. *Cross Currents* 51:2 (Summer 2001).

11. These towns are locations of colleges related to Historic Peace

Churches. *Mennonite:* Goshen, Indiana (Goshen College); Bluffton, Ohio (Bluffton College); North Newton, Kansas (Bethel College); Harrisonburg, Virginia (Eastern Mennonite University); Waterloo, Ontario (Conrad Grebel College); and *Quaker:* Richmond, Indiana (Earlham College). The latter is also the location of Bethany Theological Seminary of the Church of the Brethren.

12. Rudolph Otto, *The Idea of the Holy: An Inquiry into the Non-Rational Factor in the Idea of the Divine and Its Relation to the Rational* (New York: Oxford University Press, 1923; reprint, 1975). For an excellent recent study of Otto's classic text see Gregory D. Alles, "Toward a Genealogy of the Holy: Rudolph Otto and the Apologetics of Religion," *Journal of the American Academy of Religion* 69:2 (June 2001), 223-341.

13. David Tracy has returned to a consideration of Luther's hidden God as well as to the apophatic mystics as a way to reimagine and rethink the implications of God-talk in a postmodern, post-Holocaust world. See Tracy, "The Hidden God: The Divine Other of Liberation," *Cross Currents* 46:1 (Spring 1996), 3-16. Also see David Tracy's "The Post-Modern Naming of God as Incomprehensible and Hidden," *Cross Currents* 50:1-2 (Spring/Summer 2000), 240-247.

14. Jacques Derrida, "Adieu: Emmanuel Levinas," ed. Martin McQuillan, *Deconstruction: A Reader* (New York: Routledge, 2000), 478.

15. It is beyond the scope of this chapter to discuss how the Nigerian awareness of "the holy" impacts their hermeneutics of the life-world, nature, or creation. However, it should be noted that the same sense of both wonder and terror present in their understanding of God, not surprisingly, is also reflected in their theology of the life-world. Few American or European experiments in "ecological theology" have been able to capture this dual sense of both aesthetic awe and emotional terror in the life-world. Our poets and writers do much better. I'm thinking especially of the lovely but violent portrayals of nature and the divine in Annie Dillard's *Holy the Firm* and *The Living*. The new novellas of Maureen Howard likewise capture nature's song and violence. In *Big As Life: Three Tales for Spring* (New York: Viking, 2001), Howard takes us into the life of James Audubon, the famous painter and birder who found it necessary to kill birds for his art. Howard recalls how as a 16-year-old girl looking at Audubon's *Birds of America* in the Bridgeport Public Library she discovered "an ardor brought to information of feathers, claws, beaks, flight, color, to song and violence, which was my natural world too, though I hadn't known it."

16. In correspondence with James Reimer, he alerted me to the special issue of *Conrad Grebel Review* devoted to the work of John Howard Yoder where he takes up this critique in a more formal way. See 16:2 (Spring 1998). It should also be noted that the journal devoted a special issue to the work of Miroslav Volf; see 18:3 (Fall 2000).

17. For more on this Bonhoeffer-Auden exchange see my "First We Take Manhattan, Then We Take Berlin: Bonhoeffer's New York," cited above.

18. This statement, "God is love but not a pacifist," was made by several EYN pastors during my visit to Nigeria along with other assertions like, "God's love and judgments are violent even if we are commanded to practice

peace. Thus, we must remember that we are not God." Canadian theologian A. James Reimer has also written that, "God Is Love but Not a Pacifist," in his *Mennonites and Classical Theology: Dogmatic Foundations for Christian Ethics* (Kitchener, Ontario and Scottdale, Pa.: Pandora Press and Herald Press, 2000), 486-492.

19. A. James Reimer, p. 492.

20. Ibid.

21. I am thinking here of the constructive challenge of "a nonviolent atonement" presented by my friend J. Denny Weaver in his book, *The Nonviolent Atonement* (Grand Rapids: Eerdmans, 2001).

22. Volf made this provocative comment during a personal conversation in November, 2000, when he was lecturing at Bethany Theological Seminary and Earlham School of Religion. He begins to address this problem in the final chapter of his book, *Exclusion and Embrace: A Theological Exploration of Identity* (Nashville: Abingdon Press, 1996).

23. James Reimer, p. 492.

24. I am grateful for conversations with New Testament scholar Tom Yoder Neufeld at the Bienenberg meetings around this tension of the gospel of peace and the violence of God. His work supports my claim that this tension is present not only in the biblical texts but also in the early peace church readings of classical Christianity. See his interesting study, *Put on the Armour of God: The Divine Warrior from Isaiah to Ephesians* (Sheffield, England: Sheffield Academic Press, 1997). First Testament scholar Millard Lind likewise addresses this tension in his work, *Yahweh Is a Warrior* (Scottdale, Pa.: Herald Press, 1980).

Chapter 10

Being a Peace Church in the Colombian Context

Alix Lozano
Translation from Spanish by Rebecca Yoder-Neufeld

A new century has begun with great tasks ahead for humanity. One of these is responding to the unfulfilled promises of the neoliberal model. Poverty and marginalization are growing by leaps and bounds, generating violence in its various expressions. We must remember the words of Jürgen Moltmann: "The more accurately a church recognizes its social context, the more effectively it can become an instrument of God's justice in [that] society."[1]

In Colombia a feeling of impotence pervades people and communities, including the church. The church as well as individuals must move beyond this feeling. With the persecuted and impoverished communities, we must say, "It is necessary that the judgment come with justice" not so much to condemn, as to save, because the opportune time has come.

Faced with the tasks of humanity and the violent Colombian context, the Mennonite Church has sought to be consistent with both reality and the message of the gospel from the perspective of Hebrew *Shalom*—the biblical and gospel peace that would allow the rhythm of life to return to the country. Confronted with the panorama of violence that one lives with in Colombia, we must strive to interpret and share alternatives for peace.

THE DYNAMICS OF VIOLENCE IN COLOMBIA

Although Colombia has not always been a violent country, violence has been present in its history. The country has been in permanent endemic war, expressed in the fourteen-year war of independence against Spain, eight general civil wars, fourteen local wars, two international wars, two coups d'etat in the last century and in the present one, as well as party confrontation, generalized uprisings, and the longest internal armed conflict on the continent.[2]

Violence in Colombia is a multi-causal phenomenon, expressed in dynamics that coexist, that overlap, that feed one another, and many times live on a "culture of violence" socialized in the family, educational institutions, the workplace, and the media.[3] This social phenomenon makes itself evident in a number of ways:

Political violence is seen concretely as 40 years of armed internal conflict between the state and insurgent groups. Since the 1980s, the insurgency, the state, and the self-defense groups, known as the paramilitary groups, have been parties to the conflict.

Socioeconomic violence is the product of economic inequalities, reflected in conflicts that go beyond politics and manifest themselves in the high level of crimes against life, personal safety, and property.

Sociocultural violence is the result of the intolerance of those who conceive of persons from marginalized groups as the enemy, stigmatizing them because of race, gender, or behavior. This includes the groups of people who have been executed by the misnamed "social cleansing" organizations.

The violence of drug trafficking and the struggle for territorial control that is linked to it has displaced millions of persons, the majority being women and children.

Along with more overt violence, several other forces are wreaking havoc in Colombian society. Economic globalization imposed over the last decade has exacerbated enormous social inequalities, not only in Colombia but in all of Latin America. The defenders of economic globalization assure us that international competitiveness requires us to adopt new technologies, but we have seen the living conditions of the majority of the population worsen, excluding them from any possibility of life with dignity.

One example is privatization, presented to us as an indispensable component of openness and globalization. Public services for social well-being, such as health programs, have been labeled inefficient and bureaucratic, and gradually dismantled. Something similar is occurring with the privatization of higher education. These changes eliminate state policies designed to defend the general welfare, and reflect the elimination of social rights.

North American economic interests are at the root of the push for globalization and privatization. There is pressure for the strict fulfillment of the commitments made to the International Monetary Fund, such as the privatization of state corporations, tax hikes, and the deterioration of workplace conditions.

The U.S. government is currently promoting Plan Colombia, a strategy for strengthening the Colombian Army and eradicating coca, in the hope that the guerrillas' source of income will dry up, and they will be forced to negotiate peace. Plan Colombia is predominantly a military aid program. A massive infusion of 1.3 billion U.S. dollars has already been designated, of which 80 percent is for military support: radar, planes, helicopters, as well as the training and financing of new battalions; 12 percent is for "policies of human rights, judicial reform, and democratic systems," and the remaining 8 percent is for "alternative" development programs.[4]

Plan Colombia is extremely controversial, with aspects of its scope and content still unclear. Our questions around the plan include: Is the country prepared to receive the thousands of displaced persons that the supposed eradication of illicit crops will generate? Is the country prepared for the "vietnamization" of the armed conflict? Will strengthening armed forces known for corruption lead to wider war with more civilian deaths? Will it really contribute to the peace process?

THE CHURCHES AMID THE CONFLICT

The evangelical Christian churches in Colombia are not removed from the impact of this conflict. But in this case the persecution is not religious or the result of being evangelical, but rather because they are located in the conflict zones. Many church members and pastors have been assassinated or falsely accused of siding with the guerrillas, the paramilitary, or the army.

One must acknowledge that a minority of pastors or church leaders have allowed themselves to be influenced by the violent environment in which they live and their language is sometimes warlike, reflecting exclusion, distance from reality, or at least imprudence. On various occasions they are confronted by leaders of the armed groups, which makes them feel very alone, but their courage and constancy in difficult situations is to be celebrated.

We know of testimonies of entire churches that have been displaced with their pastors. More than 100 churches have been closed—believers, pastors, or church leaders assassinated or kidnapped. Many churches and pastors are under threat both in the countryside and in the city.

We recognize that when the church assumes a witnessing role for the cause of Jesus Christ—a clear witness for love, nonviolence, social justice, the well-being of the poorest and the marginalized, which includes persons displaced by the violence—then problems with some of the actors involved in the conflict begin.[5]

BIBLICAL GUIDELINES ON SHALOM

Reflecting on biblical texts in light of the war we suffer in Colombia and on the peace we long for, and with the purpose of orienting the work for peace, we understand that God is a God of peace; Jesus Christ is Lord of peace (Eph. 2:14-17); his Spirit is a Spirit of peace; his reign is a reign of peace (Rom. 14:17); his gospel is the good news of peace (Eph. 6;15); his children are makers of peace (Matt. 5:9).

God wants peace, an integral peace that embraces the whole person, the family, the community, the nation, the world, and creation. It is therefore imperative that in Colombia we assume a humble, but clear and committed, role in the search for peace.

The Bible says that peace is built together with social justice (Isa. 32:17, James 3:18). Through the prophet Isaiah, the Lord says: "[Is not this what pleases me]: to loose the bonds of injustice, to undo the thongs of the yoke, to let the oppressed go free, and to [end all tyranny]? Is it not to share your bread with the hungry, and bring the homeless poor into your house; when you see the naked, to cover them, and not to hide yourself from your own kin?" The result for the nation is that "[T]hen your light shall break forth like the dawn, and your healing shall spring up quickly (Isa. 58:6-8)." That is to say, peace is present when love and obedience to God are expressed as love and solidarity with the poor, the weak, and the dispossessed of society.

Peace is built on the base of truth (John 8:32). Peace cannot be based on concealment and lies. The truth about the horrors that the Colombian people have suffered must be known. The perpetrators must be identified and confronted, and faced by the victims of their actions. But truth is not sufficient; mercy is also needed. It is necessary to know the truth, not to exercise vengeance or revenge, but so that there can be repentance, forgiveness, and healing. Interrupting the cycle of violence against violence is necessary, not by burying the truth, but rather by knowing it, taking responsibility for it, and forgiving it.[6]

In summary, justice, truth, mercy, forgiveness, restoration, love, and nonviolence are necessary biblical guidelines for rebuilding the social fabric, for reconciling and restoring the Colombian community (Mic. 6:8).

As the violence intensifies in Colombia, the churches are confronted with the challenge of making a choice: Will they decide to be the church of the stranger, the displaced, the uprooted, or will they choose to turn their backs and ignore the problem? Will they simply treat violence as a sermon topic, or will they also be part of the solution to the country's problems? Will they handle the matter of peace in their programming with an understanding of the universality of the gospel and stand with those who claim the respect of their dignity as human beings? How can Colombians be a peace church in a context of violence?

Violence affects the civilian population of Colombia indiscriminately, without consideration of religious creed or gender. The culture that has been fostered is a "culture of violence"—violence whose causes and consequences we have already seen. The task of the church is to represent the alternative of peace.

THE CHURCH AS PEACE COMMUNITY[7]

What does a peace church look like in the Colombian context? We find that the implications are numerous.

A Community in Solidarity

In some countries, siding with those who suffer—the victims of discrimination—is dangerous. In many places, demonstrating sensitivity to excluded people does not enjoy the approval of the majority of Christian denominations, who appear more concerned about ecclesial models that compete for loyalties. As the church confronts the causes of the injustice that lead to different expressions of violence against people, the church must be ready to pay the price for confronting privilege and the established powers. The presence of a community that exercises solidarity with all those who suffer oppression is a community in which

- The pain of the other becomes the pain of all.
- There is space for fraternal accompaniment with those whose suffering is real.
- Persons who suffer find the necessary strength to continue life.
- Weeping with those who weep becomes a distinctive practice.

A Community That Enlivens Hope

With the means available at the present moment, we must help others continue their lives, believing and hoping for a better tomorrow. From the Christian viewpoint, hope is a collective enterprise and a community task. Hope is enlivened through a variety of means:

- Showing mercy and compassion as a Samaritan church.
- Providing an affective and effective option for the victims.
- Engaging in visible gestures for justice and human rights.
- Recovering worship and the power of celebration.
- Experiencing the power of the Word.

A Healing Community

In this context, it is not enough to simply be a community where birth and confirmation of identity are affirmed. Healing is also at issue: physical, moral, spiritual, and psychological healing. Within an affirming Christian community, an individual's possibilities for good will increase.

For persons affected by any expression of violence, the reconstruction of the social order is an urgent process to undertake and this must begin with the verbalization of what has been silenced, of what is traumatic and terrifying. Only through this verbalization of the conflict does one achieve awareness of it and in this way find a new sense of belonging. The function of the healing community, therefore, is to help the conscientization of persons who suffer violence through the social expression of fear, anguish, rage, and meaninglessness.

Since the faith community does not always have all the professional human resources available, we must nurture and strengthen support networks with other groups or faith communities, so that each community with its emphasis or special gifts may together "serve one another like good stewards of the manifold grace of God" (1 Pet. 4. 10).

A Community of "Sanctuaries of Peace"

Scripture encourages local churches to identify themselves as and declare themselves to be Peace Sanctuary Churches (Josh. 20; Deut. 19:8-13). This means being a people of peace, giving a peace message and witness, and being a space of peace. This is manifest in the following ways:

- Proclaiming the good news of forgiveness, salvation, liberation, restoration and reconciliation for all Colombians: with God, with their fellow men/women, and with themselves. It means rescuing many persons from wasted and disfigured lives to recover—with the power of the Holy Spirit and the power of transforming love in the image of God in them—the invaluable potential that each person possesses.
- Carrying out efforts for justice and peace such as assisting orphaned children and widows, displaced persons, women household heads, and all the persons affected by the violence.
- Participating in public witness such as peace vigils, times of prayer for peace, and other nonviolent local actions that advocate peace.
- Being a space of encounter and dialogue for the members of the church, the surrounding community, the actors in the conflict, the peacemakers, and also providing protection to persecuted persons whose lives are in danger. This space is a peace territory, free from all action or incursion by any armed actors, and protected by the protocols on International Humanitarian Rights.

A Community That Educates for Peace

We believe that faced with a culture of violence, peace education is necessary. The Mennonite Biblical Seminary considers pertinent its emphasis on biblical-theological training with a view to peace and nonviolence. It trains men and women leaders who in turn will help the community's awareness of the situation through workshops on the biblical basis of peace, nonviolence, peaceful resolution and conflict transformation, civic participation, human dignity, and the construction of a lasting infrastructure for peace.

CONCLUSION

I have shared with you how Colombians understand, live, and contribute to the church's role in the peace process. We believe that it must be a commitment of the world community. As Historic Peace Churches, we must accompany sisters and brothers in the third world who are struggling for change practically alone. The prophetic voice of the first world is necessary in cooperating and showing solidarity at this historical juncture.

NOTES

1. Jürgen Moltmann, *La justicia crea futuro* (Santander: Sal Terrae, 1989), 18.

2. Sánchez G. Gonzalo, "Los estudios sobre la violencia. Balance y perspectivas," *Pasado y presente de la violencia en Colombia* (Bogotá: Fondo Editorial Cerec, 1995), 19.

3. Ibid,17, 22-26.

4. Luis A. Matta Aldana, "El Plan Colombia: Desafio neoliberal contra América Latina," Foro Alternativo contra la globalización y el neoliberalismo unpublished paper (1999).

5. Guillermo Triana y R. Esquivia, *Declaratión de Cedecol a la nación*. (Bogotá: Consejo Evangélico de Colombia), Colombia, 2001 , 3.

6. Ibid., 3-4.

7. Pautas patorales de acompanamiento a personas desplazadas por la violencia en Colombia. Propuesta elaborada por la autora en trabajo de investigación para la Universidad Bíblica Latinoamericana (UBL), San José, 2000.

BUILDING
CULTURES
OF JUST PEACE

Chapter 11

Did Jesus Love His Enemies?

Daniel W. Ulrich

*T*here is apparent tension between the report of Jesus' teaching in Matthew 5:38-48 and the characterization of Jesus elsewhere in the narrative. Matthew 5:39 has often been interpreted as a call for passive nonresistance in the face of evil, and Jesus' refusal to resist arrest and crucifixion is consistent with that interpretation (26:47-56). Nevertheless, Jesus' response to his opponents on other occasions seems far from passive or nonresistant. Indeed, the conflict between Jesus and Israel's religious leaders is "acutely confrontational" on both sides throughout most of Matthew's story.[1]

Already in Galilee, Jesus calls the religious leaders "hypocrites" (5:20; 6:1-17), returns their accusations of blasphemy (12:30-32; cf. 9:3), and dismisses them as "blind guides" (15:14). The conflict escalates sharply as Jesus confronts the leaders in Jerusalem (21:12—23:39). His first act on entering Jerusalem is to challenge the operation of the temple with a provocative demonstration (21:12-17). After a series of intense debates in which Jesus reduces his opponents to silence

(22:46), he publicly rebukes them in harsh terms, calling them "offspring of vipers" and heirs to the murderers of the prophets (23:29-33). William Klassen probably speaks for many readers when he asks, "Did Jesus himself love his enemies? Matthew 23 seems to suggest that he did not."[2]

This chapter responds to Klassen's question with an attempt to clarify Jesus' attitude toward enemies as depicted in the Gospel of Matthew.[3] Matthew portrays Jesus as a model for his disciples (cf. 10:25), and he characterizes Israel's religious leaders as hypocrites on the grounds that they fail to follow their own teaching (23:3).

Therefore, an irreconcilable discrepancy between Jesus' commands and his actions regarding enemies would represent a significant flaw in the narrative. Using a strategy of "consistency-building," which involves interpreting diverse aspects of the narrative in light of each other,[4] I will argue here that both Jesus' teaching and example are consistent with the command to "reprove your neighbor" in Leviticus 19:17-18, a text that Matthew cites repeatedly (Matt. 5:43; 18:15; 19:19; 22:39). The conclusion of the chapter asks how Christians might apply Matthew's narrative ethic faithfully in today's globalized world.

REPROOF IN THE SEPTUAGINT

Matthew assumes that readers are familiar with the Septuagint. In the Septuagint as a whole, the pertinent term *elenchein* covers a broad semantic field. Possible translations include "bring to light," "expose," "demonstrate," "convince," "reprove," "convict," "punish," or "discipline." Since Matthew's only use of *elenchein* (18:15) occurs in an allusion to Leviticus 19:17-18, those verses serve as a primary background for understanding Matthew's view of reproof.

Leviticus 19:17-18 appears in the context of the Holiness Code, which is grounded in the theological presuppositions that Israelites must be holy like their God (cf. Lev. 19:2) and that God will act to preserve Israel's holiness by "cutting off" anyone who violates God's commands (19:8; 20:3,5). Leviticus does not define holiness solely in terms of cultic purity since it includes a deep concern for social justice. Indeed, social justice is a unifying theme in Leviticus 19:9-18, the immediate context of our unit.[5]

The refrain, "I am Lord," in 19:16c and 18c sets off 19:17-18 as a discrete unit with the following parallel structure:[6]

	VERSE 17	**VERSE 18**
PROHIBITIONS	You shall not hate your brother or sister in your mind.	And your hand shall not take revenge, and you shall not rage against the members of your people.
ALTERNATIVES	With a reproof you shall reprove your neighbor.	And you shall love your neighbor as yourself
MOTIVES	And you will not acquire sin because of that one.	I am Lord.[7]

This parallelism suggests that several key terms are synonyms. "Members of your people," "your brother or sister," and "your neighbor" are equivalent terms for compatriots in Israel, whose mutual obligations are emphasized through the use of kinship metaphors. The scope of the command is thus here limited to relationships within Israel, while Leviticus 19:34 also commands love for "the alien who resides among you." The prohibited actions of "hating," "avenging," and "raging" each presuppose a situation in which interpersonal conflict threatens to spiral out of control. Finally, "reproving" and "loving" are presented as synonyms, with the implication that reproof is an aspect of love. The verb translated "love" (*agapan*) points to actions rather than emotions. It means acting for the benefit of others whether they deserve it or not. Reproof is consistent with love when its purpose is to benefit others by informing them of their need for repentance and reconciliation.

The motive clause in 19:17 indicates that someone who reproves another can avoid acquiring sin on account of that person. The sin envisioned here may be related to the secret hatred, revenge, and raging mentioned in 19:17-18. In that case, the motive clause suggests that the act of reproving a neighbor may keep the conflict from escalating to the point that both parties are guilty. Another possibility is that the sin is precisely the failure to warn one's neighbor, who may incur God's wrath as a result. The sin of failing to warn others is emphasized in Ezekiel 3:16-21, where the prophet hears that he will be held accountable like a sentinel for warning the people about God's approaching judgment. If Ezekiel fulfills this crucial task, then he will no longer be responsible for the deaths of people who fail to heed the warning, and those who do heed it will live. Like Ezekiel, the Holiness Code presupposes that God will judge unjust people severely. That prospect helps to explain why the failure to reprove a neighbor may be considered a sin.

MATTHEW'S EXPLICIT TEACHING OF REPROOF

Matthew 18:15 alludes to Leviticus 19:17-18 in the context of an extended discourse on humility as greatness in the reign of heaven. [8] Matthew 18 includes a thesis statement (18:3-4; cf. 5:17-20) followed by a series of elaborations. The elaborations in 18:5-35 lift up various marks of greatness in God's eyes, including hospitality and care toward vulnerable people, self-discipline, and unlimited forgiveness. As one of these elaborations, Matthew 18:15-20 calls disciples to serve one another through caring reproof whenever one of them sins.

The kind of reproof that Matthew envisions for the church requires humility of everyone involved. The protagonist in 18:15-17 must first go alone to someone who has sinned, thus forgoing an opportunity to shame the other person publicly. Instead, the protagonist becomes vulnerable, risking sharper conflict and possible retaliation, to open the door for repentance and reconciliation. If the disciple being confronted accepts the invitation to repent, then he or she is also demonstrating the kind of greatness taught in Matthew 18. If a matter reaches the later stages described in 18:16-17, the congregation is called to demonstrate humility by openly acknowledging the sin of its members, by standing in solidarity with the victims of sin, by repeatedly calling for repentance, and by forgiving without limit those who do repent.

Matthew 18:15-20 calls for reproof within the community of disciples, not as punishment but as a way to win back someone who might otherwise be lost to God's reign. Even the decision to treat someone as a Gentile or a tax collector is not a punishment so much as an acknowledgment that the offender is no longer acting as a member of the community. The goal of reproof dictates the spirit with which it is to be carried out: humbly, patiently, and with an eagerness to forgive.

MATTHEW'S TEACHING REGARDING ENEMIES

It is intriguing that Matthew's most explicit and problematic teaching regarding enemies also includes an allusion to Leviticus

19:17-18. Could Matthew's command to love enemies also entail reproving them? A review of pertinent translation issues and analysis of Matthew 5:38-48 will help to answer that question.

The literary context for these verses is an inaugural discourse (5:1-7:29) in which Jesus teaches about the greater righteousness that is required of those who will enter God's reign. Matthew 5:21-48 describes this greater righteousness through a series of six antitheses. In each of these, Jesus cites an older interpretation of Torah followed by his own more radical pronouncement. Usually the word from Jesus continues in an elaboration that contains illustrative commands, reasons for obeying, or both. The last two antitheses, comprising Matthew 5:38-48, follow a similar pattern as they bring the series to a climax.

In 5:38-42, four secondary commands illustrate the idea of not competing with an evil person:

> You have heard that it was said, "An eye in exchange for an eye" and "a tooth in exchange for a tooth." But I am telling you not to compete with the evil person. Instead, when someone slaps you on the right cheek, turn to him the other also. And to the one who wants to sue you and take your tunic, leave to him your cloak also.
>
> And when someone compels you to go one mile, go with him two. Give to the person who asks you, and do not turn away the person who wants to borrow from you.

A study of key terms (including *ponēros, anthistēnai ,*and *echthros*) will help to clarify the meaning of these instructions. As an adjective, *ponēros* can mean "unhealthy" or "worthless," but Matthew often uses it in an ethical sense as the opposite of "righteous" or "good." Jesus repeatedly characterizes his contemporaries in Israel and especially the religious leaders as evil (9:4; 12:34, 39; 16:4). When *ponēros* functions as a noun, it can mean an evil thing, an evil person, or the evil one (i.e., Satan). In Matthew 5:39, however, *tō ponērō* almost certainly refers to a human being.

The actions named in Matthew 5:39-41 define the "evil person" more specifically as one who dominates others through unjust power. A social superior or a soldier is evil when he abuses and insults a disciple with a backhanded slap on the right cheek. A creditor is evil when using the courts to take even the shirt off a disciple's back. An imperial soldier is evil when he oppresses disciples by compelling them to lug baggage for the legal maximum of a thousand paces.

Perhaps readers are also to imagine that the person who begs in 5:42 is a pest and therefore "evil." It is more likely, however, that the command of generosity in 5:42 relates to the theme of 5:39-42 in a different way. In each of the previous examples, a disciple is being oppressed by a more powerful person. In the final one, the disciple has the upper hand and can decide whether to act like an oppressor. Through generous giving, the disciple can demonstrate that he or she is not like "the evil person," whose self-interested loans and subsequent lawsuits are so devastating for the poor.

The most difficult term in 5:38-42 is undoubtedly *mē antistēnai*, which has often been translated as "do not resist." (AV, RSV, NRSV, NIV) This translation is difficult to reconcile with the characterization of Jesus elsewhere in the narrative, however. A broad prohibition against all forms of resistance could rule out even prophetic witness and reproof. Other possible translations suggest a more limited prohibition: "do not resist *violently*,"[9] "do not *oppose . . . in court*,"[10] or "do not retaliate."[11] Unfortunately, each of these proposals has difficulty accounting for all of the illustrations that follow in 5:39a-42. *Antistēnai* has a broader range of meaning than "resist violently," and a prohibition against violent resistance or retaliation seems out of place in the situation described in 5:42. The only illustration that clearly has a judicial setting is the lawsuit in 5:40.

My translation ("do not compete") attempts to convey a nuance that is lost in other translations, namely, that the disciples must be different from their enemies. *Antistēnai* envisions a military, athletic, or forensic contest in which opponents vie for supremacy in the same arena. The competitors are mirror images of one another. Refusing to compete with evil people means that one does not mirror their oppressive actions. "Eye-for-eye" retaliation is ruled out, but so is imitation of the "evil person" in other ways, such as in one's response to beggars and borrowers. By refusing to compete with the evil person on his or her terms, the disciples can both demonstrate the greater righteousness of God's reign and resist evil creatively.

Walter Wink has helped to show the creative, assertive nature of the actions commended in 5:39b-41.[12] Far from counseling the disciples to become doormats, Jesus suggests ways in which oppressed disciples may seize the initiative, call attention to their oppression, and declare their worth as human beings. After a backhand slap on the right cheek, turning the left cheek may be a defiant gesture. It says, "You did not succeed in humiliating me. Try again, only this time you must hit me as an equal." Whether or not the oppressor accepted the invitation to strike again, he would be acknowledging the other person's refusal to be cowed.

Giving away one's clothing can also be a form of resistance. Many people in first century Palestine lost their ancestral lands and everything else they owned because of high taxes and harsh lending practices. A debtor who could only pledge an undergarment as collateral for a loan was in a desperate situation; but, when taken to court, he or she could still seize the initiative and register a dramatic protest. By giving both garments and thus stripping naked, the debtor could expose the cruelty of the entire debt system. Likewise, the disciple who insists on carrying a soldier's pack for a second mile is seizing the initiative, doing the unexpected, and possibly discomfiting an oppressor. In effect, the disciple says, "You have treated me like a pack animal, but you are wrong. My offer of a second mile is a sign of the humanity and dignity of the people whom you habitually oppress."

If Wink's interpretation is correct, then turning the other cheek, giving both garments, and going a second mile are all examples of reproof, not capitulation. Their purpose is to bring sin and injustice to light so that oppressors may be called to repentance. This interpretation is congruent with Matthew's command not to compete with an evil person, since it would be hypocritical for a disciple to reprove the sins of others while doing the same things (cf. Matt. 7:1-5). The examples in Matthew 5:39-42 are only illustrative, and Matthew would encourage readers to think of ways to resist oppressors without becoming like them. Regardless of the methods used, reproving evil people requires courage and may result in further suffering. Yet it is far from passive. It is an active, assertive form of love

Likewise, Jesus' pronouncement in Matthew 5:44 assumes that the task of loving one's enemies may include reproving them. This assumption is implicit in the allusion to Leviticus 19:17-18.[13] Matthew's reinterpretation of Leviticus 19:17-18 expands the scope of the command but does not change the kind of love that is required.

The word translated "enemies" in 5:44 is *echthros*, which as an adjective means "hostile" or "hateful." When used as a noun (as in Matt. 5:43-44), it implies that the enemy is someone with those characteristics. In 5:44 and 10:36, Matthew also associates enemies with those who persecute Jesus or his disciples. Jesus expects his disciples to go out as defenseless missionaries (10:10) to Israel first (10:6) and then to all nations (24:14; 26:13; 28:19). Their message will be a call for repentance in light of the coming reign of heaven (10:7), the same message proclaimed by John the Baptist (3:2) and Jesus (4:17). Those who heed the gospel will be baptized as a sign of repentance (28:19; cf. 3:7-8). In their mission, the disciples will follow in the footsteps not only of John and Jesus but also of Israel's earlier prophets, whose calls for repentance led to persecution (5:12; 23:29-36). John, the quintessential prophet in Matthew's story, is arrested and killed by Herod Antipas after reproving Herod about an illicit marriage (14:4).

John's fate foreshadows Jesus' arrest and crucifixion (17:11-13). Jesus warns the disciples that their treatment will be no better (10:24-25). "Wolves" will hand the innocent disciples over to councils, administer floggings in "their synagogues," and drag the disciples before governors and kings (10:16-18). Nevertheless, they should not be afraid, but view their court appearances as opportunities for divinely inspired testimony (10:19-20, 26-28). The disciples can expect persecution not only from Israel's religious leaders but also from family members (10:21-23), people in all nations (24:9), and even traitors within the church (24:9-12). They will need a long prayer-list to include all "those who persecute you" (5:44).

Thus, the mission of the disciples is the narrative context within which Matthew interprets Jesus' command to love enemies. That mission will include prophetic reproof, and, like the ministries of other prophets, it will evoke persecution. According to Matthew 5:43-48, the disciples are not to hate their persecutors but to love them in a way that includes prayer, greetings, and possibly more attempts at reproof. There is always a possibility that assertive love can still lead to repentance and reconciliation, but the disciples' efforts will be measured by their faithfulness not their success (cf. 10:39).

JESUS' EXAMPLE ACCORDING TO MATTHEW

We have seen that the story of the disciples' mission helps to interpret Jesus' command that they love their enemies. The same is true of Jesus' own story line, especially as he relates to the leaders who persecute him. Since a complete analysis of Jesus' conflict with the religious leaders is not possible here, I will focus on four traits of Jesus as portrayed by Matthew. They are reproof, vulnerability, trust in God, and forgiveness.

First, Jesus repeatedly reproves the religious leaders in keeping with their common scriptural heritage. He initiates this ministry of reproof by exposing and answering the religious leaders' secret hostility (9:3-4). He then responds directly to a criticism that they voice indirectly to his disciples (9:10-13). As Jesus' conflict with the religious leaders intensifies, they confront each other directly over matters as important as the interpretation of the Sabbath (12:1-14). Although these debates reflect sharp disagreements, they also reveal some important common ground. Both parties turn to Scripture for ethical guidance; both view reproof as a normal response to disagreement; and both apparently agree that love of God and neighbor are the most important commandments (22:34-40). These fundamental agreements may help to explain why Jesus reproves the religious leaders more often than he does the Roman authorities, even though the latter are also involved in persecuting him (cf. 27:13-14). A common ethical heritage helps reproof.

Jesus' own efforts to reprove religious leaders are a continuation of Israel's prophetic tradition. Matthew makes this relationship clear through his interpretation of the parable of the vineyard, where the owner's slaves represent prophets sent by God and the owner's son represents Jesus (22:33-46). Matthew's Jesus is more than a prophet (16:13-20), yet he acts like a prophet when reproving the religious leaders. For example, overturning tables is a prophetic sign, warning that the temple's stones will soon be overturned (21:12-13; cf. 23:38; 24:2). Jesus interprets this sign with quotations from Isaiah 56:7 and Jeremiah 7:11. The first quotation offers a vision of the temple as a place of prayer for all people, a vision that begins to be realized in Matthew 21:14-17.

The second quotation recalls Jeremiah's protest at the temple in which he likewise predicted its destruction because of its role in oppressing the poor (Jer. 7:1-15). Jeremiah's reproof is not without hope, since he suggests that God may continue to dwell in the temple if the people only change their ways. Similarly, Matthew's interpretation of the vineyard parable suggests that God has sent Jesus to the religious leaders in the hope that they would repent (21:37). Matthew's comparison between Jesus and Jonah makes a similar point (12:38-41). Like Jonah, Jesus has the difficult task of calling his enemies to repentance. In contrast to the Ninevites, the religious leaders in Matthew's story refuse to repent, but their opportunity to do so is just as real.

Matthew implies that Jesus is angry in confronting the leaders at the temple. Nevertheless, love does not preclude intense anger, and angry words can sometimes lead to healing. Even words like "you offspring of vipers" can have the redemptive purpose of shocking listeners into repentance. In Matthew 23:33, those words echo John the Baptist's cry for repentance and insist that the cry still remains unheeded (cf. 3:7-10; 21:25,32). Matthew's Jesus sometimes reproves his followers as sternly as his enemies. "Get behind me, Satan!" (16:23) sounds as harsh as "You offspring of vipers!" but there is no doubt that Jesus loves Peter. In addition, the lament in Matthew 23:37-39 shows that angry words can be motivated by love. Although Matthew does not explicitly describe Jesus as weeping (cf. Luke 19:41), readers can easily imagine tears as Jesus cries out, "Jerusalem, Jerusalem, the city that keeps on killing the prophets and stoning those who are sent to it! How often have I wanted to bring your children together as a hen gathers her chicks under her wings, but you were unwilling!" (23:37). The hen still loves her chicks. Finally, Matthew 23:39 stands like a beacon of hope at the end of such a bleak speech: "You will not see me again until you say, 'Blessed is the one who is coming in the name of the Lord.'" In other words, there is still a possibility that the people of Jerusalem will welcome Jesus' final return.

Matthew's Jesus is vulnerable in that he refuses to use weapons other than words (cf. 26:47-56). He travels unarmed and tells his disciples to do the same (10:10). His demonstration in the temple is certainly provocative, but it does not involve lethal violence (21:12-17). His only punitive miracle is directed against a tree (21:19). At his arrest, he reproves the disciple who tries to defend him with a sword, declaring that he could call on legions of angels if he wished. He chooses instead to be arrested without a fight. The chief priests' crowd does not need their swords and clubs (26:47-56).

Jesus' vulnerability reaches a climax at his crucifixion. Even so, Jesus' refusal to defend himself physically makes sense when one considers the role of God in Matthew's story. Matthew's God is intimately involved in all of creation (6:26, 30; 10:29-31), not protecting innocent people from all harm (10:16-22), but blessing those who suffer faithfully with the joy of living in God's reign (5:3-12; 16:24-26). Jesus' decision to confront his enemies vulnerably is rooted in the trust that God will not ultimately forsake him (cf. 27:46) but will raise him from the dead (16:21; 17:9; 17:22-23; 20:19; 26:32). God's fulfillment of that hope vindicates Jesus over his enemies and allows him to continue his work through the community of disciples. The presence of the risen Jesus as "God with us" empowers the disciples to follow Jesus' teaching and example as they fulfill their mission in the face of persecution (18:20; 28:16-20).

In addition to modeling reproof, vulnerability, and trust in God, Matthew's Jesus also models forgiveness of enemies. The narrative emphasizes the bloodguilt of people who had a hand in Jesus' death, including Judas, the religious leaders, the Passover crowds, and Pilate (27:3-10, 24-26). But Jesus gives his blood a new meaning in Matthew 26:26-29 when he announces that it "is being poured out in the interest of many people for the forgiveness of sins." The reference to "many" echoes Jesus' earlier declaration that his death will be a "ransom for many people" (20:28), and both sayings allude to Isaiah 53:12, where God's servant bears the sins of the people as a whole, including those who put him to death. Therefore, Jesus' blood can signify forgiveness instead of guilt.[14] The risen Jesus shows his forgiveness of the unfaithful disciples when he calls them "brothers" (28:10), and he clearly expects them to do the same for others without limits (6:14-15; 18:21-35).

This reading of Matthew's story has shown that the tension between Jesus' teaching and example regarding enemies is not as great as it may have appeared initially. When Jesus reproves the religious leaders, he is both fulfilling Leviticus 19:17-18 and continuing the tradition established by Israel's prophets. Meanwhile, Jesus' teaching does not require passive nonresistance in the face of evil. Matthew 5:38-48 allows and even encourages disciples to resist evil people by reproving them. Likewise, Matthew 18:15-20 instructs disciples to reprove one another in an effort to restore right relationships within God's family.

REPROOF IN A GLOBALIZED WORLD: PITFALLS AND POSSIBILITIES

Critical reflection and conversation are essential as we seek to apply Matthean ethics in contexts that are quite different from Matthew's story-world. Although the power of collective reproof has been evident on several occasions in the twentieth century—the movement for Indian independence, the U.S. civil rights movement, the nonviolent opposition to communist regimes in East Germany and Poland, and the struggle against apartheid in South Africa—this approach is not without pitfalls.

People who speak forthrightly against oppression are likely to be persecuted, especially when they follow Jesus' example of vulnerability. Unfortunately, the cost of resisting evil prophetically is often borne disproportionately by those who are oppressed, and that cost may be higher for those who resist without resorting to lethal violence. As someone who has so far lived in relative safety, I hesitate to suggest a course of action that may cause others to suffer. Even so, I understand Matthew's ethic as a challenge to resist evil collectively, prophetically, and lovingly. Since "love" means acting for the benefit of others, I do not believe that it is possible for human beings to love their enemies while also planning to kill them.

If people who reprove others are in danger of being persecuted, the opposite danger is equally troubling. Those who reprove may become the persecutors. Tragically, this danger has been realized through centuries of Christian anti-Semitism, fueled in part by a misuse of Matthew's rhetoric against the religious leaders. Professing Christians have also persecuted other religious groups, including other Christians, with great violence. Matthew's response to Christians who persecute others would probably be to reprove them sternly. Matthew 23 points in that direction since it begins with a warning that the disciples must not become like the religious leaders in the story. Even so, there is not always a clear line between reproof and persecution or between violence and nonviolence. For those on the receiving end, an attempted reproof can feel like hatred rather than love.

Even when words of reproof are well-intentioned, they are easy to misunderstand. This pitfall is especially apparent in an age when communication is increasingly rapid, global, and impersonal—quite different from the face-to-face interaction that Matthew presupposes. Misunderstandings, often rooted in cultural differences, can lead to escalating conflict rather than to repentance and reconciliation.

Given the many risks involved in reproving others, silence may seem the wisest course. But silence is rarely a faithful answer to injustice, and it does nothing to correct misunderstandings. Instead of remaining silent and hoping that our suffering neighbors will do the same, Christians are encouraged by Matthew's ethic to engage in mutual reproof. This ministry requires hearing and speaking the hard truths that can lead toward repentance.

When Christians decide to reprove others, a few precautions will help to guard against the potential pitfalls. First, there may be less potential for misunderstanding when reproofs are communicated face-to-face between people who share a common language and culture. Wherever possible, local people who have experienced oppression should take the lead in planning public demonstrations or other collective acts of reproof. Of course, Christians from other cultures may be called to stand in solidarity with people who are reproving injustice. In some cases, the attention and support of Christians around the world can help to limit persecution.

Since internal divisions continue to hamper the church's witness, there is an ongoing need for ministries of reconciliation within the church. There is also a need for interfaith dialogues in which all participants have an opportunity to explain their beliefs and ethical systems. Christians need to know the narratives that serve as the basis for Christian ethics, but we must not assume that people of other faiths share the same narratives or ethical standards. Reproofs are most likely to be "heard" when they are grounded in the hearer's own faith. If people from other faiths become disciples of Jesus, then there is a basis for further instruction in discipleship, including the practice of reproof.

Finally, as the immediate context of Matthew 18:15-20 suggests, those of us who would reprove others should begin by correcting ourselves. Humility, compassion, and eagerness to forgive are all essential ingredients of loving reproof according to Matthew. If we approach others in that spirit, we may find that they listen and that they also have important messages for us.

NOTES

1. Jack Dean Kingsbury, *Matthew as Story*, 2nd. ed. (Philadelphia: Fortress, 1988), 120. I use "Matthew" as a convenient name for the anonymous author of the Gospel of Matthew.

2. William Klassen, "'Love Your Enemies': Some Reflections on the Current Status of Research," in *The Love of Enemies and Non-Retaliation in the New Testament*, ed. Willard M. Swartley (Louisville, Ky.: Westminster/John Knox, 1992), 13.

3. This literary study does not attempt to reconstruct a pre-canonical form of the Jesus tradition, nor to discuss the attitude of the historical Jesus toward his opponents.

4. On the term "consistency-building" used to refer to a reader's competent processes of filling in gaps in literary narrative, see Wolfgang Iser, *The Act of Reading: A Theory of Aesthetic Response* (Baltimore: The Johns Hopkins University Press, 1978), 34, 67, 129.

5. Jacob Milgrom, *Leviticus 17-22: A New Translation with Introduction and Commentary*. Anchor Bible, vol. 3a (New York: Doubleday, 2000), 1655.

6. Ibid., 1646.

7. All biblical translations are the author's and are anthropologically gender-inclusive where the retrievable intent of the biblical text warrants.

8. Regarding this theme, see Daniel W. Ulrich, "True Greatness: Matthew 18 in Its Literary Context" (Ph.D. diss., Union Theological Seminary, Richmond, Virginia, 1997), 25-31, 201-202.

9. Walter Wink, "Neither Passivity nor Violence: Jesus' Third Way (Matt. 5:38-42 par.)" in Swartley, 115 (emphasis original).

10. Robert Guelich, *The Sermon on the Mount: A Foundation for Understanding* (Waco: Word Books, 1982), 220 (emphasis original).

11. Hans Dieter Betz, *The Sermon on the Mount* (Minneapolis: Fortress, 1995), 280.

12. Walter Wink, " Third Way," 102-125.

13. The allusion to Leviticus 19:2 in Matthew 5:48 is further evidence of Matthew's assumption that readers are familiar with this part of the Septuagint.

14. Timothy B. Cargal, "'His Blood be Upon us and Upon Our Children': A Matthean Double Entendre?" *New Testament Studies* 37 (1991), 112.

Chapter 12

Paul as Mediator[1]

Moisés Mayordomo

Recently conflict resolution has become an important theoretical as well as practical issue on the agenda of various social sciences. In many cases representatives from the Historic Peace Churches have contributed positively to the growth of interest. It is my impression, however, that biblical studies so far have been less evident within these important developments. Therefore, I will offer a contribution from this field, working with the following basic definition of "conflict":

A conflict is the product of incompatible goals and nonnegotiable priorities between different parties within a commonly shared field of action.

This definition aims to be neutral in the sense that conflicts do not necessarily have to be viewed as intrinsically negative. A conflict can also represent an opportunity to bring about important personal changes or social transformations. "Conflict resolution" is not so much a matter of making a conflict nonexistent but of minimizing its pernicious aspects while at the same time maximizing a conflict's positive potentials.

UNITY IN THE EARLY CHURCH?

For many Christians the early church shines as a model of unity and spiritual power. [2] And indeed some passages in the New Testament may lead us to this conclusion. The Acts of the Apostles shows a marked interest in church unity. Luke tells us that the followers of Christ "all joined together constantly in prayer" awaiting the coming of the Spirit (Acts 1:14). After Peter's Pentecost sermon "they continued to meet together in the temple courts. They broke bread in their homes and ate together with glad and sincere hearts" (2:46). A little later we learn that "all the believers were one in heart and mind. No one claimed that any of his possessions was his own, but they shared everything they had" (4:32). Even when faced with an inner discord concerning law obligations for Gentile Christians, the leaders of the church assembled and quickly came to a decision which "seemed good to the Holy Spirit and to us" (15:28). [3]

Some of the later writings of the New Testament speak of the Christian faith as a unified tradition handed over once and for all by the apostles (Jude 3; Eph. 3:4f). We also find predictions that in the future false teachers will cause divisions in the church, which seems to imply that the first generations of the church were free from inner controversies (Acts 20:29f; 1 Tim. 4:1; 2 Tim. 3:1, 8-9; 1 John 2:18; Jude 1:17f; 2 Pet. 3:3f).[4]

The Christian writers of the following centuries strengthened the ideological construction that early Christianity was the golden age of harmony. Many important and influential church leaders claimed the backing of a sacred past with one unified apostolic tradition to fight against what they considered dangerous theological heresies.[5] This led very early to the sharp distinction between heresy and orthodoxy.

It seems as if all the conflicts early Christians had to face came either directly from outside—in the form of social stigmatization, vilification or straightforward persecution—or from "outsiders" who tried to cause damage from within the community: heretics, false teachers, sectarians, schismatics, "wolves in sheep's clothing" (Matt. 7:15). Although the first Christians may appear to us, for the most part, as a unified group living in total harmony, is this really the case?

INNER-CHURCH CONFLICTS

The apostle Paul writes in his letter to the Galatians: "When Peter came to Antioch, I opposed him to his face, because he was clearly in the wrong" (Gal. 2:11). This description of a direct conflict between

Paul and Peter has been a tough nut to crack in the history of interpretation. Readers of all periods have had problems accepting an open conflict between the two pillars of the early church and have thus tried to tone down the conflict potential. Theologians as influential as Origen, John Chrysostom, and Jerome believed that Peter and Paul made the whole scene up for pedagogical reasons.[6] Modern historical exegesis cannot read the texts along these harmonizing lines.

Even a superficial look at the New Testament shows that inner conflicts seem to have been not the exception but very much the rule. We find many conflicts referred to explicitly. One of the first emerges in the Jerusalem church between "Hebrews" and "Hellenists" (Acts 6:1-7), because the widows of the Hellenists "were being overlooked in the daily distribution of food" (6:1).[7] Christians from Judea and Christians from Antioch had a problem concerning the binding nature of the Jewish law for Gentile Christians. This dispute led to the so-called Jerusalem Council which ended with a compromise acceptable at least to some of the involved parties (Acts 15; Gal. 2). Paul and Barnabas, two close missionary partners, had a "sharp disagreement" about the suitability of John Mark as their junior partner (Acts 15: 36-41).

The conflict between Paul and Peter arose when Peter refrained from participating in the full fellowship between Jewish Christians and Gentile Christians in Antioch as a result of a visit of Jewish Christians from Jerusalem (Gal. 2:11-15). Influenced by Peter, even Barnabas and others began to follow his example.[8]

Coming to the church in Corinth, we find a real "conflict factory." We have ample evidence for the existence of different disputing parties who won their identities by appealing to certain founding figures such as Peter, Paul, and Apollos (1 Cor 1:10ff; 3:5-9). Corinthian Christians tried to "resolve" their conflicts by going to the secular courts (6:1-7). This was highly problematic because lawsuits tended to favor the rich. A deeper-level conflict emerged among the "weak" and the "strong" (chs. 8–10). Another concerned the symbolic representation of gender roles in worship (11:2-16). Still another—a very serious one—had to do with differences between rich and poor during the Lord's Supper (11:18-34). The Corinthians also argued about the value of the more spectacular charismatic gifts (chs. 12–14) and the future resurrection of Christians (ch. 15).

Besides these explicitly mentioned conflicts we find many additional ones which are mirrored in other letters of the New Testament. The epistle of Paul to the Romans reflects a conflict between Gentile

Christians and Jewish Christians (chs. 14–15).[9] Second Corinthians not only reflects a very serious conflictive encounter between Paul and one member of the Corinthian congregation (2 Cor. 2:3-11; 7:6-11), but also a dispute with infiltrated "wrong apostles" who claim by their many ecstatic experiences to be better apostles and servants of Christ than Paul (chs. 10-13).

The epistle to the Galatians presupposes that Christian Judaizers managed to convince the Gentile Christians in Galatia to maintain some identity markers of Jewish faith, such as food regulations and circumcision (Gal. 1:6-9; 3:1; 6:12-17). Paul shows no signs of compromise with them. Similar conflicts lie behind the redaction of the letters to the Philippians (cf. 3:2-21) and the Colossians (cf. 2:6–3:6), the second epistle to the Thessalonians (cf. 2:1-3), 1 John (cf. 2:18-19; 4:1-6), 2 Peter (cf. chs. 2–3), the letter of James (cf. 2:1-2,6-7; 4:1-9), the short letter of Jude and the letters to the seven churches in the Apocalypse of John (cf. chs. 2–3).

THE AMBIVALENCE OF CONFLICTS

This gallery of inner-church antagonisms is not intended to have a depressing effect on us. On the contrary, we can learn from it.

It is helpful to note that conflicts in early Christianity were not just the product of enmity from the non-Christian environment or from infiltrated false teachers, but were also generated within the Christian communities themselves. The mere existence of inner-church conflicts in our day is not necessarily an indication of decay from the construction of a "pure" first generation of Christian faith. The existence and inevitability of conflicts leads to the conclusion that pluralism was a factor of Christian faith from its very beginnings—as it still is!

Conflicts do not automatically have to lead to negative results. They are inherently ambiguous. On the one hand, they may destroy every form of communication and community. But on the other, they may be the trigger for positive developments within a Christian community, such as the participation of the Hellenists in church leadership in Jerusalem (Acts 6), the compromise concerning the Gentiles and the law (Acts 15), and, not least, the redaction of many if not most writings of the New Testament. In a text which has puzzled many interpreters, Paul emphasizes this ambivalence: "In the first place, I hear that when you come together as a church, there are divisions among you, and to some extent I believe it. No doubt there *have to be* differences among you to show which of you have God's approval" (1 Cor. 11:18f).

This leads to a working hypothesis: Bearing in mind that every group which over time does not manage to channel conflicts into positive paths loses its strength and cohesion, we may assume that the early Christians must have had characteristic ways of conflict-management. This aspect of community life surely played a role in the astonishing growth of Christianity within the Roman society—a cultural environment which had no established ways of handling interpersonal conflicts creatively and nonviolently.[10] I would like to test this hypothesis with a biblical example.

PAUL AS MEDIATOR
BETWEEN THE "STRONG" AND THE "WEAK"

Before entering into exegetical details, we should consider the question whether biblical studies can contribute something to our modern problem of conflict resolution at all. The fact that in the pages of the New Testament polemical statements abound,[11] and that many of our churches today suffer from unresolved conflicts, does not give very much credit to church and theology with regard to effective conflict management. It may appear wiser to leave the field to the "experts": sociologists, psychologists, conflict theorists, specialists in political and economical affairs, and professional mediators. However, it is not a matter of having to decide between a "biblical way of conflict resolution" (if that existed) and a social scientific way, but of searching for ways of shared responsibilities and helpful interactions between them.

Since the apostle Paul has the reputation of being a highly conflictive person, I would like to present him as a "model mediator" by directing attention to two similar struggles between "strong" and "weak" in the churches in Corinth and Rome (1 Cor. 8-10 and Rom. 14–15).[12]

ANALYSIS OF THE CONFLICT

The problem: In Corinth the conflict between "strong" and "weak" has to do with whether a Christian can eat meat that has been used as a sacrifice in a heathen temple. In Rome the problem is more far-reaching. Should a Christian maintain a vegetarian diet, refrain from alcohol, and observe a certain cultic calendar (Rom. 14:2-6, 20-21)?

The position of the "weak": The "weak" in Corinth are convinced that a Christian should under no circumstances eat meat sacrificed to the idols (10:25, 27f). Their view is apparently grounded in a certain fear. They are afraid of exposing themselves to the influence of the powers of evil by the mere fact of eating the food offered to the idols. The "weak" in Rome seem to be the promoters of the conflict. They are not afraid of ungodly powers, but they try to live according to certain Jewish concepts of ritual purity (14:14,20) and propagate this moral conviction to all others.

The position of the "strong": The "strong" in Corinth eat, without any scruple, meat sacrificed to the idols (8:9; 10:25-30). Some of them even go so far as to share in temple meals (8:10; 10:14, 20f). The "strong" do not hide away but try to live openly according to their theological convictions. They act willingly to induce others to express their Christian freedom the same way they do (8:10). This attitude not only scandalizes their brothers and sisters (8:9, 13), it also leads them to a serious crisis of conscience (8:8, 10). The "strong" value their personal freedom more highly than the "other man's conscience" (10:29). Their motto is: "Everything is permissible" (6:12; 10:23).

Similarly, the "strong" in Rome are by no means convinced that attaining to certain ritual laws of purity has any spiritual value in itself. As Gentile Christians they are no longer bound to the law of Moses.

PRACTICAL ASPECTS OF PAUL'S MEDIATION

First of all it is important to notice that Paul has a personal stance in these hotly debated issues. In terms of theological content he shares the position of the "strong" (1 Cor 8:4-7; Rom 14:14; 15:1). It is a theological knowledge which can easily be deduced from Paul's preaching of the gospel. If Christians belong to God, this implies that they have been completely freed from the powers opposed to God and from the tyranny of human laws.

In this case, however, Paul is not trying to resolve the conflict as an outward authority who decides between right and wrong. Instead he speaks as a pastor searching for the best solutions on the basis of the gospel. It is not a matter of correct theology but of attitude toward others. The following table presents a brief summary of his advice.

	Advice for the "strong"	Advice for the "weak"
Higher priorities:	Love is more important than knowledge, the building up of the community is more important than personal freedom. "Knowledge puffs up, but love builds up." (1 Cor. 8:1b)	Paul does not try to convince them theologically. To the contrary, he exhorts them not to act against their conscience, even if others do otherwise (Rom 14:5,23; 1Cor. 8:7).
Empathy for the other:	The "strong" should not deliberately provoke the "weak," especially if they put at risk their "weak" faith by expressing their freedom (1Cor. 8:9-13). They should not judge and look down on their weaker brothers and sisters (Rom 14:1-4,10-13).	The "weak" should not criticize and judge the "strong." Everyone is responsible for himself and herself before God (Rom 14:24,10-13).
Pragmatic aspects:	The "strong" should live some of their convictions on a more private level (Rom 14:22).	Paul wants the "weak" in Corinth to avoid extreme positions which may burden their everyday life. He encourages them to buy meat in the market and eat in the houses of non-Christians without asking for the origin of the meat (1 Cor. 10:25-28).

To summarize, in terms of practical mediation Paul tries to move the conflict from the level of a purely theological dispute about certain insights and beliefs to the level of interpersonal communication and relationship.

THEOLOGICAL ASPECTS OF PAUL'S MEDIATION

Paul's pastoral aim is not to decide whose theology is more consistent with the gospel, but to create a common basis for the different parties.

The Ethical Basis: Love

The concept of Christian love is comprised of many ethically and theologically relevant aspects. In the present context, one is especially relevant: the sacrifice of my own freedom for the sake of a higher goal. Paul gives as an example athletes who deprive themselves of many conveniences to obtain the victory (1 Cor. 9:24f). Paul himself lives according to this principle for the sake of his mission (1 Cor. 9:20-23). Similarly, he wants his readers to see the building up of the community as the prior goal, whereas personal freedom and theological insights are relegated to second place. The "strong" and the "weak" should reach a compromise not simply on the basis of pragmatism, but motivated by Christian love. Love puts a new and commonly shared goal on the agenda of a Christian community. In view of this goal all existing incompatibilities become more or less secondary.

The Theological Basis: Gratitude

"He who regards one day as special, does so to the Lord. He who eats meat, eats to the Lord, for he gives thanks to God; and he who abstains, does so to the Lord and gives thanks to God." (Rom. 14:6). Giving thanks to God is a natural expression of a pure conscience and shows a person's ethical orientation toward God. Gratitude brings about a change of perception. Two Christians in the same community can thank God for exactly the opposite things (one for the meat, the other not for the meat), but more importantly they both are sharing a common activity and an inner attitude of thankfulness. This is an active form of living inner-church pluralism in tolerance.

The Christological Basis: The Death of Christ.

"So this weak brother, *for whom Christ died,* is destroyed by your knowledge" (1 Cor 8:11). "If your brother is distressed because of what you eat, you are no longer acting in love. Do not by your eating destroy your brother *for whom Christ died*" (Rom. 14:15). The death of Christ plays a decisive role for different reasons.

Empathic solidarity. Christ's death is the ultimate paradigm for God's unconditional love toward every human being. Individualistic interpretations of this soteriological exchange stand in the way of discovering the tremendous social dimensions of the cross. If Christ gave his life in exchange for the "strong" as well as for the "weak," this shows that everyone has the same value before God and it gives Christians an impulse for mutual empathy. The cross is not only a sign of God's solidarity with sinners but also an impetus for our solidarity toward each other.

Consideration. Christ's death shows the "cost" of salvation. Therefore, every behavior which may put at risk the other's faith should be reduced to an acceptable minimum. Theological differences lose their importance when compared to a person's spiritual well-being. The cross moves us to mutual consideration, especially for the "weak."

Interdependence. The death of Christ makes clear that existence *for* others is absolutely essential to Christian faith. The gospel is in the end not a matter of theological insights, although they have their relevance and value, but a matter of living. Christian freedom is not independence from the others but interdependence within the new social reality of the Christian church. Within this complicated net of relationships many personal and theological conflicts will arise, but in the end the individuals are more important than the opinions they hold. The cross can, thus, help us to accept a person without giving in to the temptation to judge others by their deeds and personal opinions.

CONCLUSIONS AND FURTHER THOUGHTS

The Bienenberg consultation consultation dealt with two great words: *theology* and *culture*. Although there have been many attempts to see culture and theology as an antidote against conflicts,[13] a look at early Christianity makes us aware that conflict is a decisive factor for developing both Christian culture and Christian theology. The church in our present globalized world displays a richness of differences and struggles which may be used creatively rather than destructively. The example of Paul as mediator gives us some insights into early Christian conflict management, insights which we may refine on a practical level with modern approaches. But there is also a genuinely theological basis to inner-church conflict handling, namely the cross of Christ as a symbol for social transformation.

Once their destructive mechanisms are set into motion, conflicts can make us believe that the reality we have to accept is one marked by negativity. The cross is so important for this issue not because it makes conflicts disappear, but because it embodies the greatest conflict we can imagine, the one between life and death, strength and weakness, wisdom and foolishness (1 Cor chs. 1–2). This paradoxical reality, that lies at the very heart of Christian identity, has not yet developed its full potential for coping creatively with inner-church conflicts. If our dreams of creative peacemaking are being threatened by extinction there is one place to look: the cross of Christ.

NOTES

1. I would like to thank my colleague Julia Müller-Clemm for reading and thinking through this paper. Bible quotations are from the NIV.

2. The romantic view that the origin of a movement is especially pure and that all later developments entail a process of decline has effected a great influence on this popular view; cf. Stefan Alkier, *Urchristentum. Zur Geschichte und Theologie einer exegetischen Disziplin.* (BHTh 83; Tübingen: Mohr, 1993).

3. Luke's stress on unanimity can also be deduced from his pronounced use of the Greek adverb *homothumadón* ("with one mind, by common consent, unanimously"): Cf. 1:14; 2:46; 4:24; 5:12; 8:6; 15:25 (as textual variants in 2:1; 20:18).

4. J. C. Fenton, "Controversy in the New Testament," in E. A. Livingstone (ed.), *Studia Biblica 1978* (JSNT. S 3; Sheffield: JSOT Press 1980), III, 97-110:97-99.

5. Irenaeus writes in his *Against the Heresies* I, 10,1-2: "The Church although scattered through the whole world even to the ends of the earth has received the faith from the Apostles and from their disciples. Since the Church has received this preaching and this faith, as we have said, although she is scattered through the whole world, she preserves it carefully, as one household: and the whole Church alike believes in these things, as having one soul and heart in unison preaching these beliefs, and teaches and hands them on as having one mouth. " H. Bettenson, trans., *The Early Church Fathers* (Oxford: Oxford University Press, 1969), 92.

6. Cf. Ralph Hennings, *Der Briefwechsel zwischen Augustinus und Hieronymus und ihr Streit um den Kanon des Alten Testaments und die Auslegung von Gal. 2,11-14.* (Supplements to Vigiliae Christianae 21; Leiden: Brill, 1993).

7. We may fairly assume that this was the tip of the iceberg of a more deeplevel conflict between Palestinian Jewish Christians who spoke Aramaic and Jewish Christians who had spent much of their life in the diaspora and spoke Greek—the so-called "hellenists." Albeit they shared a common experience, they expressed themselves in different languages which also means that, right from the beginning of the church's existence, there were differences in culture and theological emphases.

8. This is a very critical moment in the enterprise Paul devoted his whole life to: the full inclusion of the Gentiles into the church. There seems to be no deep theological difference between the two apostles but a marked difference in attitude. With respect to this issue Peter may appear to be more pragmatic and flexible than Paul. From Paul's perspective Peter and Barnabas are not assuming the consequences of the Gospel.

9. Historically we may assume that it was a conflict between Gentile Christians who stayed in Rome after the expulsion of the Jews under the emperor Claudius (49 A. D.) and the Jewish Christians who returned after Claudius' death (54 A. D.). The struggle was probably due to the problematic role of the Jewish law for the expression of Christian faith.

10. In the Roman society there was no official police and the sophisticated legal system was in theory open for all Roman citizens, but in practice only a small number could afford to go to the courts. We find some exhortations to resolve interpersonal conflicts between friends, but once we come to the normal struggles of every-day conflicts there was a propensity for using verbal and physical violence. Roman society did not take over some of the older Greek ways of mediating in personal and political conflicts.

11. E. g. Matt. 23; 2 Cor. 11:15; Phil. 3:2; 2 Pet. 2:10-22; 1 John 2:18; Rev. 2:9, 13-14, 20; 3:9.

12. Cf. Thomas Söding, "Starke und Schwache. Der Götzenopferstreit in 1Kor 8-10 als Paradigma paulinischer Ethik," *Das Wort vom Kreuz: Studien zur paulinischen Theologie* (WUNT 93; Tübingen: Mohr 1997), 346-369.

13. Cf. Aleida Assmann and Dietrich Harth, eds., *Kultur und Konflikt* (Frankfurt: Suhramp 1990).

Chapter 13

A Feminist Theological Perspective on Conflict Resolution

Debbie Roberts

HISTORIC QUOTATIONS
FROM THE CHURCH OF THE BRETHREN

"No [Ana]Baptist will be found in war."
—*Alexander Mack, Sr.* Basic Questions, *1713*

"We cannot see or find any liberty to use the sword, but only the sword of the Spirit, the Word of God."
—*1785 Brethren Annual Meeting*

"The doctrine of nonresistance is a fundamental doctrine of the Christian religion."
—*The Brethren Tracts and Pamphlets, 1892*

"It is our conviction as humble followers of Christ, that all war is sin."
—*1935 Brethren Annual Conference*

"We believe that such commitment [to Jesus Christ] leads to the way of love and of nonviolence as a central principle of Christian conduct, knowing full well that, in so doing, violence may fall upon us as it did upon Jesus."
—*1970 Brethren Annual Conference, "War"*

"Violence takes many forms: war, crime, oppression, denial of justice, and violation of personhood. The voice of the Church of the Brethren usually has been clear and unequivocal regarding non-participation in war, the most obvious expression of violence in our global community. Often the church has been less clear regarding more subtle expressions of violence, even benefiting from the injustice and violence that others suffer.

"Is it not time for us in the church to examine ourselves and our faith and to work forthrightly for liberation, justice, and peace in ways that respect the life and potential of every person and the whole human family?"
—*1977 Brethren Annual Conference, "Justice and Nonviolence"*

"Continuing the work of Jesus. Simply. Peacefully. Together."
—*Brethren motto*

The above quotations exemplify a shift from what those identified as Brethren do not do, to what they in fact do.[1] The issue of war broadens into nonparticipation in injustice, which is also violence. A careful analysis of the current practice of conflict resolution suggests a similar shift is needed in that field. My intention here is to review the current practice and contemporary critiques of conflict resolution, and to suggest the applicability of key concepts from the metaphorical feminist theology of Sallie McFague in offering insight toward such a shift.

MY INVESTMENT IN THIS CONVERSATION

I am the campus minister and direct the peace studies program at the University of La Verne in California. The university is rooted in the Church of the Brethren, one of the Historic Peace Churches. Even though it is not a "Christian" university, in terms of required chapel or religion courses, its mission statement is embedded in Church of the Brethren values and beliefs, and the Brethren tradition of service, peace, and community building is strongly emphasized.

I do not remember when I became interested in peacemaking. I do recall that the first time I heard the words "peace" and "Jesus" in the same sentence was when I was introduced to the Church of the Brethren as a peace church in my freshman year of college. I remember feeling that I had come home.

It is in this spirit of community building, service, and peace that I practice ministry and teach peace studies courses. In recent years I have found myself questioning the conflict resolution techniques and theory that I teach and in which I have been trained. Conflict resolution continues to gain popularity as an academic as well as a professional discipline. But in my experience, its methodology sometimes does not work very well, and occasionally does not work at all.

Most of the accepted sources of learning and training in conflict resolution come from white, male, Eurocentric contexts; thus they carry certain presumptions that require critical appraisal. Feminist theological discourse can contribute valuable understandings to the current discipline and practice of conflict resolution, especially regarding its shortsightedness for those who have attempted to engage it but for whom it did not work. Sallie McFague's deconstruction and reconstruction of the concept of resurrection, and her emphasis on Thou-Thou relationships, may offer a helpful corrective, particularly in the case of conflicts that originate from an imbalance of power.

SITUATING CONFLICT RESOLUTION

A standard popular resource on the Western notions of conflict resolution that helps to frame Western theory and methodology is the text *Getting to Yes*.[2] The book holds that conflicts are natural phenomena of life, that we often play the role of negotiator, whether consciously or not, and that it is not *whether* or not we have conflicts—we do, or whether or not we negotiate—we do, but *how* we handle those two facts of life that is of consequence. The authors argue that important negotiating tactics are to separate the people from the problem, to explore the common interests that underlie stated positions, and to develop options that may more readily offer a win-win outcome. The core of the book begins with a description of "hard" and "soft" bargaining, offers a critique of those methods, then discusses the advantages of an alternative model which the authors call "principled bargaining."

"Soft" bargaining proceeds from the assumption that the participants are friends who honor the primacy of that relationship, and therefore subordinate all considerations, including self-interested positions, to reaching an agreement. In the authors' terms, this kind of bargaining is "soft" on the problem as well as on the people. "Hard" bargaining, on the other hand, views the other participant as an adversary and has victory as the primary goal. Hard bargaining proceeds from self-interested positions and employs tactics of pressuring, threats, or demands to force compliance to one's wishes. Hard bargaining is "hard" on the problem as well as on the people.

In contrast to these approaches, the authors suggest a third way, "principled bargaining." The main feature of this approach is to view the participants as problem solvers (rather than as either friends or adversaries) who are "hard" on the problem but "soft" on the people with whom they are in conflict or with whom they are bargaining. This sets up the authors' strategies of separating the people from the problem, focusing on interests rather than positions, and brainstorming options for mutual gain.[3] The advantage of principled bargaining is the possibility that exists for reaching a win-win solution, whereas, under the other two methods, one or both parties will always lose (hard bargaining) or will leave the table without feeling the problem is solved (soft bargaining).

CRITIQUES OF CURRENT
CONFLICT RESOLUTION THEORY AND METHOD

For those engaged in conflict who are bargaining from a level playing field, it may be true, as Fisher and Ury posit, that win-win outcomes are possible. To note that a level playing field is possible is also to note that a level playing field is not always the case.

In considering emotions, for example, Fisher and Ury suggest that at times "feelings may be more important than talk."[4] Others hold that emotions are always more important than talk. More often than not, one cannot vent for an hour or two and then be done with it. Neither can one always avoid reacting to emotional outbursts. Using the Holocaust as a case in point, both venting and reactions to emotional outbursts may go on for years, possibly for centuries. Another concern is the emphasis on win-win outcomes. One example is the apartheid government in South Africa. What kind of mutual gain would have been acceptable in that situation? The negotiation principle of separating people from the problem is also problematic.

> It may be impossible to separate the person from the problem because the problem may be the person. Focusing on interests rather than positions is no guarantee that matters will be made any easier; things may get worse when focusing on the underlying interests to the negotiation... Finally, objective criteria may not be available, especially if one is dealing with highly subjective matters such as feeling.[5]

The popular approach does nothing to contribute to an understanding of the situational and structural dynamics of conflict. Rather, it only molds public debate over conflict, which is in reality a cultural discourse, not a neutral one. [6]

In a feminist assessment of negotiation theory typically used in business, professional, and international contexts, Deborah Kolb and Linda Putnam suggest that current conflict resolution analysis "is characterized by attributes and behaviors that are more commonly associated with masculinity than with femininity."[7] Particular characteristics are allied with masculine worldviews, such as self-interest, competitiveness, and rationality. These attributes are generally more prominent than those associated with feminine worldviews, such as connection, collaboration, and feelings. The conventional framework of negotiation analysis fails to account for the hierarchical social structure in which it is placed. Within this structure, which determines the expectations for successful negotiation, the successful negotiator will be autonomous, and strategies and tactics for negotiation will be viewed in relation to outcomes.

Most theories of negotiation hold agency in high regard. Agency, understood as self-interest within an individualistic orientation, is a central attribute of a good negotiator. The opposite of agency is community. However, negotiators who act from a sense of community are likely to have their actions judged less effective, because negotiation is a means to an end. Negotiators are encouraged to build trust with their adversaries to help a settlement that is beneficial to themselves. Relationship building, then, is not a value for its own sake; rather, it is valued because of the settlement it furthers.

In a critique of Western conflict resolution theory and practice, Paul E. Salem charges from an Arab perspective that "the Western community of conflict resolution theorists and practitioners operate within a macro-political context . . . which colors their attitudes and values."[8] This context is often unconscious, and is largely related to the West's dominant position in the world. For Salem and many other "outsiders," it is common to view Western international conflict resolution policies as merely "stratagems for defusing opposition to and rejection of the status quo."[9] In other words, the West understands whatever exists due to its influence and/or intervention as good. Conflict itself in this Western international context is seen as negative, and every attempt is made to diffuse conflicts before they get "out of hand."

According to Salem, Western conflict resolution relies on the assumption that pain is bad and pleasure/comfort is good. It follows that discomfort/pain/suffering is inconvenient, at the very least, and should be eliminated. However, from other perspectives the negative side effects of conflict may not be nearly as significant as the value of the struggle itself if it succeeds. Western conflict resolution's emphasis on the necessity of resolving conflict because of the discomfort it brings may not be relevant in a social setting in which discomfort is widespread.[10] People in non-Western settings who are used to living with discomfort may give less importance to the discomfort generated by conflict than they do to the justice of the dispute.

Most conflict resolution practice begins with exercises in which both parties are encouraged to "open up" to each other. But from the point of view of members of other cultures, such opening up may disrupt valued formal roles and alienate participants from the negotiation process.[11]

In a similar vein, group process is lifted up as desirable within the Western context, even though there are often forces working in that process to prearrange a particular outcome. Thus, for an "outsider," working together may become suspect, as control is given to a group in whom he or she may have little trust.

Finally, Salem raises the issue of the questionable outcome of an agreed-upon negotiation in the absence of an enforcer able to transcend the limits of an unknown situation. Some may prefer a conflictual, but familiar and predictable situation to attempts to construct a new, less conflictual but also less predictable one.[12]

A related question arises regarding the emphasis on efficiency in conflict resolution theory and methodology. A penchant for efficiency pervades Western culture, where "time is money," in contrast to time being relationship. A similar critique of current conflict resolution theory encourages practitioners and others to employ analytic tools that operate outside the system, then to use those tools to reconstruct it. What Sharon Welch calls an "ethic of risk" may be a resource in this regard. Welch's ethic includes beginning with interests and emotions, not to determine specific outcomes, but rather to place on the table a more truthful reality.[13] Hers is a relational ethic in which honesty of process would be the central focus of attempts to resolve conflicts.

We may also raise a concern regarding the role of the "neutral" mediator in a conflict. Negotiators come out of contexts that are never completely neutral. Mediators bring assumptions and values of their own. Their visions and expectations for assisting in the resolution of the conflict emerge from their own histories and training in particular contexts. But a further question arises: should a mediator be neutral? When we consider the enormous diversity of conflicts, both in terms of the contexts out of which they come as well as the players in those contexts, can there be a universal principal underlying the attempt to resolve them? What is the just role for a mediator when the playing field is not level?

Conflict resolution theory and practice have become mired in white, male, Eurocentric descriptions that at times do not adequately respect the diversity or the possibilities for relationship of those in conflict.

I assert that the concept of relationship is rightfully integral to the theory and practice of conflict resolution. We need new models for methodology, but we also need to imagine differently, to allow conflict resolution to have a heuristic quality. For example, we might imagine a theory that embraces both connection and difference at the same time, or one that looks at the role of neutrality and impartiality in conflict resolution. Sallie McFague's resurrection theology points to a position that can provide a helpful base for such exploration.

METAPHORICAL THEOLOGY

Sallie McFague posits that to make the Christian faith relevant for our time, we need new metaphors and concepts for expressing God's presence and power.[14] Metaphors direct us to concepts, and characterize both what is and what is not. They assume that our talk is indirect. That is, words or phrases refer indirectly to that which we are trying to describe, for "in certain matters there can be no direct description."[15]

However, we are tempted over time to understand metaphor as model, fixing it with definition rather than suggestive possibility. Traditional metaphors can become too adequate. When metaphors become fixed definitions, they no longer invite questions and accompanying possibilities. A good example is the metaphor of God the father. In becoming a fixed concept, "if God is seen as father, human beings become children, sin can be understood as rebellious behavior, and redemption can be thought of as a restoration to the status of favored offspring."[16] If the metaphor's intention is to simply give a shock, along with a jolt of recognition, then the metaphor of God as father is no longer doing its job. Metaphorical language attempts to express a relationship. It is not that relationship itself.

An important aspect of metaphorical theology is that it is heuristic by nature. Through metaphor, one experiments and tests, thinks in an as-if fashion, imagines possibilities that are novel, dares to think differently. Metaphors experiment with images that are always and only partly right. "To say that metaphorical theology is experimental is to emphasize its as-if quality . . . of finding out for itself."[17]

THE METAPHOR OF THE LOVING EYE

In McFague's view, traditional metaphors that hierarchicalize our relationship with the sacred, with each other, and with the earth are in dire need of new imagination if those relationships are to reveal God's way with the world through the incarnation of Jesus. The Christian vision is the story of Jesus as a destabilizing, inclusive, nonhierarchical vision, and it is indeed this new vision that we need. The Christian vision is inclusive, reaching out to the weak and disenfranchised. This inclusivity extends to embrace the earth itself. In Jesus' table fellowship, the emphasis is always on inclusivity; the invitation is not to a few but to all. In Jesus' parables, stories that say something about the unfamiliar, suggesting egalitarian relationships and an end to categorizations of insider/outsider, when extended to the cosmos proclaim "the end of the conventional, hierarchical, oppressive dualism of human/nonhuman."[18]

McFague's emphasis on the nonhierarchical nature and intent of God is developed through her metaphorical discourse on the arrogant eye versus the loving eye. The arrogant eye interprets our relationship to the world and to each other as a subject-object dualistic model. Since Westerners value mind and reason over nature, it stands that "whatever falls on the top side of the dualism has connections with reason and whatever falls on the bottom side is seen as similar to nature. Thus, male/female, white/people of color, West/East, heterosexual/homosexual, educated/illiterate, rich/poor all illustrate the reason/nature dichotomy."[19] As well, distance between the two parties is exaggerated. The arrogant eye is the eye of the subject, the eye of the one who understands power as power over another, the eye of reason, and the eye that arrogantly denies there is any problem with this kind of imagery.

The loving eye, on the other hand, understands all presence as embodied rather than abstract and rationalistic. The loving eye is based in the sense of touch. "The first thing that mammals do with their newborns is touch them." The loving eye is based in a concrete rather than an abstract understanding of the self: "I am touched and touch, therefore I am" rather than "I think, therefore I am."[20]

Whereas the arrogant eye is a subject-object model, the loving eye is a subject-subject model. McFague calls us to pay attention to the differences between these two, in part to help us acknowledge that "in the beginning is relation," while also recognizing the otherness of the other.[21] McFague's ecological model suggests "a way of being in the world rather than a way for an individual to find God."[22] Seeing and knowing others rightly requires embracing both connection and difference at the same time. An embodied knowledge, beginning with the sense of touch, encourages us to see the world differently, as embodied parts who occupy specific bodies in specific locations. In this way, metaphorical theology contributes toward a new way of understanding the relationship between God and the world, between humans and humans, and between humans and nonhumans, as well.

RESURRECTION

McFague's discourse on resurrection takes up this notion of embodied knowledge in her description of resurrection's inclusivity, making it a worldly rather than an otherworldly reality. Her interpretation is in keeping with understanding the gospel "as a destabilizing, inclusive, nonhierarchical vision of fulfillment for all of creation."[23] McFague reminds us that a critical aspect of Jesus' story as paradigmatic of God's relationship with the world is that the relationship continues after Jesus' death. "The resurrection is a way of speaking about an awareness that the presence of God in Jesus is a permanent presence in our present. The appearance stories capture this awareness better than do the empty tomb narratives with the associated interpretation of the bodily resurrection of Jesus."[24] The empty-tomb narratives suggest we are not fully in God's presence until our bodies ascend to another world to join Jesus. But the appearance stories suggest that whatever resurrection is, if interpreted as permanent presence, it is inclusive, it takes place in every present, and is the presence of God to us, not our translation into God's presence.[25]

McFague's invitation here is to consider that the resurrection of Jesus is God's promise to be permanently present, "bodily present to us, in all places and times of our world."[26] McFague then invites us to imagine and experiment with the metaphor of the universe as God's body, which underscores interdependence and mutuality. The notion of the world as God's body suggests further that God loves bodies: in loving the world, God loves a body.[27]

Imagination is key. That is all we can finally do, imagine. Our fullest knowing is precisely that which our imagination allows: nothing more, nothing less. If we can imagine that bodies are worth loving, then our attitudes and actions toward human beings, including human beings in conflict, change.

RESURRECTION AS JUSTICE

In *Life Abundant*, McFague writes, "in [Jesus'] life and death I learn who God is, and I learn that the God revealed here is incarnate also everywhere else. Jesus as the Christ means God's way with, in, and for the world. Finally, in Jesus' resurrection I can hope that the love of God for the dispossessed and oppressed will not die but live again for us and in us."[28] This kind of resurrection theology is not impartial. It cares.

McFague asks the question, "How can we understand resurrection in a way that emphasizes the destabilizing, inclusive, nonhierarchical vision of fulfillment?"[29] A metaphor of the world as body carries the promise of God to be with us always, where we are in our world. If we understand resurrection as God's ongoing, caring presence with us, we also have the obligation to reciprocate that care to life in all its forms. This means making decisions and choosing lifestyles that are truly pro-life, that promote community and mutuality. We awaken to the full liberative power of the sacred when we lift resurrection out of its future and make it attainable now.

With this view of resurrection in mind, we identify each life and each life form as a "Thou" and are led to strive toward justice at all times. With this view of resurrection in mind, we see that current theory and practice of conflict resolution does not offer sufficient care to those involved in conflict.

SALLIE MCFAGUE'S CONTRIBUTION
TO CONFLICT RESOLUTION THEORY

As noted above, conflict resolution theory and practice have become mired in too-limited descriptions that do not adequately respect the diversity nor the possibilities for relationship of those in conflict. They do not embrace a nonhierarchical, inclusive vision.

Built on McFague's resurrection imaginary, negotiation and mediation techniques would begin with a loving eye, an attitude of subjects having something both to teach and to learn from other subjects. Context and history would be integral to this process, as would an awareness of the changing character of possible conflict resolution paradigms. An effective resolution in one case would not necessarily bear on the next conflict.

McFague's construal of resurrection and her emphasis on Thou-Thou relationships supply a lens through which to analyze currently accepted practice and theory of conflict resolution, and a way to look at the inadequacy of such theory and practice in dealing with conflicts that originate from an imbalance of power or those in non-Western contexts. With McFague's metaphorical, resurrection, justice-oriented contribution in mind, I look forward to the possibility of a healthier conflict resolution paradigm in the future.

NOTES

1. Quotations compiled by Ronald J. McAllister, Provost, Elizabethtown College, Elizabethtown, Pennsylvania.

2. Roger Fisher and William Ury, *Getting to Yes: Negotiating Agreement Without Giving In,* ed. Bruce Patton (New York: Houghton Mifflin Co., 1981).

3. Ibid.,13.

4. Ibid., 29.

5. Alan Tidwell, *Conflict Resolved?* (London: Pinter, 1998), 26.

6. Neutrality is one condition of a good mediator according to Fisher and Ury, Ibid.

7. Deborah Kolb and Linda Pitman, "Through the Looking Glass," in *Workplace Dispute Resolution: Directions for the 21st Century* (East Lansing, Mich.: Michigan State University Press, 1997), 232.

8. Paul E. Salem, "In Theory: A Critique of Western Conflict Resolution from a Non-Western Perspective," *Negotiation Journal* (October, 1994), 361.

9. Ibid., 362.

10. Ibid., 364.

11. Ibid., 366.

12. Ibid., 368.

13. Sharon D. Welch, *A Feminist Ethic of Risk* (Minneapolis: Fortress Press,

1990), 3.

14. Sallie McFague, *Models of God: Theology for an Ecological, Nuclear Age* (Philadelphia: Fortress Press, 1987), 31.

15. Ibid., 34.

16. Ibid.

17. Ibid., 37.

18. Ibid., 51.

19. Sallie McFague, *Super, Natural Christians: How We Should Love Nature* (Minneapolis: Fortress Press, 1997), 88.

20. Ibid., 91, 92.

21. Ibid., 98.

22. Ibid.,103.

23. McFague, *Models*, 60.

24. Ibid., 59.

25. Ibid., 60.

26. Ibid.

27. Ibid., 74.

28. Sallie McFague, *Life Abundant: Rethinking Theology and Economy for a Planet in Peril* (Minneapolis: Fortress Press, 2001), 20.

29. McFague, *Models*, 57.

Chapter 14

"The Sacred Nature of Places":[1] Understanding Land as a Contribution to Peacebuilding

Elaine Bishop

INTRODUCTION

The understandings of land held by individuals and peoples throughout the world are a result of their experiences of land mediated by culture. These understandings may then become a source of latent and active conflict.

Long-term peace building is an essential component of the process of overcoming violence and building a culture of peace. This involves "programmes designed to address the causes of conflict and the grievances of the past and to promote long-term stability and justice."[2] To be effective, this must address issues of land. Consequently, a critical task for the Historic Peace Churches must be to engage with, and to facilitate others' participation in, understanding land within and beyond our own cultural experiences and to address the issues of justice that this raises.

LAND RIGHTS AND THE DECADE TO OVERCOME VIOLENCE

Ian Fraser writes,

> In 1975, at the end of my stint for the World Council of Churches, I was asked whether I could put my finger on a dominant theological concern common to the many countries I had visited. I replied without hesitation: "the ownership and use of land."[3]

In 1982 the World Council of Churches' Central Committee issued a "Statement on Land Rights."[4] This focused on Indigenous Peoples from the Americas, Australia, and Aeotearoa/New Zealand. It named the conflict arising from the "colonial invasion [of indigenous lands]. . . by nations with predominantly Christian populations" and the resulting conflicts over occupation and control of land.[5] It challenged member churches to address this.

In 1989 the WCC Programme to Combat Racism convened *Integrity of Creation: Land Is Our Life*, a global consultation of Indigenous Peoples with churches and the Chairman-Rapporteur of the United Nations Working Group on Indigenous Populations. The Darwin Declaration issued by that consultation stressed the crisis for Indigenous Peoples who "have had our lands invaded by land-greedy nations and local, individual collaborators, and the invaders have established themselves in our lands, subjugating us to their will ever since."[6] The declaration challenged the WCC and churches around the world to address issues of indigenous land rights. N. Barney Pityana articulated the basis of WCC's involvement:

> The concern of the World Council of Churches about the issue of land rights of the Indigenous Peoples the world over is not merely a matter of political expediency. It arises out of a spiritual commitment that wrestles with the need to establish the justice of god (sic) and the implications of that search for the people of faith in our times and their witness in society.[7]

DIFFERING EXPERIENCES OF LAND IN CANADA

Land and its associated substance, water, are the fundamental bases of life.[8] Land is integral to complex varieties of activities and identities associated with human and other life on Earth.

My research looks at relationships between land and peace. I am using situations in Canada and Scotland to inquire into some of the cultural and spiritual dynamics of issues concerning land.

FIRST NATIONS

Canada is often perceived as a country with an abundance of land and water. Yet conflicts over who controls the land and the consequent issues of where and what activity takes place on it between "First Nations"[9] peoples and the successors of the newcomers over land are rife. This was identified by the United Nations Human Rights Committee in 1999, for the fourth year in a row, as "the most pressing human rights issues facing Canadians."[10]

First Nations peoples identify this conflict over land as being spiritual and cultural. It encompasses others within creation that share the land:

> Indigenous spirituality around the world is centered on the notion of our relationship to the whole of creation. We call the Earth "our mother." The animals are "our brothers and sisters." Even what biologists describe as inanimate, we call our relatives.
>
> This calling of creation into our family is a metaphorical construction that describes the relationship of love and faithfulness between human persons and the creation. Our identity as creatures in the creation cannot be expressed without talking about the rest of creation, since that very identity includes a sense of interdependence and connectedness of all life.[11]

Land is essential to the life and identity of the people. "If our land dies, we die," states a Teme Augami Anishinabai chief.[12] Robbie Dick, an Eeyou Astchee chief explains that

> It is impossible for my people to even think of the idea that the land they use will not be there. They cannot conceive that this can happen. If it happens, we will lose part of our life. Because our land is our life.[13]

The relationship to land entails responsibilities for right relationships and actions. The relationship encompasses future generations.

An Innu spokesperson says that

> Our religion teaches us that the land has been loaned to us by Tshishe-Manitu, the Great Spirit. We are the caretakers of this beautiful territory that we have been given to live on. It is our duty to pass it on, undamaged, to future generations until eternity.[14]

The worldview of the Dene

> is a worldview that encompasses far more than the need to make a living and use resources effectively. The relationship between Dene and animals is a very spiritual one, based on equality and respect.[15]

This way of living is not a matter of the management of the natural environment but of seeking to understand it and live within it.

NEWCOMER DOMINANT CULTURE

The English understanding of land was introduced to Canada when Britain won possession of New France in 1759, and proceeded to make it hospitable to British settlers through the imposition of English law.[16] This law integrated an understanding of land as commodity with an hierarchical ownership system based on tenure. In this system the term "tenure" refers to the relationship between tenant and lord. Each parcel of land was held by the tenant mediately or immediately from the British monarch.[17]

These newcomers came seeking better conditions than they had left. But many found the land inhospitable. To them the tree cover of North America was hostile and menacing.[18] They experienced the forest as enemy.[19]

COLLISIONS BETWEEN UNDERSTANDINGS OF LAND

This perspective, separating the land from the forest and the diverse ecosystems that are part of it, is alien to aboriginal understandings. Collisions between these profoundly different perspectives continue to result in conflicts throughout Canada. In a recent dispute between the Lubicon Cree Nation in Northern Alberta and Union Oil of California (Unocal), the Unocal values were straightforwardly aimed at a strong return on financial investment, serving their self-understood responsibilities to shareholders and to those involved in their operational activities. The Lubicon perspective was equally straight-forward from their point of view. In the words of Chief Ominayak, "The Lubicon people are not prepared to allow Unocal to operate a sour gas processing plant across the road from the area where our people have lived for countless generations and where we've been seeking to have a reserve established for over 50 years."[20]

Vine Deloria offers one interpretation of such contrasts:

> Within tribal traditions there is a real apprehension of and ap-preciation of the sacredness of land, and more specifically, for the sacred nature of places. . . . We experience the uniqueness of places and survey the majesty of lands. There we begin to medi-tate on who we are, what our society is, where we came from, quite possibly where we are going, and what it all means. Lands somehow call forth from us these questions and give us a feeling of being within something larger and more powerful than our-selves. . . . Unfortunately, most whites lack the historical per-spective of places simply because they have not lived on the land long enough. In addition, few whites preserve stories about the land, and very little is passed down which helps people identify the special aspect of places.[21]

Deloria's observation about the lack of historical connection may explain one aspect of conflict about land in Canada. Examination of the situation from Scotland, however, suggests that some "white" peoples do have stories and deep relationships to land.

SCOTLAND

Conflict over land and land ownership has been a central theme in the history of Scotland.[22] For the old clans of Scotland, kinship and land were integrated, providing social meaning as well as liveli-hood.[23] Feudalism, when introduced over 800 years ago, created pat-terns of land ownership based on contractual relationships between the monarch and the nobility—land in exchange for loyalty, including financial, political, and military support.[24] In the late eighteenth and nineteenth centuries, feudal landowners made decisions concerning land management that resulted in many areas, particularly in the Highlands and Islands, being depopulated. People who worked the land were forced off to provide space for a more profitable occu-pant—sheep. Some migrated to cities. Others emigrated. To provide access to cheap labor for fishing and the harvesting and processing of kelp, landowners in the Highlands disrupted emigration. They established crofts, plots of land too small to support a family, to accommodate workers.[25]

Feudal land ownership was finally abolished by the reconstituted Scottish parliament[26] in 2000.[27] As a consequence of this extended period of feudalism, in Scotland land and associated wealth and power remain profoundly unequally distributed.[28] Issues of "how land is owned (the system of land tenure), the pattern of ownership, who owns the land [and] how the land is used . . . different aspects of power relationships within society" result in land reform being a crucial issue throughout Scotland.[29] Wightman argues that ending feudal landholding may not serve the deeper issue of justice. Without further radical transformation of land management, including issues of tenure, land values, information about landowners, succession, and issues of urban land use, it may strengthen rather than resolve current inequalities.[30]

HOW DOES THIS HISTORY
TOUCH THE HISTORIC PEACE CHURCHES?

Members of Historic Peace Churches living in Canada are part of this history. We have benefited from our occupation of land, its richness and its wealth. Access to land was one of the reasons that Quakers moved into Canada. Emigration after the war of independence from what became the United States of America enabled them to combine their desire to remain loyal to the British crown with obtaining land.[31] Land was also one of the reasons Mennonites came to North America.[32]

Both groups have responded to land rights conflicts. In 1974 both reacted to an armed occupation by Ojibwa warriors of Anicinabe Park, Kenora, Ontario. This jolted some Quakers into realizing that "[Quakers], too, had been paying little attention to the concerns of aboriginal people until violence seemed to threaten."[33] Since that time Canadian Quakers have had a committee working in collaboration with Indigenous Peoples and Elders, addressing land rights and other issues through education and political action. Mennonite Central Committee (MCC) Canada has been working with Aboriginal Peoples in North America since 1972.[34] In 1992, 500 years after the European invasion of the Americas, more popularly "celebrated" as "500 years after discovery," MCC (both the Canadian and joint Canada/United States bodies), approved formal apologies to the

First Peoples of the Americas and committed themselves to working for justice, including resolution of land rights. The apology created some tension among Mennonites. In response to the suggestion that Mennonites have no reason to apologize, John H. Redekop argued that Mennonites, along with millions of others in Canada, benefited from First Nations being moved off their lands.[35]

Mennonites and Quakers also have worked on aboriginal land rights collaboratively with ecumenical and aboriginal partners. Both became members of Project North, an ecumenical coalition started in 1975. In 1987 church leaders, including Quakers and Mennonites, signed a document, "A New Covenant." This envisioned a new relationship between Indigenous Peoples and the newcomers based on respecting aboriginal rights to be distinct peoples, to an adequate land base, and to self-determination.[36]

In 1989, Project North was relaunched as the Aboriginal Rights Coalition (ARC). In 2000, ARC was a partner in the Canadian Ecumenical Jubilee Initiative (CEJI) which launched a campaign on global land rights. Issuing a call "Respecting the Land and its Peoples" CEJI plans to address environmental degradation created by the actions of Canadian corporations on indigenous lands around the world and government collusion with this through policy and funding.[37]

My research has found little to suggest historic or present corporate involvement of Scottish Quakers in land issues. Mennonites do not have representation in Scotland.

SPIRITUALITY/THEOLOGY OF LAND

One of the challenges of exploring land across cultures is finding a language that transcends the profoundly different perspectives grounded in each culture. Nuances of meaning may not survive translation from one language to another. "Theology" and "spirituality" are two concepts used here to explore some understandings of land across this divide.

"Theology" is here defined as "discourse about God."[38] The theology explored in this chapter is Christian. "Spirituality" is defined here as "of or concerning the spirit as opposed to matter; concerned with sacred or religious things."[39]

Land is invisible in most Christian theology. An exception has been the liberation theology of Central and South America. Thomas Hanks describes land as "the fundamental biblical substratum (agrar-

ian society) for human life and economic productivity."[40] Leonardo
Boff links "the cry of the oppressed with the cry of the Earth."[41]

In North America, Walter Brueggemann argues that land is the
central theme of the Bible. He speaks of land as gift from God.[42] The
gift entails responsibilities—justice and righteousness. The land also
has life of its own, beyond providing for the needs of peoples. The gift
creates temptations. He describes the Old Testament as an history of
the Hebrews engaging with that gift, of their being tempted into unjust and unrighteous behavior that results in the landed becoming
landless and then becoming landed again as God again gifts the people with land. Brueggemann goes on to suggest that land also is critical to understanding the New Testament. The proclamation of the
new age includes, he argues, reference to new land arrangements.[43]

In the Scottish context, Donald E. Meek draws parallels between
the history of oppression of the Highland people and the history of
oppression of the Hebrews and Jews.[44] He describes sermons, publications, and actions of lay and ordained activists in the land reform
movement of the late 1800s. Making reference to Old and New Testament stories, these materials and actions emphasized themes such as
God's ownership of the land given to humans for their sustenance,
and the greed of landlords.

Theology of land continues to develop. The Earth Bible Team advocates a hermeneutic of suspicion. It argues that the writers of Scripture may have represented the interests of their human group rather
than those of the Earth.[45] Raising concerns about ways in which Western dualism may affect interpretation of Scripture, the team articu-
lates six principles of ecojustice:

- *Intrinsic Worth.* The universe, Earth and all its components,
  have intrinsic worth/value.
- *Interconnectedness.* Earth is a community of interconnected living things that are mutually dependent on each other for life
  and survival.
- *Voice.* Earth is a subject capable of raising its voice in celebration and against injustice.
- *Purpose.* The universe, Earth and all its components, are part
  of a dynamic cosmic design within which each piece has a
  place in the overall goal of that design.
- *Mutual Custodianship.* Earth is a balanced and diverse domain
  where responsible custodians can be partners, rather than
  rulers, to sustain a balanced and diverse Earth community.

- *Resistance.* Earth and its components not only suffer from injustices at the hands of humans, but actively resist them in the struggle for justice.[46]

The team advocates creating new interpretations of Scripture through the lens of these principles, "detecting features of the text that may help retrieval of traditions about Earth or the Earth community that have been unnoticed, suppressed, or hidden."[47]

As I have worked with, and learned from, Aboriginal elders for over twenty years, I have come to see the articulation of these primarily oral faith traditions as most adequately described by the concept "spirituality" rather than as "theology." George Tinker identifies a central difference between Aboriginal and Western cultures: "Native American spirituality and values, social and political structures, and even ethics are rooted not in some temporal notion of history, but in spatiality. This is perhaps the most dramatic (and largely unnoticed) cultural difference between Native American thought and Western intellectual tradition. The question is not whether time or space is missing in one culture . . . but which is dominant."[48]

Yet it is possible for those in one tradition to experience the other. Sharon Butala, in coming to know an area in southern Saskatchewan in which she was living, described a transition in her understanding of that land:

> I began to see, in place of emptiness, presence: I began to see not only the visible landscape but the invisible one, a landscape in which history, unrecorded and unremembered as it is, had transmuted itself into an always present spiritual dimension.[49]

CONCLUSION

The Decade to Overcome Violence offers opportunities for churches around the world to take part in long-term peacebuilding. Addressing local, regional, and international land rights issues must be part of this. Yet, understanding land across cultures is complex, engaging issues of land, culture, and theology/spirituality.

This limited exploration of land and the relationship between humans and land identifies some places to begin. Land belongs to and is the gift of God. Justice and righteousness must be the bases for relationships between land and humans. Land has its own voice which needs to be heard separate from human land use.

Major challenges remain. Land has received little attention in dominant theology. Brueggemann does not address the fact that the land into which God led the Israelites was occupied. The understanding of land as "commodity" does not encompass a relationship to God. Exploring theology from the perspective of Earth is in its early days. Challenges exist in developing mutual understanding and respect between Christian theology and First Nations spirituality.

McKay suggests that allowing people to reflect on the spirituality of First Nations, linking themes to those explored in theology, may create a basis for understanding. Some Canadian churches in ARC have experienced this. In working with Aboriginal peoples they have learned that justice in the social order is inextricably linked with a recovery of the integrity of creation.[50]

Exploring different faith perspectives of land with others who share that land may thus serve several purposes. It may deepen the faith life of our communities. It may build relationships with others. It may contribute to ways of living more lightly on the Earth. All of these can contribute to the long-term peacebuilding needed if the Decade is to be effective.

NOTES

1. Vine Deloria, Jr., "Reflection and Revelation. Knowing Land, Places, and Ourselves" in Vine Deloria, Jr., *For This Land: Writings on Religion in America* (New York: Routledge, 1999), 251.

2. Simon Fisher, et al., *Working with Conflict: Skills and Strategies for Action* (London: Zed Books Ltd., 2000), 14.

3. Ian Fraser, "Probe: Land, Food, and Power," *Coracle* 3:50 (2000), 13.

4. World Council of Churches Central Committee, "WCC Central Committee Statement on Land Rights," *PCR Information: Reports and Background Papers*, 25 (1989), 74-77.

5. Ibid., 94.

6. Integrity of Creation: Land Is Our Life Consultation, "Darwin Declaration, Indigenous Nations in Global Crisis," *PCR Information: Reports and Background Papers*, 25 (1989), 75.

7. N. B. Pityana, "Director's Preface," *PRC Information* 25 (1989), 5.

8. D. Hillel, *Out of the Earth: Civilization and the Life of the Soil* (Berkeley: University of California Press, 1992), 3.

9. Several terms are used in Canada when identifying Peoples and Nations living there prior to the arrival of European colonizers. "First Nations" and "Aboriginal Peoples" are used by many of those previously called "Indians." On the West Coast some of these peoples still choose to call themselves "Indians." The peoples of the far north call themselves "Inuit." The Inuit are generally not included in the terms First Nations or Aboriginal Peoples. Canadian

government terminology identifies four "categories" of Original Peoples. Those Aboriginal Peoples with whom it has a formal treaty relationship, it calls "status" and those without such a relationship "non-status." It recognizes as separate groups Inuit and Métis, those people of mixed aboriginal and other descent. "Indigenous Peoples" is the term used in the international arena to describe all these peoples.

10. Lorraine Land, "Emerging Trends and Issues in Aboriginal Rights Support Work" (Unpublished Paper, 1999), 7-11.

11. Stan McKay, "Calling Creation into Our Family," in *Nation to Nation: Aboriginal Sovereignty and the Future of Canada*, ed. Diane Engelstad and John Bird (Concord, Ont.: House of Anansi Press Limited, 1992), 29.

12. Gary Potts, "Last-Ditch Defense of a Priceless Homeland," in ed. Boyce Richardson, *Drum Beat: Anger and Renewal in Indian Country* (Toronto: Summerhill Press, 1989), 201.

13. Grand Council of the Crees (Eeyou Astchee), *Never Without Consent: James Bay Crees' Stand Against Forcible Inclusion into an Independent Quebec* (Toronto: ECW Press, 1998), 117.

14. Daniel Ashini, "David Confronts Goliath: The Innu of Ungava Versus the NATO Alliance" in Richardson, 50.

15. J. Barnaby, "Culture and Sovereignty," in Engelstad and Bird, 40-41.

16. Desmond Morton, *A Short History of Canada* (Edmonton, A.B.: Hurtig Publishers, 1983), 22.

17. *Mabo and Others v. Queensland*, No. 2 (1992), 175, CLR 1 F.C. 92/014 #48.

18. James Hunter, *A Dance Called America*: *The Scottish Highlands, the United States, and Canada* (Edinburgh: Mainstream Publishing, 1994), 91.

19. Morton, 30.

20. V. Gibson, *Resources, Conflict, and Culture: The Sour Gas Plant Dispute Between Unocal Canada and the Lubicon Cree Nation* (Edmonton, A. B.: University of Alberta, 1996), 110.

21. Deloria, 251-253.

22. Andy D. Wightman, *Who Owns Scotland?* (Edinburgh: Canongate Books, 1996), 1.

23. Robert A. Dodgshon, *From Chiefs to Landlords: Social and Economic Change in the Western Highlands and Islands, c.1493-1820* (Edinburgh: Edinburgh University Press, 1998), 8-13.

24. Andy D. Wightman, *Scotland: Land and Power, the Agenda for Land Reform* (Edinburgh: Luath Press Limited, 1999), 16.

25. James Hunter, *The Making of the Crofting Community* (Edinburgh: John Donald Publishers Ltd., 1976), 6-21.

26. *Abolition of Feudal Tenure*, etc. (Scotland) Act 2000 (asp 5), 1.

27. Scotland's independent parliament was adjourned March 25, 1707, when the Act of Union was passed, to much public opposition in Scotland, uniting the parliaments of Scotland and England. It did not meet again until devolution was implemented in 1999, with new parliamentarians of the Scottish parliament taking their oaths on May 12.

28. Wightman, *Scotland: Land and Power*, 27-42.

29. Ibid., 44-45.

30. Ibid., 65-104.

31. G. Finnegan, "People of Providence, Polity, and Property: Domesticity, Philanthropy, and Land Ownership as Instruments of Quaker Community Development in Adolphustown, Upper Canada, 1784-1824," in *Faith, Friends, and Fragmentation: Essays on Nineteenth Century Quakerism in Canada*, ed. A. Schrauwers (Toronto: Canadian Friends Historical Association, 1995), 13-24.

32. John H. Redekop, "Why Apologize to Native People in 1992," in *The Teachable Moment: A Christian Response to the Native Peoples of the Americas* (Winnipeg, Man.: Mennonite Central Committee Canada, 1992), 13.

33. Jo Vellacott, "The Origins of the Canadian Quaker Committee on Native Concerns," *The Canadian Friend* 92:1 (1996), 14.

34. Mennonite Central Committee Canada, "Statement to the Aboriginal Peoples of the Americas in 1992, 500 Years After Columbus 'Discovered' the Americas," in *The Teachable Moment*, 11.

35. Ibid., 11.

36. *A New Covenant: Towards the Constitutional Recognition and Protection of Aboriginal Self-Government in Canada, A Pastoral Statement by the Leaders of the Christian Churches on Aboriginal Rights and the Canadian Constitution*, 1987.

37. Canadian Ecumenical Jubilee Initiative, *Respecting the Land and Its Peoples*, (Toronto: Canadian Ecumenical Jubilee Initiative, 2000).

38. Alister E. McGrath, *Christian Theology: An Introduction*, 2nd. ed. (Oxford: Blackwell Publishers Ltd., 1997), 141.

39. S. Tullock, ed., *The Reader's Digest Complete Wordfinder* (London: The Reader's Digest Association Limited, 1994), 1497.

40. Thomas D. Hanks, *God So Loved the Third World: The Biblical Vocabulary of Oppression* (Maryknoll, N.Y.: Orbis Books, 1983), 62.

41. Leonardo Boff, *Cry of the Earth, Cry of the Poor* (Maryknoll, N.Y.: Orbis Books, 1997), xi.

42. Walter Brueggemann, *The Land: Place as Gift, Promise, and Challenge in Biblical Faith* (Philadelphia: Fortress Press, 1977).

43. Ibid., 170-175.

44. Donald E. Meek, "The Land Question Answered from the Bible; The Land Issue and the Development of a Highland Theology of Liberation," *Scottish Geographical Magazine* 102:2 (1987), 84-89.

45. The Earth Bible Team, "Guiding Ecojustice Principles," in *Readings from the Perspective of Earth*, ed. N. Habel (Sheffield: Sheffield Academic Press, 2000), 39.

46. Ibid., 42-53.

47. Ibid., 39.

48. Freda Rajotte, *First Nations Faith and Ecology* (Toronto: Anglican Book Centre and United Church Publishing House, 1998), 23.

49. Sharon Butala, *The Perfection of the Morning: An Apprenticeship in Nature* (Toronto: HarperCollins Publishers Ltd., 1994), 113.

50 Peter Hamel, "The Aboriginal Rights Coalition," in *Coalitions for Justice*, ed. Christopher Lind and Joe Mihovic (Ottawa: Novelis, 1994), 30.

Chapter 15

Intercessors for Reunification: Toward a Peacebuilding Church in Korea

Sang Gyoo Lee

INTRODUCTION

Since World War II, Korea, along with the Middle East, has been one of the most dangerous and conflicted places in the world. The Cold War, the main source of tension, is over and a certain amicable mood between the North (DPRK—Democratic Peoples Republic of Korea) and the South (ROK—Republic of Korea) has emerged in recent years due to the South's "Sunshine Policy." However, aggressive military tensions and threats still remain which may lead not only to armed conflict between the two Koreas but also to a nuclear conflict on the peninsula and in Asia.

Thus, the tension in Korea is an international problem, involving the United States, Russia, China, Japan, and other Asian countries. Today, the greatest threats to peace we see are regional conflicts that can escalate to unmanageable global proportions, including nuclear confrontation. The ongoing hostility between North and South is not only a regional issue but also a global problem. Therefore, peacemaking on the Korean peninsula is important for world peace.

In this chapter I will draw attention to Korea by reflecting on its context. Rather than a detailed recounting of the complex historical relations between North and South, I will focus on the role churches can play and the challenges for peace theology. In this discussion, "the role of Korean church" refers to the role of the South Korean church toward the North.

HISTORICAL BACKGROUND OF THE DIVISION

To aid our common understanding of the Korean context, let me briefly survey the historical background of the division of Korea and subsequent conflict between North and South.

Although Korea has been referred to as "the land of morning calm" (so-called by the meaning of her old name, *Chosun*), she has seldom experienced peace and tranquility. Throughout her recorded history, which goes back to 2333 B.C., the decisive changes in Korean national life have taken place to the accompaniment of battle music.

The famous American author Pearl Buck once wrote, "Korea is the gem of the orient and a noble people live there." However, due to her geographic position, Korea was destined to become a bone of contention among her powerful neighbors. From time to time across the centuries, either China or Japan has controlled Korea. In the late nineteenth century these two nations fought over Korea, and in the early twentieth century the Russians fought the Japanese over Korea. The Japanese defeated the Russians in 1905 following their victory over China in 1895, and finally occupied and formally annexed Korea in 1910 and ruled for thirty-six years (1910-1945). A bitter period of oppression and resistance ensued.

On August 15, 1945, World War II ended with the Allied victory. Japanese imperialism was vanquished. With liberation from the Japanese, Koreans looked forward to the restoration of a unified, independent national state. This ambition was frustrated, however, by the arbitrary US-Soviet decision to divide Korea at the 38th parallel. As the Cold War between the superpowers deepened, this division assumed an increasingly permanent appearance and the hostile attitude intensified. In 1948, separate governments were established in the North and South. They then engaged in a struggle for legitimacy and sovereignty culminating in the Korean civil war in 1950.

The Korean War lasted for three years and, comparatively speaking, Korea suffered more death and destruction than any other nation in modern history. Four million Koreans were killed; ten million were separated from their families; six hundred thousand women lost their husbands; and fifty thousand children were orphaned. Since the 1953 Armistice agreement, a fragile truce has been in effect. For the last fifty years, the division between North and South has not only been preserved, but entrenched. The division provoked open hostilities and military confrontation between the two sides.

Koreans, North and South, share the same blood, a strong sense of national identity, a common experience of oppression and struggle, and a fervent desire for unity. Yet they have become the most ideologically divided and physically separated nation in the world.

Today, the nation still remains divided, with twenty-one million Koreans living in a very isolated socialist system in the 122,000 square kilometers of the North, and forty-two million Koreans living in a capitalist system in the 99,000 square kilometers of the South.

CONFLICT AND CONFRONTATION
BETWEEN NORTH AND SOUTH

Following the division between North and South, there have been endless skirmishes and military clashes during the past half century. According to a government report, since the 1953 armistice there have been 2,800 North Korean provocations or attacks and 538 soldiers have been killed in conflicts. The border between North and South Korea remains the most heavily militarized frontier in the world. Perhaps one million soldiers on both sides face each other along the so-called "Demilitarized Zone" in an environment of tension and hostility. Technically, a state of war remains in effect, as a peace treaty has never been signed. North Korea is suspected of having developed its own nuclear weapons. Some 37,000 U.S. troops are stationed in the South, guarding against invasion from the North.

The experiences of the Korean War and today's military readiness are clear indications to all Koreans that any future war on the peninsula would result in great suffering and total destruction for both sides. Politically, therefore, the withdrawal of nuclear arms from the peninsula, troop reductions on both sides, and peace talks to ease political tension and military confrontation have become major issues.

Following the North-South division, peacebuilding on the Korean peninsula became an urgent task for all Koreans. However, the discussion of "reconciliation" or "peace" with each other was strongly forbidden by both governments. Both governments—the one led by *KIM, Il-Sung* in the North and the one led by *RHEE, Syng-Man* in the South—pursued reunification by military force. Absolutely no room was allowed to discuss reconciliation or peace with each other. To do so was considered an act of treason or foreign espionage. Although government authorities discussed reunification, such dialogue was primarily for political use and did not genuinely pursue reunification. In 1972, for example, three principles for achieving reunification—that it be achieved independently, democratically, and peacefully—were articulated and adopted by both North and South and endorsed by the United Nations. These agreed upon principles have been cited in numerous concrete proposals over the years, but they have been used to maintain and support the political power or regime. Thus real progress on reunification has been frustrated, for which each side blames the other.

In recent years, more hope for reunification has at times emerged. In 1988, the Korean church declared 1995 the jubilee year of national reunification. In 1994, North Korean dictator KIM, Il-Sung died, while in the South, President KIM, Dae-Jung made it clear his government would promote economic cooperation and civilian exchanges with North Korea regardless of political and security tensions on the Korean peninsula. In June, 1998, the Hyundai Group founder JUNG, Ju-Yung crossed the border into North Korea with five hundred head of cattle. And in August, 2000, and again in 2001, some families separated for fifty years were finally able to meet each other in Seoul and in Pyongyang, raising worldwide interest in the Korean situation.

TOWARD A PEACEBUILDING CHURCH

As noted before, Koreans continue to suffer conflict from the division between their two highly militarized countries. Koreans have experienced neither peace nor justice since the division.

Korean reunification means for Koreans the following three things: (1) the historical and geographical recovery of Korea as a single country, (2) the recovery of the Korean nation, that is, national reconciliation of Korea and (3) the recovery of peace and justice.

From the time of the division to the 1970s, the Korean church was positively involved neither in reunification issues nor in peacebuilding on the Korean peninsula. Rather, it was relegated to the status of a servant of the dictatorial government. During this period the South Korean government strengthened its anti-communist stand, while the Korean church supported and accepted the government's policy.

The church's action was based on two reasons. First, many Christians who fled the North as war refugees experienced persecution under the communist government and carried an anti-communist stance. Secondly, the Korean church was strongly influenced by the RHEE, Syng-Man government's anti-communist policy. Thus, Christians in South Korea had anti-communist attitudes and North Korea was viewed as the object of destruction, not of peaceful coexistence. Talking about "peace with the North" was itself regarded as a violation of "Anti-Communist Law," that is, as antigovernment activity.

However, since the 1980s, despite government oppression, the Korean church has begun to engage in issues of national reconciliation and reunification. Because it has been impossible for the Korean church to have direct contact with the North, South Korean Christians have invited international church communities to help with the process of building opportunities for dialogue. This process took definite shape in 1984 when the World Council of Churches convened a consultation on "Peace and Justice in North-East Asia: Prospects for a Peaceful Resolution of Conflicts," in Tozanso, Japan. The Tozanso consultation was followed by a series of conferences or meetings.

At Glion, Switzerland, in September, 1986, and in November, 1988, Christians from North and South Korea met for the first time since the division. Mostly significantly, in February, 1988, the National Council of Churches of Korea (KNCC), issued an historic document entitled *Declaration on National Reunification and Peace* that aroused international interest regarding the peaceful reunification of the Korean peninsula.

It is evident that this series of efforts by the Korean church to achieve reunification has contributed to awakening awareness of its role in the conflict transformation and peaceful reunification of the Korean Peninsula. Nevertheless, the Cold War climate can still be sensed in areas of tension and conflict. In North Korea, many people are hungry and some fifty thousand refugees are at extreme risk of life. It is therefore not surprising that now, more than ever, the peaceful resolution of conflict has become an important issue for the churches in South Korea.

We do not have to assume the role of mediators in all conflicts, but we need to explore the role of the Korean churches in this context. We need to remind Korean Christians of their responsibility to reconcile, mediate, and to bridge the gap that separates North and South.

For Korean churches to be ambassadors of Christ in this challenging context, along with repentance of our sins of disobedience, unbelief, hatred, fighting, and war, we must perform a twofold public role. We must assume a prophetic role in the proclamation of peace and reconciliation, and also become agents of peace and intercession.

REPENTANCE OF SINS

First of all, we as Christians of Korea must confess before God and our people that we have sinned. We, disciples of Christ, have been called to labor as "apostles of peace" (Col. 3:15), but have participated in fighting, war, and killing each other. We must confess our guilt and sin, our violation of God's commandment to "love your neighbor as yourself" (Matt. 22:37ff.). We have long harbored a deep hatred and hostility toward one another. We have committed the sin of endorsing the reinforcement of troops and further rearmament in the name of preventing another war. We must confess and ask for God's mercy.

ASSUMING A PROPHETIC ROLE

As Kingdom citizens, Korean church communities must witness to the significance of peace and proclaim that peace is a noble vision worth pursuing by all humanity. Paul describes the ministry of the Christian community as a "ministry of reconciliation" (2 Cor. 5:19) and the letter to the Ephesians confesses Christ as "our peace" who has broken down the dividing walls of hostility (Eph. 2:14). Yet, in Korea, due to the conflict and armed stand-off between North and South Korea since 1945, the idea of reconciliation or peace on the Korean peninsula has been entirely disregarded by the government and by the churches. Jesus Christ, in His Sermon on the Mount, calls the peacemakers blessed (Matt. 5:9). But this has not been seriously considered in the Korean context.

First of all, Korean churches are responsible to teach the significance of peace and the value of *shalom* in community. This is a basic and fundamental task of the Korean church which is called to witness to the "gospel of peace." Individual Christians and the Christian com-

munities have the duty to spread the gospel of peace and reconciliation. The Korean churches, like other churches in the world, must
share a common conviction that they are responsible for peace and
conflict transformation. When Korean Christians place importance
on reconciliation and peace in human affairs, then we will be able to
come to grips with the world around us, discern the fundamental issues in our Korean context, and be able to witness to the reality that
things can be different.

Korean churches are, I believe, responsible for initiating and developing a theology of peace. The most tragic phenomenon in Korea
is that the church does not emphasize building peace in our society of
conflict. As mentioned earlier, the discussion of "peace" or "peaceful
coexistence" has been virtually ignored or, worse still, simply used as
political propaganda. Pacifism has not been given any voice. Rather,
it has been considered a subversive idea that undermines national security. At this time, we in the Korean church have a prophetic man-
date to teach, exhort, persuade, encourage, and stimulate the noble
value of peace and peaceful coexistence. Accordingly, peace studies
or peace theology, as a foundation of discussion on the conflict transformation and peaceful unification of Korea, must be pursued.

We need a holy boldness and confidence to willingly speak out,
challenge, and confront the spirits of the age and to seek new directions. This is the prophetic posture of cultural engagement, through
critique and renewal for the sake of Christ's Kingdom, which should
characterize the Christian community.

A MEDIATING ROLE

The other role of the Korean church in transforming conflict and
peacefully reunifying Korea is to serve Koreans as an intercessor. Not
only Koreans, but all followers of Christ, are called to be agents of
change and reconciliation wherever the Lord leads us to serve.

To prevent war, reduce tensions, and promote peace on the Korean peninsula, the Church must continually be engaged in promoting mutual understanding, cooperation, and national reconciliation.
The reunification of Germany can serve as an example and precedent
for Korean reunification.

First, for the sake of the peaceful reunification of Korea, it is imperative that we build trust between North and South. The Korean
church must make special efforts to reduce and overcome hostility
and hatred, thereby creating an atmosphere of forgiveness and recon-

ciliation. The division of Korea created a mutually antagonistic mood and posture for both North and South Korea. Each has been described by the other as an enemy, or the servant of one of the imperial super-powers.

The division created an ideological structure preventing Koreans from seeing each other as their nation's other part. In this context, Christians are required to do their part for national reconciliation. In a sense, political and territorial reunification is relatively easy compared to the reunification of a divided people. In this respect, *MUN, Yung-Hur,* a Christian political scientist, encourages the churches to overcome the "division of heart" in the Korean nation before seeking the reunification of Korea.

Second, Korean Christians need to approach Korean reunification by demonstrating love for North Koreans through relief work or material aid. In North Korea, millions have died of starvation while the government pours funds into the military. More than fifty thousand North Koreans hover between life and death. Love in action for North Koreans means sharing material goods. Without sharing food with those who hunger there can be no peace. Love expressed through the sharing of goods can transcend ideological conflicts, will help recover the nation's sense of commonality, and can become a seed toward building peace and reconciliation.

Third, Korean churches should be engaged in teaching and facilitating a paradigm shift. *Pax Romana* is not and cannot be the ideal way to maintain peace on the Korean peninsula. In the *pax Romana* paradigm, peace depends on a military strength superior to all real and potential enemies. This paradigm presumes that peace can be maintained by military superiority or war. The Korean church, called to serve a mediating role, must teach people that authentic peace cannot be secured by way of military contest or war, and that peaceful coexistence is possible. The idea that eternal peace can be secured by superior power will only produce military reinforcement which will inevitably result in another war. We are challenged to speak out and declare that the *pax Romana* tradition has not been and cannot be the solution to the Korean context.

Fourth, the Korean Christian community needs to work together with international church organizations for the reduction of military forces, weapons, and facilities, thereby reducing tension and ultimately avoiding military confrontation. Reducing and eliminating this major threat to peace and the reunification of the Korean peninsula is also part of the church's role as mediator.

CONCLUDING REMARKS

If the Korean church expresses interest in conflict resolution and engages in an active role as a bridge builder, I believe it will greatly influence the reunification process. In light of reunification, peace on the Korean peninsula can be considered as an end in itself. And in light of peacemaking, reunification can also be considered as an end in itself.

Peace is justice, particularly in the Korean situation. Justice implies forgiveness rather than retaliation. Justice is reconciliation, not mutual confrontation.

Peace is needed because of the sinfulness of human nature, and is possible because of Christ who is our Peace and because of the Spirit of Peace, who speaks to our consciences.

I believe there is an urgent need to promote and develop peace theology and peace studies in the Korean context. Despite the danger, suspicion, and disbelief, Christian efforts for peacemaking on the Korean peninsula are imperative and, I believe, are commanded by God.

It is our hope that the conflict, confrontation, weapons, and war be eliminated and that people be able to live together in peace and justice.

Chapter 16

Peace in the Tiger's Mouth

Alastair McIntosh

A gentle Buddhist monk from Thailand [who had been persecuted] for or-
ganizing controversial social justice activities in his home country . . .
came one day and silently left a beautiful rice paper brush and ink draw-
ing on the floor of our simple abode in the forest. It was of a rampant tiger
with the caption, "The best place for meditation is in the tiger's mouth."[1]

In this chapter I will suggest that *community* is the soil in which peace
unfolds. Peace is the building of community in a triune relationship—
with one another, with the creation, and with God. This is achieved
not by denying power, or necessarily by renouncing it, but often by
engaging with it amid conflict—in the "tiger's mouth." The calling to
engage, however, must not be of this world. It must be moved by the
grace of God, the preferential concern of which is for the poor of the
earth and the broken in nature.

TRIUNE COMMUNITY

Community is a condition of belonging that results from living in
growing consciousness of interconnection. It is, as Paul put it, the

"church" as "members one of another" (Rom. 12:5). Jesus said that we are all branches of one vine. If we cut ourselves off we will, as sure as a branch dies without water, wither and be good only for the metaphorical fire (John 15). Similar principles of interconnection are found in all mystical religions. "Consider my sacred mystery. I am the source of all beings, I support them all, but I rest not in them," says Krishna in the *Bhagavad Gita*. "Thirty spokes share one hub," is how the *Tao te Ching* puts it. "All Muslims are as one person," says the *Hadith*, the oral tradition of the Prophet Mohammed (peace be upon him).

In the Christian tradition, "sin" can be defined as the breaking of God's community. We might see the three temptations of Jesus on the mountain as representing pressure to break community in each of its primary fields of expression (Luke 4, Mt 4). Had Jesus used his power to change stones into bread he would have violated, and so misused, the laws of nature. For him to have assumed landed power by acquiring kingdoms would have wronged human social structures. And for him to have put God to the test by leaping from the pinnacle would have been an abuse of spiritual power.

A deep understanding of community integrates both the social and natural environments that comprise "human ecology" into an all-embracing spiritual environment. Simultaneously immanent and transcendent, such an human ecology constitutes the totality of reality. It gives humankind an integral role in a universe bound together by love. Love articulated out into the universe, made incarnate, is justice. But for this to "roll down like waters" (Amos 5:24), spiritual justice must underlie social and ecological justice.

Spiritual justice may be understood as the avoidance of spiritual delusion. If social justice concerns our affairs with one another, and ecological justice our relationship with the rest of the creation, spiritual justice concerns right relationship in worship. Worship, in the broadest and deepest understanding of the concept, is about how we fundamentally orient our lives. It is a perceptual matter, being concerned with how we *see* reality, with what happens when the scales fall from our eyes. In living life worshipfully we lift our eyes to God. We make God the measure by which all else is judged. Spiritual justice means seeing life reverentially, seeing with eyes that accord with God's love, and not with eyes set upon some lesser "god" such as money, status, or a human leader. As social and ecological justice follow on from spiritual justice, and as community and therefore peace arise at the confluence of all three faces of justice, it follows, as the prophets repeatedly saw, that the most fundamental barrier to creating a peaceful world is idolatry. In this sense the seemingly glib assertion that "all wars have religion at their heart" is deeply true. All wars idolize violence; the religion in question is idolatrous.

In being community and so becoming the church, we have to make choices of whether to become more dead or alive. If need be, we must leave the dead (note, *the dead*, not the living) to bury their own dead, shake the dust from our feet, and walk on through the desert until we come to where community is alive (Deut. 30:19; Luke 9:60; Mark 6:11). This refusal to collude with the deadness of everyday life, the "banality of evil," the idolatry of necrophilia, implies a continuous commitment to "turn back the streams of war" as peace workers.[2]

WAR AND EMPATHY

War, the antithesis and negation of community, comes about when understanding of the interconnection of all life has never been developed in the first place, is inadequately developed, or has broken down. As such, war derives from a perceptual failing, from a deficit of conscious awareness about reality. War reflects a fragmented worldview; one that considers "collateral damage" to be an acceptable possibility, rather than seeing it as an oxymoron in what is "One World" that can have no externalities to the economic or military equation. If we could but see and experience our membership, one of another, as one body, we would no more harm that which surrounds us than we would willingly cause harm to our own corporeal body. Yes, it is true that self-harm is a common psychopathology. But it is precisely that— a psychopathology. Except in specific sacrificed testimonies of witness, as sometimes expressed in making certain types of protest or in shows of mourning, self-harm is invariably connected to a loss of self-worth. As such, the resolution of war connects with the wider work of salvation that seeks to "salve" our sense of who we are.

The ability to experience interconnection with the other derives from *empathy*. Empathy is the fruit of spiritual presence. War can only be sustained in an absence of empathy. It results from a deficit of presence, which is to say, of connection with wider and deeper reality in consciousness. Empathy is the capacity to feel for and with the other. It is a gift of grace. It is revealed and not something that can be forced. It can only be opened out to, asked and waited for, by becoming confessionally more present to our lack of presence with the other.

Peace is therefore built from the recognition that war has a socially emergent property. War derives from lack of mutual presence in a society's members. Its presenting symptoms may be geopolitical, but its roots are psychospiritual. "Do you know where wars come from?" asks the Indian Jesuit Anthony de Mello. "They come from projecting outside of us the conflict that is inside. Show me an individual in whom there is no inner self-conflict and I'll show you an individual in whom there is no violence." [3] This is what makes deep peace work spiritual work. We should not despair at having to undertake peace work, or at the hugeness of the task. We should not fear when we find ourselves in the mouth of the tiger, because that is where God needs us to be. That is where presence will be sharpest. That is why conflict, spiritually understood, can be so good for meditation. It challenges us to seek the strength that can bring us spiritually alive through unthinkable situations. It challenges us to work out our own salvation in the context of the troubled social and natural environments in which we find ourselves living. It brings liberation.

Gustavo Gutiérrez sees liberation as a threefold process. First, he says, there is "liberation from social situations of oppression and marginalization." That is to say, liberation at levels that affect family, community, and political and economic institutions. Next there is the need for "personal transformation by which we live with profound inner freedom in the face of every kind of servitude." This is psychological and spiritual development—liberation from our internal blockages, hang-ups, and various uptightnesses. And thirdly, there is what he calls liberation from "sin." Gutiérrez describes this level of liberation as that "which attacks the deepest root of all servitude; for sin is the breaking of friendship with God and with other human beings." Liberation, he concludes, "gets to the very source of social injustice and other forms of human oppression and reconciles us with God and our fellow human beings." It sets us free at social, psychological, and spiritual levels of experience. "Free for what?" Gutiérrez asks. "Free to love," he concludes, adding that "to liberate" means "to give life." [4]

CONFESSING POWER

Power is germane to conflict; therefore, the dynamics of power must be faced by peace workers. Too often in justice and peace movements, power is denied, forgetting that power denied is power abused. This is the cause of much strife within our movements.

Power is the capacity to bring about change in the structure of reality. As such, power and the making of community cannot be separated. Power, including our personal power, must therefore be confessed. We must live in conscious acknowledgment of it so that we are fully accountable to one another and can yield power when that is appropriate. Our communities must be *confessional communities*, predicated on mutual psychological honesty.

In his trilogy, *Naming the Powers, Unmasking the Powers,* and *Engaging the Powers,*[5] the American theologian Walter Wink explores the principle that power is central to the spiritual expression of life. Power constellates or crystallizes reality. It might be seen as *the will to be*. We are familiar with power's exterior expressions in people, institutions, buildings, nations, and natural processes such as the growth of a tree. But it has also, according to Wink, an interior dynamic.

This interiority is, Wink suggests, "spirituality." Such spirituality underlies the outward manifestation of things. Outward forms of reality are shaped by their inner spirituality. This is not to deny the importance of molecular structures, genetic sequences, and the laws of physics. It is simply to say that spirituality is at their root. Spirituality accounts for their emergent properties—features that arise from systems that would not have been predictable from only the sum of their component parts. Consider, for example, the Periodic Table of the Elements as a template for the material world. Spirituality, can be seen as the difference between an aggregation of carbon, water, and a few other components, and what constitutes an human being. It is the difference between C_2H_5OH, the chemical formula for alcohol, and a cup of wine sacramentally representing the spirit of life.

The implications of understanding the interiority and exteriority of power are profound for the peace activist. The following matrix illustrates this. It was developed for a lecture I give annually at the Joint Services Command and Staff College, Britain's foremost school of war. The matrix suggests a spectral relationship between conventional applications of military force, and the Gandhian "truth force" that spiritual activism employs. It acknowledges that both the peace activist and the serving soldier may be participants in a connected process. As a generalization, and one that is not always valid, both the soldier and the peace activist think of themselves as working for peace, and each knows that this involves engaging with power. The difference between us, and it can be a decisive life-or-death difference, lies in how we go about it. At the end of the day, we might remember, God told David that he could not build the temple because "you have shed so much blood in my sight on the earth" (1 Chron. 22:8).[6]

Based on Wink's theology, the matrix on the opposite page suggests that power has an interior, spiritual, or intrinsic face and an exterior, physical, or incarnate face. This interior/exterior "dynamic," as I have called it, is shown on the downward y axis.

Through these dynamics, power can be expressed at levels of being that are capable of being physical, psychological (of which I distinguish two types), and "spiritual."[7] This is shown moving right along the horizontal x axis. Peace, I suggest, is a process by which the expression of power in the human world shifts left to right along this spectrum.

Just as persons are, in terms of Christian theology, "fallen," in the sense that they fall short of their God-given potential, so too the "powers that be" (Rom. 13:1, KJV) governing the inner spirituality of institutions and nations are "fallen." They therefore necessitate constant calling back to their God-given potential. At the level of nationhood, Walter Wink consequently distinguishes between the fallen *personality* of a nation and the higher *vocation* or "calling" of nationhood—a nation representing a community of people at the macro level. Wink says that

> In a little-known essay of 1941, [Martin] Buber acknowledges that every nation has a guiding spiritual characteristic, its genius, which it acknowledges as its "prince" or its "god." The national spirit unfolds, matures, and withers. There is a life cycle for every nation. Every nation makes an idol of its supreme faculties, elevating its own self as absolute, and worshipping its own inner essence or spirit as a god. But to be limited to oneself is to be condemned to die. When the national spirit decays and disintegrates, and the nation turns its face to nothingness instead of participating in the whole, it is on the verge of death. . . . Whenever the state makes itself the highest value, then it is in an objective state of blasphemy. This is the situation of the majority of the nations in the world today, our own included.[8]

Swiss psychologist C. G. Jung saw the ideologies and symbols of nationhood as important because they mediate power from the collective unconscious of a people into political action. In one of his last essays, *The Undiscovered Self,* he wrote of the danger that, "Where love stops, power begins, and violence, and terror." And, he maintained, "The individual who is not anchored in God can offer no resistance on his own resources to the physical and moral blandishments of the world." Jung continues,

LEVEL OF POWER	PHYSICAL	PSYCHOLOGICAL TYPE I	PSYCHOLOGICAL TYPE II	SPIRITUAL
Dynamic	Coercion by hard sanction of terror—death, torture, loss, detention, injury, shock.	Persuasion through soft sanction of fear—prison, fines, social conformity, obedience.	Persuasion through convincement leading to empowerment, especially at community level.	Transformation—empowerment from within, satyagraha, autopoesis—comes from the soul.
Interior Face	Power over others by use or threat of brute force, violence against the person or property—authoritarian.	Power over others by strength of rules, law, ideology, governance, motivational manipulation—authoritarian to authoritative.	Power with others—solidarity, education as "leading out," courtesy, trade, governance, advocacy, conscientisation—autoauthoritative.	Power from within—grace, vocation, self-realization, a prophetic and liberation theology—spiritual authority, as self-authored from beyond mere ego.
Exterior Face	Armed forces, violent revolution, monkey-wrenching, saboteur action, industrial action such as strikes and boycotts.	Police law & order, tax authorities, institutional discipline, manipulative marketing, sects, threat of industrial action, whistleblowing, social conditioning.	Democratic political processes & open government, schools & universities, industry lobby groups, trade unions, religious & nongovernmental organisations.	Touching of hearts, creativity/art, wholistic worldview, joy, nonviolence, witness, martyrdom, fun—both individual and collective through community.

SPECTRUM OF SOCIALLY EXPRESSED POWER

We are living in what the Greeks called *Kairos*—the right moment—for a "metamorphosis of the gods," of the fundamental principles and symbols. This peculiarity of our time, which is certainly not of our conscious choosing, is the expression of the unconscious man within us who is changing. Coming generations will have to take account of this momentous transformation if humanity is not to destroy itself through the might of its own technology and science. . . .

So much is at stake and so much depends on the psychological constitution of modern man. Is he capable of resisting the temptation to use his power for the purpose of staging a world conflagration? Is he conscious of the path he is treading, and what the conclusions are that must be drawn from the present world situation and his own psychic situation? Does he know that he is on the point of losing the life-preserving myth of the inner man which Christianity has treasured up for him? Does he realize what lies in store should this catastrophe ever befall him? Is he even capable of realizing that this would in fact be a catastrophe? And finally, does the individual know that *he* is the makeweight that tips the scales?[9]

REDEEMING POWER

What are the implications of redeeming power for those who acknowledge that we work in a "fallen" world? Based upon a biblical exegesis of the "principalities and powers," Wink derives the following formula:

> The Powers are good.
> The Powers are fallen.
> The Powers must be redeemed.[10]

We can illuminate the challenge of this if, as Wink intends, we substitute for "the powers" the name of a person, institution, or nation that we know. Conflict between others and ourselves can then be seen in a framework that understands strife both as inevitable but also potentially as mutually redemptory. It can help us to face our enemies without hatred, with love; to search for ways to free their higher God-given vocation while, at the same time, allowing them to challenge ours. After all, Jesus never said not to have enemies. He had plenty himself. He only recommended trying to love them.

In Wink's schema of naming, unmasking, and engaging the powers, the first stage—naming—aims to place handles upon psychospiritual processes that are otherwise difficult to see. In the Bible, these processes had names like *Moloch*, *Mammon*, and the *Golden Calf*. Wink suggests that such principalities, "angels," or "gods" remain present in the idolatry of modern life. We do not notice them because we have been persuaded to think that they belong to a bygone age, yet they dominate many of the structures of our lives. We see them in the worship of such obsessions as war, money, power, drugs, corporations, and sex.

"Naming the powers" entails recognition and, therefore, the restoration of a *visible* power dynamic. This is because naming calls into presence—it makes features of reality manifest in consciousness. Once that is established, once we are more spiritually awake to that which is, we can proceed with "unmasking the powers"—that is to say, stripping off the disguises and camouflage to expose the means by which the psychodynamic principles in question cause degradation and corruption. For example, nuclear weapons and their massive cost can be seen as being psychologically similar to the worship of Moloch, that Old Testament fire-filled stone god into whose arms the children were sacrificed to purchase prosperity. Or to take another example, it can sometimes be useful to *personify* the spirit of a greed-led economy by using Jesus' Aramaic term, Mammon—the worship of which, he said, was incompatible with loving God.

Only after naming and unmasking can we attempt "engaging the powers." This aims not to destroy power, which was originally a God-given organizing force, but to *redeem* it from a "fallen" or degraded state. Wink sees nonviolence as central to this task. If violence is used to combat what he calls the "domination system" of oppression it will ultimately fail, because the domination system actually feeds on violence. More violence is how violence clones itself. Wink, therefore, refers to the theory that violence can be redemptive as the "Myth of Redemptive Violence." If social transformation is to be effective, he says, it has to avoid being sucked back into the cycle of violence.

For these reasons, if peace is to become a long-term condition of society and not merely the temporary absence of war, it is imperative to shift along what I called, above, the "spectrum of socially expressed power." It is necessary for nations to learn how to evolve from coercive forms of governance that express "power over" others, through persuasive techniques that express "power with" them, and on into the autopoetic transformative mode of "empowerment within." This spectral shift is required to achieve effective consensual governance. As it raises the application of power from a physical level of being, through psychological ones, to the spiritual, it moves toward progressively greater degrees of recalling the world to a higher vocation. This is the practical work of redemption. The former U.S. president, Jimmy Carter, understood this very clearly. He writes:

> Historically and currently, we all realize that religious differences have often been a cause or a pretext for war. Less well known is the fact that the actions of many religious persons and communities point in another direction. They demonstrate that religion can be a potent force in encouraging the peaceful resolution of conflict.
>
> Personal experience underlies my conviction that religion can be significant for peacemaking. The negotiations between Menachem Begin, Anwar el-Sadat, and myself at Camp David in 1978 were greatly influenced by our religious backgrounds. . . . [Such] cases suggest that the world's religious communities possess moral and social characteristics that equip them in unique ways to engage in efforts to promote peace. . . . [We] must recognize the growing importance of religious factors for peacemaking and develop ways, both informal and formal, to cooperate with religious leaders and communities in promoting peace with justice.[11]

These arguments are not to belittle the insightful views of our Mennonite friends against constantinianism. They do, however, suggest that if a nation can be understood as a community at a macro scale, it is difficult to see how the church, as the body of membership one of another, can or should avoid having an impact upon it. There are various ways in which that can be achieved and the discredited model of the "Holy Roman Empire" is but one.

RENEWING THE EVANGELICAL COUNSELS

I opened with a discussion of the triune nature of community—community with nature, community with one another, and community with God. I paralleled these with the three temptations of Christ, and followed that through with an exegesis of power. I will close by suggesting that a further parallel can be drawn with the so-called "Evangelical Counsels"—poverty, chastity, and obedience.

Poverty calls for right relationship with the earth, including the richness of enjoying the fruits of Providence. It is about cultivating the simplicity of sufficiency rather than the obesity of surplus. It means frugality rather than destitution. As Jesus showed when he made the equivalent of 900 bottles of wine in John's gospel, or when he accepted the costly anointing oil, and when his parents (presumably) accepted on his behalf the wise men's gifts of gold, myrrh and frankincense, poverty does not mean the compulsive-obsessive denial of serendipitous luxury. It simply means having good things in right proportion, in right relationship, and as Jesus clearly saw in his parables about feasting, it is actually the poor who can most appreciate good things!

Chastity strictly speaking means "purity." It is only synonymous with celibacy if, for some reason, sex is inappropriate. Chastity might be thought of as right relationship with one another—for example, through cultivating psychological honesty. As such, chastity is a prerequisite for rich sexual fulfillment.

And obedience is simply obedience to God, to the deepest life-force within. It is also worth noting that this is not the same as obedience to any worldly power. Rather, it is relationship to the deepest level of our inner selves—to that of God within, as the apostle Paul pointed out (Gal. 2:20). Earlier English usage better captures a Taoist or Dharmic sense of the word, as when Shakespeare speaks of "floating . . . obedient to the streame." Obedience is thus a rhythmic process of moving in harmony of Being with Creation's continuous unfolding.

FIELD OF COMMUNITY	TEMPTATION OF CHRIST	EVANGELICAL COUNSEL
Community with the Creation—"Soil"	Turn stones into bread (Abuse natural power)	Poverty—simple lifeways
Community with one another—"Society"	Take control of kingdoms (Abuse social power)	Chastity—honest relationship
Community with God—"Soul"	Force divine intervention (Abuse spiritual power)	Obedience—seek God within

Poverty thereby protects against the abuse of nature's power; chastity against the abuse of social power; and obedience against the abuse of spiritual power, as the preceding matrix summarizes:

Lastly, the power of community to build peace and give life can be very real. On January 25, 2002, as I edited the publication version of this chapter, Scotland's *Herald* newspaper ran an obituary of Church of Scotland minister Ernest Gordon, Dean Emeritus of Princeton University. Gordon had nearly died during World War II from beatings in a Japanese POW camp on the River Kwai. But it was through creating community in the camp that his life, and humanity, remained intact.

"It was awful," he testified, "yet it helped to reaffirm your faith in humanity. . . . All of us had experienced something approaching grace. I think we all began to realize that bitterness was not an option. Although no one would ever forget what happened, some of us discovered we could forgive."

NOTES

1. Katrina Shields, *In the Tiger's Mouth: An Empowerment Guide for Social Action* (Philadelphia: New Society, 1994), xiii.

2. This expression is associated in Celtic tradition with St. Bride. It is substantially from Celtic perspectives on spirituality that I draw the triune schema presented here. I explore this in a less condensed way in *Soil and Soul: People Versus Corporate Power* (London: Aurum Press, 2001.)

3. Anthony de Mello, *Awareness* (New York: Image Doubleday, 1992), 182.

4. Gustavo Gutiérrez, *A Theology of Liberation: History, Politics, Salvation* (London: SCM, 1988), xxxvii-xxxviii, 24.

5. Walter Wink, *Naming the Powers: The Language of Power in the New Testament; Unmasking the Powers: The Invisible Forces that Determine Human Existence; Engaging the Powers: Discernment and Resistance in a World of Domination* (Philadelphia and Minneapolis: Fortress Press, 1984, 1986, 1992).

6. God, of course, had been skeptical from the outset about the feudal, patriarchal, and militaristic consequences of Israel acquiring for itself a king (1 Samuel 8:10-22).

7. The danger of this schema dualistically separating the spiritual from the material can be avoided by seeing each advancing level of awareness as incorporating the earlier expressions, thus the spiritual would incorporate both the physical and the psychological levels.

8. Wink, *Unmasking the Powers*, 95-96.

9. Anthony Storr, *Jung: Selected Writings* (London: Fontana, 1983), 360, 402-403.

10. Wink, *Engaging the Powers*, 10.

11. Eds. Douglas Johnston and Cynthia Sampson, *Religion, the Missing Dimension of Statecraft* (Oxford: Oxford University Press, 1994), vii-viii.

Appendix 1

HPC Epistle from Bienenberg

To: Our brothers and sisters in the Historic Peace Churches and in the wider ecumenical fellowship of Christians

From: The International Historic Peace Church Consultation, "Theology and Culture: Peacemaking in a Globalized World," at Bienenberg Theological Seminary, Switzerland, June 25-29, 2001

Greetings in the name of the Prince of Peace.

We, members of the Historic Peace Churches—Mennonites, Friends, and Church of the Brethren—are gathered in Bienenberg, Switzerland, to assess our contemporary theologies of peace and justice in preparation for the Decade to Overcome Violence. We come from all parts of the world, although we lament the disproportionately small participation of those from outside Europe and North America. We come with a commitment to listen to each other, to honor our differences and celebrate our commonalities, and to work together for the culture of peace which is God's will for our broken world.

AFFIRMATIONS

Together we affirm the following:
- Essential to the good news of the gospel is the teaching, exam-

ple, and Spirit of the crucified and risen Christ, who calls us to witness to the transforming power of God's kingdom of peace, justice, and reconciliation—for this nonviolent way of life is at the very heart of the gospel.

- The good news of the gospel is more than a renunciation of violence in the struggle for justice and reconciliation. It is a call and a gift to seek to develop a culture of peace that creatively addresses and overcomes the many causes of violence in the contemporary world.
- The good news of the gospel calls us to regard seeking justice as central and integral to a nonviolent way of life. The commitment to nonviolent love and to the struggle for justice belong to one another and are not to be separated.
- A careful study of the Scriptures discloses this unity of nonviolent love, the struggle for justice, reconciliation, and the creative search for a culture of peace. In the Sermon on the Mount, love for the adversary includes reproof and creative confrontation of evil, but does not include competing with the violent methods of evil. In the New Testament account, the early church did not avoid confrontation for the sake of the Truth.
- We are called to find creative nonviolent ways to address situations of conflict in the search for justice. These include solidarity with the victim, binding the wounds of the oppressed, addressing the needs of the poor, seeking genuine understanding and empathy with all partners of the conflict, efforts for reconciliation when possible, learning to forgive, and genuine love of enemy.
- We are called to witness in the hope and anticipation that God may use our witness to bring reconciliation and a culture of peace with justice. Therefore, the effectiveness of our witness is always an important consideration, but not the only consideration. We are called to a patient and persistent trust that God will make use of our obedience in ways that often surpass our understanding. The willingness to accept suffering is, therefore, a part of our witness for peace.
- We are called to experience the providential intercession of the Spirit that may carry us through situations where the use of violence, even as a last resort, has been renounced.
- Our witness proceeds from worship, prayer, study, and discernment within the discipline of the community of faith. At

the same time our witness reaches out to the civil societies and ecological environments within which we all live. Peace in its depth includes spiritual, communal, and political dimensions as well as care for the earth.

- The different ways of understanding these affirmations in our various doxological, theological, and ecclesial traditions serve to strengthen them, rather than to weaken our commitment to them. Indeed, the affirmations themselves express our belief in a reconciliation that allows for difference.

CONFESSION

At the beginning of the twenty-first century, does the title "Historic Peace Churches" fit the Church of the Brethren, Mennonites, and Friends? In many places, we have become indistinguishable from the society around us. Some of us would challenge the extent to which we identify with and conform to our respective states. Is our peace witness simply historic, or does it stand as a challenge to the modern forms of national religion? Our churches' peace witness arose within contexts of suffering and persecution.

Today, many of our churches, especially in the North, exist in a position of privilege in our societies, and no longer speak from the vantage point from which our ethic arose. This fact, far from calling into question the radical nature of the gospel, could instead stand as a call to repentance. Many of us have been too inattentive to our brothers and sisters who live in situations of real suffering, whether in the Southern Hemisphere or in the North, and even within our churches and homes. We do not seek suffering for its own sake; yet too many of us practice a comfortable and conformist ethic of peace, which is incompatible with God's mission to overcome the evils of this world. We deplore the apparent inability of this very consultation to more fully reflect the realities in which many of our churches in the Southern Hemisphere find themselves.

COMMITMENT TO
THE DECADE TO OVERCOME VIOLENCE

We who are gathered here express our commitment to the Decade to Overcome Violence, and to all ecumenical work which serves the cause of peace, justice, and reconciliation. We urge our churches, whether they are members of the World Council of Churches or not, to commit to active engagement with other Christians in the service of God's will for peace. We intend to continue the discussions begun here this week, and to broaden the participation to include those who are not here. We intend to share the gifts of our tradition with the ecumenical community of churches through the Decade. We intend to make this a time of renewal and energy for our active nonviolent work for peace, justice, and reconciliation.

As we begin this Decade to Overcome Violence together with the ecumenical fellowship of churches, we make the following commitments:

- We wish to deepen our understanding of the peace God wishes to give us, the righteousness with which God graces us, and the justice God requires of us.
- Our witness for peace and our calling to Christian unity are two aspects of the same gospel imperative "that all may be one" (John 17). We admit that we have not always ourselves understood or embodied the necessary link between reconciliation among Christians and the Christian ministry of reconciliation in the world. We pray that, through the Decade to Overcome Violence, we can discover that a commitment to nonviolent peacemaking need no longer be a church-dividing issue.
- The search for peace is not the possession of the peace churches, but is a deep common yearning of all Christians, people of other faiths, and all of humanity. We recognize that, in committing to ecumenical dialogue and action for peace, we are called to lay aside any prideful tendencies within ourselves to lay special claim to this concern. Instead, we are called to listen humbly to the earnest commitments of others to peace. We must understand and willingly embrace the fact that through ecumenical encounter, we too may be changed. Indeed, a vulnerability and openness to the "other" is constitutive of the peace witness we profess.
- We commit ourselves to urge our respective institutions, with their resources, to engage fully in the ecumenical dialogue and action of the Decade to Overcome Violence. Now is the time to bring forward our gifts with a spirit of generosity.

SUGGESTIONS FOR THE DECADE TO OVERCOME VIOLENCE

From our perspective as members of peace churches, we offer the following suggestions for the Decade to Overcome Violence:

- For the churches of our traditions, a commitment to nonviolent action for justice and reconciliation is a mark of the church, a point of confessional status. We suggest pursuing an ecclesiological approach to nonviolence, following on the WCC's recent work in Ecclesiology and Ethics. We strongly affirm the statement from that study, that "ethic is intrinsic to the nature of the church," and suggest this might be a fruitful avenue for building ecumenical consensus in the Decade.

- Much of the world's energy and resources are channeled into preparing for and engaging in violent attempts to resolve conflict, and in misguided attempts to create security. The governments of the world continue to outdo themselves in arming for war. In addition, much creative imagination and energy is absorbed by the interpersonal, social, structural, economic, cultural, and ecological dynamics of violence. We all suffer from a lack of energy and resources for creative nonviolent conflict transformation. Through this Decade, we urge that significant resources be devoted to experimental methodologies for positive alternatives to violence, so that our "no" to violence can be followed by the "yes" of love, justice, and transforming power.

- Our experience in peacemaking has taught us that overcoming violence is very difficult. We, therefore, suggest committing ourselves to use resources from beyond ourselves, to pray for the courage of our convictions, and to practice patience so as not to impede God's spirit of peace.

CONTINUATION FROM THIS CONSULTATION

The participants here this week are clear that this is not an isolated experience, but is rather one chapter in a story which began long before us, and will continue into the future. We feel the need for more consultations of a similar nature. More fundamentally, we feel the need to continue together, to witness together, to share our differences in love, to embody the reconciliation we seek to call forth in the world, and to strengthen ourselves and the entire community of Christians in our shared ministry of peacemaking.

May you be blessed by the One who calls us to be peacemakers.

Appendix 2

Just Peacemaking: Toward an Ecumenical Ethical Approach from the Perspective of the Historic Peace Churches

**A STUDY PAPER FOR
DIALOGUE WITH THE WIDER CHURCH[1]**

We, the undersigned members of the Historic Peace Churches, have gathered together from South America, North America, Asia, Africa, and Europe June 25-29, 2001, for an International Historic Peace Church Consultation, "Theology and Culture: Peacemaking in a Globalized World," at Bienenberg Theological Seminary, Switzerland. We affirm our commitment to the statement of the First Assembly (Amsterdam 1948) of the World Council of Churches (WCC) which held that:

> War as a method of settling disputes is incompatible with the teaching and example of our Lord Jesus Christ. The part which

war plays in our present international life is a sin against God and a degradation of man.

We speak with one mind in our yearning for the churches to enlarge this commitment to reject all violence. We believe that violent coercive force as a method of settling disputes is incompatible with the teaching, example, and Spirit of Jesus Christ. We, therefore, endorse with enthusiasm the World Council of Churches' "Decade to Overcome Violence: Churches Seeking Reconciliation and Peace." We deeply appreciate this commitment of the churches of the world, and we pledge ourselves to learn from the insights of the many churches within the WCC, even as we share from our Historic Peace Church traditions.

We recognize that at the beginning of the twenty-first century we face the scourge of violence not only or even primarily in the form of war in the international system, but as a pervasive problem that challenges us at many levels: the new proliferation of local and regional wars within and between nations that unleash destructive conflict on civilian populations; acts of genocide committed in ethnic, racial, and religious conflicts; state terrorism, torture, and the violation of fundamental human rights; economic disparity and exploitation that violates above all the poor and the marginalized; gender inequality, sexual exploitation, and violence within our families; and the assault on the natural environment that threatens to undermine the very web of life that sustains God's created order. All these are degradations of God's *shalom* on earth.

We begin with a confession of our own complicity in this violence. We have often failed to live up to our commitment to the Spirit of Jesus Christ. We have often been silent and failed to act on behalf of those who are suffering the scourge of injustice and violence. We do not always know exactly what constitutes justice—or peace—in a given situation; we lack wisdom in addressing the complex issues of our time. In particular, we share with the wider church and the larger world the perplexities of addressing the complex issues raised by conflicts such as those in Rwanda, Iraq, the Middle East, Somalia, Southern Sudan, Kosovo, Colombia, South Africa, and many other places.

It is in this spirit that we express our concerns about the recent document received by the WCC Central Committee, and recommended for further study: "The Protection of Endangered Populations in Situations of Armed Violence: Toward an Ecumenical Approach."[2] We offer our response to the document in the form of the following five points:

1. A biblically and theologically grounded pacifism regards seeking God's justice as central and integral to a nonviolent philosophy of life. To state the issue as if we have to choose between nonviolence and justice is a false dichotomy.

One of the biggest stumbling blocks to principled nonviolence among many Christians is the *assumption* that a nonviolent philosophy fails adequately to address questions of justice. The argument goes something like this: in a world of radical evil, pacifists choose nonviolence over justice, when both moral imperatives cannot be met. Non-pacifist Christians argue that priority should be given to justice instead, and that the use of force may be justified in protecting or securing justice.

Over the past century there has been a radical transformation in the understanding of the integral relationship of justice and nonviolence in a biblically and theologically based pacifism. Our churches have developed from traditions of nonresistance and non-participation in war toward active nonviolent peacemaking, which involves not only nonresistance and conscientious objection to war, but also active participation in the relief of suffering, building the institutions of peace, and working to remove the causes of war. This is grounded in a view of Jesus as the one who incarnated the rule of God by healing and transforming lives, by engaging the principalities and powers, and by confronting violence with the cross. In turn, our view of Jesus is grounded in our experience of the Spirit of Christ in our midst and our practices of nonviolent peacemaking today.

The biblical and theological vision of justice is based on God as a God of justice who is active in the world in a restorative way—to make right the broken relationships between God and humans, humans and humans, and humans and the natural order. An embodied, Jewish Jesus engages the political and social context of his time as an agent of radical social change. Jesus' acceptance of the cross is the price Jesus pays for his engagement of the powers and his radical nonconformity. The cross is not a defeat by the powers, but is God's nonviolent overcoming of evil through the power of the Slain Lamb. *Shalom* is a holistic vision of God's healing power that restores the human relationship to all that is: to our own bodies, to the earth, and within the social order.

Jesus challenges the systems of patriarchy, exploitation and greed, violence and political domination. In their place, he embodies practices of mutuality between men and women, an economics of sharing and equality, and a politics of nonviolent transformation. Jesus' teaching in the Sermon on the Mount "to seek God's kingdom and God's righteousness" is a call to restore just relations among us personally, societally, and with God. The moral imperatives of the Sermon on the Mount are not impossibly high ideals, but rather a call to concrete acts of justice (e.g. "go be reconciled") that is made possible by God's liberating grace that frees us from bondage to anger and hatred. As we follow God's light, we are shown how to live in the "virtue of that power and life that takes away the occasion of all wars" (George Fox).

Injustice is a major cause of violence. To make peace, we must strive for justice. The vision of justice we set forth here is holistic and social, rooted in the biblical vision of *shalom*. It should be distinguished from the narrative tradition of justice rooted primarily in Lockean and Enlightenment views that emphasize individual autonomy and freedom, the protection of private property, the right to exploit the environment, and narrow views of human rights as primarily the protection of individual liberties like freedom of speech and association. The biblical tradition of covenant justice with its emphasis upon social solidarity and its holistic vision of salvation is carried on more adequately in Catholic traditions of social responsibility, in early, free-church Puritan traditions of religious liberty and covenant responsibility, in some secular versions of social democracy, and in comprehensive visions of human rights that include political, economic, cultural, and environmental considerations.

2. We can identify a number of normative practices for seeking justice within principled pacifism.

To state the issue as if principled nonviolence has no way to respond to injustice fails to recognize widely available, and often used, peacemaking practices for seeking justice. These peacemaking practices can be supported both by those who are pacifists and those who accept "just war" reasoning.

It is not sufficient simply to argue theologically or conceptually that justice is integral to a pacifist vision. We have to go beyond concept and theory to show that there are available actual practices for implementing justice nonviolently. Furthermore, we should invite persons of diverse points of view to observe and study these practices in order that we might learn from our successes and mistakes, and be able to make better judgments in the future in our efforts to seek justice. One of the important characteristics of nonviolent peacemaking is that it is open to empirical observation and scrutiny by the wider community, not hidden in the recesses of intelligence agencies and covert operations. The following is an illustrative (not exhaustive) list of five available practices that have been tried and can be studied to determine how these nonviolent practices contribute to justice.

1. *Nonviolent forms of defense and social transformation.* There is by now a huge repertoire of case studies and practices of nonviolent transformation. Walter Wink calls for a "revisioning of history" to break the monopoly of an androcentric history written by the victors which is largely a chronicle of kings and dynasties, wars and empires, a study of the successes and failures of violence rather than careful observation and reporting of how peace has often been made or preserved nonviolently.[3] The Quaker sociologist Elise Boulding has recently published an alternative history, *Cultures of Peace: The Hidden Side of History.*[4]

A distinction between violence and coercion is one dimension of moral reasoning in practicing nonviolent action that requires further investigation. How do nonviolent actors employ coercive force in preserving or seeking justice, yet avoid irreparable harm to persons? We have seen how so-called "nonviolent" economic sanctions (such as those against Iraq) have produced irreparable harm, because the sanctions do not distinguish between the leader that the international community wanted to punish and the mass of people who live in the society, who bear the brunt of the sanctions.

Some beginning efforts along these lines would be to study the experience of groups who carried medical supplies to North Vietnam during the Vietnam war, and those who have worked to bring humanitarian supplies to people in both Cuba and Iraq. What is there to learn about conflicts and third-party interventions from these examples, which were protests against U.S. policy as well as against leaders in the countries opposed by the U.S. and its allies?

2. *Citizen corps of observers/interveners/advocates as a "presence" in situations of conflict* (e.g. Christian Peacemaker Teams, Witness for Peace, and so forth). We do not yet have a comprehensive theoretical and empirical analysis of the impact of such groups in conflict situations, but there is a growing body of experience with these ventures. Their actions have included accompaniment, public witness against injustice, giving public exposure to injustices that authorities have tried to hide, testimony to government officials, and more.

There is much to learn from systematic study of such actions. Could the development of corps of interveners, called on to be a "presence" in emergency situations, be one answer to crises like Kosovo or Rwanda? Could such peacekeeping forces be established in cooperation with the United Nations? Through our volunteer services, people also provide a presence and support local efforts at reconciliation, attempting to prevent recurrence of violence in communities.

3. *Acknowledging responsibility for violence and injustice and seeking repentance and forgiveness* (e.g. the Truth and Reconciliation Commission in South Africa). We are now able to identify a growing body of literature on the theory and practice of forgiveness and reconciliation. How do we break the cycles of violence through the "healing of memory"? We humans cannot "forget" the atrocities that happen to us, but how can we help people "remember" in ways that can break the cycles of violence and lead to healing? The Middle East immediately comes to mind as one place where this matter of "right remembering" is so critical for healing, and where any further use of violent force only escalates hostilities. How does the church, through a politics of compassion that addresses the experience of victims, help implement the words of Hannah Arendt:

> Without being forgiven, released from the consequences of what we have done, our capacity to act would, as it were, be confined to one single deed from which we would never recover; we would remain the victims of its consequences forever, not unlike the sorcerer's apprentice who lacks the magic formula to break the spell.[5]

4. *Training persons in the use of cooperative conflict methods and strategies* (e.g. conflict transformation programs in Brethren, Mennonite, and Quaker colleges, universities, and seminaries which train people in culturally appropriate methods of conflict management and transformation, the Alternatives to Violence Project, and other training initiatives). We can begin to see the results of these efforts in programs of the Mennonite Central Committee, the Church of the Brethren Ministry of Reconciliation, the Quaker Peace and Social Witness program, and the Canadian and American Friends Service Committees. As we identify key persons in governmental and nongovernmental organizations who are actively involved in nonviolent forms of conflict resolution and peace building in places like El Salvador and Central Africa, we can expect this work to expand further.

There is a vast body of literature on theory and practice in this arena. One example is the work of John Paul Lederach, a practitioner who has reflected on the nonviolent resolution of conflict in settings such as Central America and Africa.[6] Another is the handbook prepared by the Responding to Conflict Programme.[7]

5. *The church's witness and advocacy on behalf of the marginalized and those whose lives are threatened by injustice* (e.g. the campaign to end sanctions in Iraq; the support of Christians in Colombia who believe U.S. aid for violent solutions to the drug war are misplaced; the effort to bring a balanced perspective on the Middle East conflict by representing the plight of Palestinians living under occupation; the voices of the voiceless in Guatemala). William T. Cavanaugh shows how a "Christendom" theology during the time of the Pinochet dictatorship in Chile undermined the church's capacity to resist the state apparatus of torture and defend the plight of the tortured.[8] The separation of the "spiritual" and the "temporal" undermined the church's ability to engage the powers of this world. Cavanaugh argues that only in following Jesus and "bodying" Jesus' life politically and socially in the Eucharist can the church "resist" the powers and stand with and advocate for the tortured. To summarize:

> The Eucharist builds a visible social body capable of resisting the state's strategy of disappearance. The Eucharist anticipates the future kingdom, re-members Jesus' conflict with the powers of this world, and brings both future and past dimensions of Christ into the present in the form of a visible body. The result is a "confusion" of the spiritual and the temporal, an invasion of worldly time and space by the heavenly, and thus the possibility of a different kind of social practice.[9]

In other words (which can be shared by non-eucharistic traditions as well), the capacity to be a genuine advocate on behalf of the most vulnerable is made possible by the recovery of the church's own identity in the story of Christ's suffering and passion at the hands of the principalities and powers.

3. The use of violent force as a "last resort" to secure justice creates conditions that inhibit the achievement of justice. Too often we work under the false assumption that, if we cannot find a nonviolent solution to a conflict, the use of violent force will take care of the problem.

The following statement is typical of the reasoning of most Christians: "War may be necessary under certain circumstances to protect the innocent and limit even greater evils."[10] But it is the commitment to the possibility of the "exception," the "last resort" use of violent force, that is so problematic, because the exception in actual practice tends to become the "rule."

Such thinking is especially dangerous when dealing with military force. We question whether armed intervention can really provide the "space" for more normal political processes to develop and flourish. Presumed "humanitarian" intervention may mask egoistic self-interests and the partisan political agendas of the parties who presume to intervene. Some members of the wider church have questioned whether our pacifism confronts the true depths of evil in the world or in human nature. We respond that our understanding of the problem of evil may be more searching than the understandings of those who are ready to promote military action with moralistic language.

Again, because we must be prepared for the exception, enormous intellectual and economic resources are committed to preparing for that possibility. Witness the amount of resources nations (or alliances like NATO) put into defense spending to prepare for the possibility that force must be used. With regard to the church, once it has granted the "exception," it has morally compromised itself such that it lacks the moral leverage to resist the preparation for the use of violent force. Implicitly, the church has accepted the assumption that violent force is inevitable, and since it is inevitable, we must support the preparation for that possibility.

"Last resort" thinking cuts short imaginative thinking and creative action to find alternative ways to make peace. It is very easy to become complacent in our thinking, simply to mouth the platitudes of policy makers who try to convince us "that there was nothing else we could do." Usually the alternatives are put as follows: we either had to engage in the use of violent force, or let things continue as they are (do nothing). The logic that leads to the "last resort" of war is often fatally flawed, as flawed as parents' resort to spanking to discipline their children. Nothing else has worked; we have tried every peaceful means to solve the conflict. So now, like the parent who resorts to a spanking, we will try the use of violent force. The assumption is that force will work, since no other method worked.

In fact, there is an uncertainty here: the presumed certainty of good results from force is often exaggerated, and later not borne out by the facts. In conflicts involving two parties who both justify the use of force to accomplish their just cause, if there is a declared "winner," we know that half the actors were wrong in their calculations right from the start.

The "last resort" continues rather than breaks the cycle of violence. It reinforces the concentration of power in the hands of those who have the money and resources to secure weapons (guerrilla groups, nation states, alliances of nations). In locating the resources for addressing conflict with "elites" who have the resources and technology, we undermine the very structures of civil society (the power of the people). How do we develop the infrastructures of civil society so as to sustain democratic institutions? We again cite the work of Elise Boulding, who helps us imagine and construct a "culture of peace." [11]

By definition, the reliance on armed force to settle issues locates power and decision making in "elites," no longer under the direction and control of people. Democracy is enhanced when people take responsibility and action to shape their own lives and seek the common good through civil processes and institutions. Democracy is preserved when people act democratically, when they assert their power in the context of associations to shape the common good. This also preserves freedom, contrary to the commonly held myth that the willingness to use violent force preserves freedom.

For example, we can see how the huge defense establishment in the United States, and the economic self-interest of that establishment to preserve itself and grow, inhibits the capacity of elected officials to make rational decisions about security issues. The Strategic Missile Defense System, we suspect, has almost nothing to do with questions of security (though that is the "rationale" which masks the reality), but almost everything to do with the need for policy makers to "deliver" on their promises of economic well-being to that elite constituency that has "bought" them and got them elected. (It should also be noted that U.S. militarism functions as a "security blanket" for many of America's allies, who may need to rethink their own security issues.) Unfortunately, the church's use of "last resort" thinking undermines its moral leverage and capacity to resist the principalities and powers. So the church, worldwide, rather than offering an imaginative alternative, "legitimates" the very structures that perpetuate the cyclical forces of violence.

4. We call on the churches to emphasize the distinctive witness to the world that flows from our commitment to the Spirit of Jesus Christ and our identity as the body of Christ in the world.

We are disappointed that the language of the WCC study document is dominated largely by political analysis and prudential calculation about when resort to armed intervention might be justified, and what restraints should be placed on it. Within the framework of the assumptions of the document we do respect the way the statement carefully places restraints on the use of force. But we question whether the dominant language of the document can really help to develop an ecumenical ethical approach as suggested by the subtitle. Furthermore, we are disappointed that the document, which is intended to lead the Christian church in moral/ethical discernment, seems to assume that the primary actors in addressing these complex issues are agencies like NATO and/or the United Nations Security Council. We do, however, see the importance of the church working with the United Nations and of strengthening international law.

We also see the validity of the differentiation between moral and theological views, and political analysis and argument. While we acknowledge the importance of political analysis and prudential calculation in the overall assessment of how we address these complex issues, we still feel the need to indicate how our political recommendations arise from our understanding of what it means to be the body of Christ committed to Jesus Christ.

5. Both pacifists and those who reason with "just war" principles should make more modest claims about their ability to guarantee success. Though both traditions seek justice, neither tradition can guarantee that justice will be accomplished. Both traditions involve faith visions about how to "secure" a future in which justice is more likely to be achieved. The pacifist commitment to nonviolence is ultimately grounded in an eschatology of trust in the victory over evil of God revealed in Jesus' life, teachings, death, and resurrection.

Both the claim of just war theorists to secure justice through the "last resort" of armed force and the pacifist claim to secure justice through nonviolence must guard against the arrogance of exaggerated claims. Both positions ultimately rely on an eschatology, an understanding of the way God moves forward in history. Neither position can guarantee success. In fact, there may be some conflicts in which there is no available human solution. When societies have long been addicted to hatred and violence, we may not be able to avoid violence and suffering. We could invest all our resources in trying to find "last resort" interventions, but to no avail. We have to admit that we, and God as well, live with the consequences of the free decisions which we humans have made. God does not automatically prevent the judgment that is a consequence of human sin.

Ultimately, a Christian vision of life is based on the conviction that in the life, death, and resurrection of Jesus Christ we have a vision of the kingdom of God. In Christ we have a revelation of the way God's sovereign power works in history, a vision of the nonviolent cross as the way in which God's victory over evil is accomplished. This is the foundation for our work as Christians. Ultimately, our work as peacemakers is not based on our ability to be successful, but is invested in means of action grounded in our trust in the way of Jesus, our calling to be the body of Christ, and the guidance of the Holy Spirit. May we truly "embody" that vision, and repent of all arrogant trust in our own schemes to make history come out right.

Signatories:
(Bienenberg Participants)
Claude Baecher
Annis Bleeke
Neal Blough
Helmut Doerksen
Peter Dula
Fernando Enns
Arnold Neufeldt-Fast
Lon Fendall
Kristen Flory
Duane Friesen
Hans Jakob Galle
Eden Grace
Douglas Gwyn
Helmut Harder
Judy Zimmerman Herr
Robert Herr
Gabe Hoekema
Scott Holland
Chris Huebner
Harcourt Klinefelter
Andrea Lange
Sang Gyoo Lee
Moisés Mayordomo
Alastair McIntosh
Lauree Hersch Meyer
Donald Miller
Alfred Neufeld
Tom Yoder Neufeld

Ben Richmond
Debbie Roberts
Laura Short
Alex Sider
Siaka Traore
J. Denny Weaver
Alfred R. van Wijk
Wilfried Warneck

NOTES

1. This study paper is based on a paper read at the Bienenberg consultation by Duane Friesen, subsequently published as "The Moral Imperative to Do Justice Within Christian Pacifism: Tensions and Limits," *Mennonite Quarterly Review,* Vol. 76, No. 1 (January, 2002), 63-71. The paper which appears here was reworked from Friesen's paper by participants in the consultation, in response to the WCC study paper on humanitarian military intervention, and signed by persons who attended the consultation.

2. "The Protection of Endangered Populations in Situations of Armed Violence: Toward an Ecumenical Approach," Potsdam, Germany (29 January, 2001). Recommended for study and comment to WCC member churches by the International Affairs Department.

3. Walter Wink, *Engaging the Powers: Discernment and Resistance in a World of Domination* (Minneapolis: Fortress Press, 1992), see especially 243-257.

4. Elise Boulding, *Cultures of Peace: The Hidden Side of History* (Syracuse, N.Y.: Syracuse University Press, 2000).

5. Hannah Arendt, *The Human Condition* (Chicago: University of Chicago Press, 1958), 237.

6. John Paul Lederach, *Building Peace: Sustainable Reconciliation in Divided Societies* (Washington, DC: U.S. Institute of Peace, 1997); and *Preparing for Peace: Conflict Transformation Across Cultures* (Syracuse, N.Y.: Syracuse University Press, 1996).

7. *Working with Conflict: Skills and Strategies for Action* (London: Zed Books, 2000).

8. William T. Cavanaugh, *Torture and Eucharist* (Oxford: Blackwell, 1998).

9. Ibid., p. 251.

10. Father Stanley Harakis, *In Communion,* Orthodox Peace Fellowship Occasional Paper (May, 1992), cited in *Transforming Violence: Linking Local and Global Peacemaking,* ed. Herr and Zimmerman Herr, (Scottdale, Pa.: Herald Press, 1998), 27.

11. Elise Boulding, *Building a Global Civic Culture: Education for an Interdependent World,* (New York: Columbia University Press, 1988).

Appendix 3

"Theology and Culture: Peacemaking in a Globalized World"

**International Historic Peace Church Consultation
Bienenberg Theological Seminary, Bienenberg, Switzerland
June, 25-29, 2001**

Morning Worship led each day by John Rempel and Patricia Daly

I. PEACE THEOLOGY AND THE BIBLICAL TRADITION

Consultation Opening
Fernando Enns (Mennonite), Germany, "Welcome to Bienenberg: Introduction/Setting the Context" (pp. 29-41)

Biblical Tradition and Early Christianity
Neal Blough (Mennonite), France, "From the Tower of Babel to the Peace of Jesus Christ: Christological, Ecclesiological, and Missiological Foundations of Peacemaking" (pp. 45-61).

Daniel Ulrich (Church of the Brethren), USA, "Resistance, Reproof, and Love for Enemies in Matthew's Narrative Ethic" (pp. 157-170).

Konrad Raiser (WCC), Geneva, "Welcome and Remarks from the WCC" (pp. 19-28).

Moisés Mayordomo (Mennonite), Switzerland, "Conflict Resolution and Human Reconciliation in the Early Church" (pp. 171-181).

Evening Forum
"John Howard Yoder and Beyond," panel discussion
Chris Huebner (Mennonite), Canada, "How to Read Yoder: An Exercise in Pacifist Epistemology," published in *Mennonite Quarterly Review* 76:1 (January 2002), 49-62.

Alex Sider (Brethren in Christ), USA, "To See History Doxologically: Miroslav Volf's and John Howard Yoder's Competing Conceptions of the Place of Memory in the Politics of Forgiveness."

Peter Dula (Mennonite), USA, "The Disavowal of Constantine in the Age of Global Capital" (pp. 62-77).

Peace Theology
Duane Friesen (Mennonite), USA, "The Moral Imperative to Do Justice Within Christian Pacifism: Tensions and Limits," published in *Mennonite Quarterly Review* 76:1 (January 2002), 63-71.

Harry Huebner (Mennonite), Canada, "The Politics of Memory and Hope" published in *Mennonite Quarterly Review* 76:1 (January 2002), 35-48.

Debbie Roberts (Church of the Brethren), USA, "Peace and Mediation: A Feminist Perspective" (pp. 182-193).

J. Denny Weaver (Mennonite), USA, "Critically Embodied Nonviolence" (pp. 109-123).

II. PEACE THEOLOGY AND CONTEXT

Context: Violence and Nationalism
Patrick Bugu and Scott Holland (Church of the Brethren), Nigeria and USA, "Reconciliation or Pacifism? The Church of the Brethren in Nigeria" (Bugu) (pp. 124-131, scheduled, unable to attend); "The Gospel of Peace and the Violence of God" (Holland) (pp. 132-146).

Alix Lozano (Mennonite), Colombia, "What It Means to Be a Peace Church in the Context of Violence" (pp. 147-154).

Alfred Neufeld (Mennonite Brethren), Paraguay, "Historical Roots and a Culture of Violence" (pp. 78-94).

Sang Gyoo Lee (Independent/Mennonite), Korea, "The Role of the Korean Church for Conflict Transformation and the Peaceful Reunification of the Korean Peninsula" (pp. 206-214).

Context: Religious Pluralism
Prem Bagh (Mennonite), India, "Christian Peace Theology in the Indian Inter-Faith Context."

Bedru Hussein (Mennonite), Ethiopia, "Methodologies for Making Peace and Pursuing Justice in Ethiopia" (scheduled: unable to attend).

Context: Gender and Ethnicity
Ann K. Riggs (Quaker), USA, "Theology and Culture: The Claim of Ethnicity and Gender on Faith and Understanding" (pp. 97-108).

Context: Land
Elaine Bishop (Quaker) UK, "The Sacred Nature of Places: Understanding Land as a Contribution to Peacebuilding" (pp. 194-205).

Alastair McIntosh (Quaker), UK, "Healing Nationhood" (pp. 215-226).

III. FOUNDATIONS FOR ECUMENICAL DIALOGUE

Building on Our History
Gene Hillman (Quaker), USA, "Quakers and the Lamb's War: A Hermeneutic for Confronting Evil," published in *Quaker Theology* 4 (2002), 148-160.

Helmut Harder (Mennonite), Canada, "Peace and the Mennonite Confessional Tradition."

Ecumenical Directions
Lauree Hersch Meyer (Church of the Brethren), USA, "Peace Theology and Foundations for Ecumenical Dialogue" published in *Quaker Theology* 5 (2003), 55-66.

John Rempel (Mennonite), USA, "The Unity of the Church and the Christian Peace Witness," published in ed. Jeffrey Gros and John D. Rempel, *The Fragmentation of the Church and Its Unity in Peacemaking* (Grand Rapids: Eerdmans, 2001), 34-47.

Responding to the WCC Central Committee, Jan/Feb 2001 Berlin Meeting: reporting from participants. (See study paper response, pp. 232-243).

Geneva Meetings at the WCC
Programs and papers as presented in consultation can be found at www.peacetheology.org.

The Index

The Contributors

Elaine Bishop has been warden of the Quaker Meeting House in Glasgow, Scotland, and pursuing a Ph.D. through Sunderland University in England on the topic of "Peace and Land: A Challenge to Quakerism." Elaine holds a B.A. from Queens University (Kingston, Ontario), a B.Ed. from Lakehead University (Thunder Bay, Ontario), and an M.S.W. from Carleton University (Ottawa, Ontario). She has worked with women and children survivors of abuse and homelessness, been coordinator of Canadian Friends Service Committee, and spent four years working with the Lubicon Cree Nation. Elaine is a former clerk of Canadian Yearly Meeting and past chair of the Aboriginal Rights Coalition (Project North), now part of the KAIROS Coalition of the Canadian Council of Churches.

Dr. Neal Blough is director of the Paris Mennonite Centre and professor of church history at the Faculté Libre de Théologie Évangélique (Vaux sur Seine). His Th.D. degree from the Protestant Faculty of Theology at the University of Strasbourg is on Pilgram Marpeck's Christology.

Patrick Bugu is a minister in the EYN Church of Nigeria (the Church of the Brethren in Nigeria). He is principal of the Kulp Bible College, Adamawa state. He is a graduate of the Theological College of Northern Nigeria, and completed a Th.M. at Bethany Theological Seminary (Richmond, Indiana) in 2001.

Peter Dula has served with Mennonite Central Committee (MCC) in Burundi, Africa, and is a doctoral student in theology and ethics in the Duke University Graduate Department of Religion, Durham, North Carolina. He currently serves as a member of MCC's Peace Committee.

Dr. Fernando Enns is director of studies for the Ecumenical Institute of Heidelberg University. He is a Mennonite delegate to the

World Council of Churches (WCC) and a member of the WCC Central Committee. He also serves currently as vice-chairperson of the Association of German Mennonite Congregations.

Dr. Duane K. Friesen (principal author of the "Just Peacemaking" study document) is professor of Bible and religion, Bethel College (Newton, Kansas). He holds a Th.D. from Harvard Divinity School in Christian social ethics, and is author of *Christian Peacemaking and International Conflict: A Realist Pacifist Perspective* (Herald Press, 1986), and *Artists, Citizens, Philosophers: Seeking the Peace of the City* (Herald Press, 2000).

Dr. Scott Holland teaches peace, public, and cross-cultural theology at Bethany Theological Seminary, in partnership with Earlham School of Religion in Richmond, Indiana. He is contributing editor to *Cross Currents: The Journal of the Association for Religion and Intellectual Life.*

Dr. Sang Gyoo Lee studied at Kosin University (B.A., Th.M.), Korea Theological Seminary (M.Div.) at Presbyterian Theological College (Melbourne, Australia), and the Australian College of Theology (Th.D.). He has served as director of the Institute for Christian Thought (1993-97), dean of academic affairs (1993-97), senior chaplain (1997-2000), and is currently professor of church history at Kosin University in Pusan, Korea. His publications include *History of Presbyterianism in Korea* (Division of Christian Education, PCROK, 1988) and *A Walk Through the History of the Reformation* (Sung Kwang Pub. Co., 1997) and such articles as "The Christian Church in North Korea, 1945-1950," "The Resistance Against the Shinto Shrine Issue," "The Just War Tradition," "Calvin and Anabaptist Radicals," "Wealth: Blessing or Bane?" and "Democratization and Unification Movements in Korea."

Alix Lozano was born in Bucaramanga, Colombia, South America. She holds a M.Th. and serves as director of the Seminario Bíblico Menonita de Colombia in Bogota. She has participated in various areas of ministry in the Mennonite Church of Colombia, including pastoring, teaching, and working with women who suffer violence. She writes for religious journals in Colombia on women and violence, and family violence.

Dr. Moisés Mayordomo was born in 1966 in Barcelona, Spain, and grew up in Germany. He studied theology in Giessen, London, Heidelberg, and Bern, finishing in 1997 with a doctoral dissertation in New Testament studies. Currently he is assistant professor for New Testament studies in the University of Bern, Switzerland, and a member of the Mennonite church in that city.

Alastair McIntosh is a Scottish Quaker, writer and campaigning academic at Edinburgh's Center for Human Ecology. He is author of many papers on theology, ecology, community, economics (see www.AlastairMcIntosh.com), and of the books, *Healing Nationhood* (Curlew Productions, 2000) and *Soil and Soul: People Versus Corporate Power* (Aurum Press, 2001). He is a leading figure in land reform, has conducted a major national values discernment exercise in association with Scotland's new parliament, and each year addresses 400 senior military officers on the theme of nonviolent direct action at the Joint Services Command & Staff College.

Dr. Alfred Neufeld, the son of Mennonite immigrants to Filadelfia, Paraguay, studied theology in Basel, Switzerland, and in Fresno, California. He worked for fifteen years at the Instituto Bíblico Asunción (Paraguay). He holds a Doctor of Missiology degree from Basel and currently is dean of the theology faculty of the Universidad Evangélica del Paraguay, an academic confederation of Mennonite, Mennonite Brethren, and Baptist Bible seminaries. His doctoral thesis covered the area of fatalistic beliefs and worldviews in Paraguayan cultural history.

Dr. Konrad Raiser served as the General Secretary of the World Council of Churches from 1993-2003. He was professor for ecumenical studies at Bochum University, and is a member of the Evangelical Church in Germany.

Dr. Ann K. Riggs holds a Ph.D. from the School of Religious Studies at the Catholic University of America, Washington, D.C., and M.Div and M.Th. degrees from the Divinity School, Duke University, North Carolina, a Methodist institution. She is coauthor of *Introduction to Ecumenism* (Paulist Press, 1998) and coeditor of the journal, *Quaker Theology*. She has worked in the Secretariat for Ecumenical and Interreligious Affairs of the United States Conference of Catholic Bishops, Washington, D.C., and currently serves as Associate General Secretary for Faith and Order of the National Council of the Churches of Christ in the U.S.A.

Debbie Roberts is currently campus minister at the University of LaVerne (California), where she also directs the peace studies minor. She earned her Th.M. from Bethany Theological Seminary, Richmond, Indiana and her M.Div. from Seattle, Washington. She is currently in a Ph.D. program in women's studies in religion at Claremont (California) Graduate University.

Dr. Daniel Ulrich is associate professor of New Testament studies at Bethany Theological Seminary, Richmond, Indiana. He is ordained in the Church of the Brethren, and a former pastor of the Easton (Maryland) Church of the Brethren. He holds an M.Div. degree from Bethany Theological Seminary, and a Ph.D. from Union Theological Seminary, Richmond, Virginia.

Dr. J. Denny Weaver is professor of religion and the Harry and Jean Yoder Scholar in Bible and Religion at Bluffton (Ohio) College and editor of the C. Henry Smith Series. He holds a B.A. from Goshen (Indiana) College, an M.Div. from Associated Mennonite Biblical Seminary (Elkhart, Indiana), and a Ph.D. from Duke University (Durham, North Carolina). Recent publications include *Anabaptist Theology in Face of Postmodernity: A Proposal for the Third Millennium* (Pandora Press U.S., 2000), *The Nonviolent Atonement* (Eerdmans, 2001), and (co-edited with Gerald Biesecker-Mast), *Teaching Peace and Nonviolence and the Liberal Arts* (Rowman and Littlefield, 2003).

The Editors

Dr. Fernando Enns teaches systematic theology and ecumenical studies at Heidelberg University in Germany. A pastor in the German Mennonite Church, he also serves as vice-chairman for the Association of Mennonite Churches in Germany. Dr Enns holds a Doctor of Theology degree from the University of Heidelberg.

Dr. Enns is active in ecumenical circles, both in Germany and internationally. He currently serves as a delegate of the German Mennonite Churches to the National Christian Council of Germany, and to the World Council of Churches. Since 1998 he has been a member of the Central Committee of the World Council of Churches. He was instrumental in the WCC's action to adopt the current "Decade to Overcome Violence," at the Eighth WCC Assembly in Harare, Zimbabwe, in 1998, and serves as a member of the reference group for the Decade within the council.

Dr. Enns and his wife Renate live in an ecumenical student center at the University of Heidelberg, where he also serves as Director of Studies for the Ecumenical Institute.

Dr. Scott Holland is Associate Professor of Peace, Public, and Cross-Cultural Theology at Bethany Theological Seminary, in partnership with Earlham School of Religion in Richmond, Indiana, Unites States. As an ordained minister in the Church of the Brethren, he has served pastorates in Ohio and Pennsylvania. He is a contributing editor to *Cross Currents: The Journal for the Association of Religion and Intellectual Life*. He holds an M.A. from Ashland Theological Seminary, and a Ph.D. from Duquesne University.

Dr. Ann K. Riggs is a Quaker theologian who works ecumenically. Following some time as a staff person for the United States Conference of Catholic Bishops, in ecumenical relations, she currently serves the National Council of the Churches of Christ in the USA as Associate General Secretary for Faith and Order. In this capacity she guides various study processes among the diverse churches that participate in Faith and Order discussions.

Dr. Riggs holds a doctorate from the Catholic University of America. She writes on issues of theological anthropology, Quaker theological understandings, and ecumenical conversations as well as art history and sacred art. She serves as a consultant to the World Council of Churches Faith and Order Commission.

A member of the Friends General Conference, Dr. Riggs lives with her daughter near Washington, D.C.